The Economic and Legal Effectiveness of the European Union's Anti-Money Laundering Policy

Brigitte Unger

Professor of Public Sector Economics, Utrecht University School of Economics, The Netherlands and Director of the Institute of Economic and Social Research WSI in Düsseldorf, Germany

Joras Ferwerda

Assistant Professor, Utrecht University School of Economics, The Netherlands

Melissa van den Broek

PhD Candidate, Utrecht University School of Law, The Netherlands

Ioana Deleanu

PhD Candidate, Utrecht University School of Economics, The Netherlands

Edward Elgar
Cheltenham, UK • Northampton, MA, USA

Published by
Edward Elgar Publishing Limited
The Lypiatts
15 Lansdown Road
Cheltenham
Glos GL50 2JA
UK

Edward Elgar Publishing, Inc.
William Pratt House
9 Dewey Court
Northampton
Massachusetts 01060
USA

A catalogue record for this book
is available from the British Library

Library of Congress Control Number: 2013949876

This book is available electronically in the ElgarOnline.com
Law Collection Subject Collection, E-ISBN 978 1 78347 277 2

ISBN 978 1 78347 276 5

Typeset by Servis Filmsetting Ltd, Stockport, Cheshire
Printed and bound in Great Britain by T.J. International Ltd, Padstow

Contents

Preface

Anti-money laundering policy is now about 25 years old. Many actors have been involved, many efforts have been made and much money has been invested in this policy area. It seems time to stand still for a moment and to investigate whether all these efforts and costs have had a positive effect. Have the legal efforts achieved their intended goals? And has the investment in police, public prosecution, reporting systems and supervision had a positive impact on combating laundering and terrorist financing? This book assesses the economic and legal effectiveness of anti-money laundering in the 27 EU Member States.

This book is based on research undertaken by the Utrecht University School of Economics and School of Law, the Netherlands; the University of Wollongong, Australia and the University of Economics and Business Administration, Vienna. The research project on which this book is based was funded by the European Commission, Directorate-General (DG) Home Affairs (JLS 2009/ISEC/AG/087).

The authors would first like to thank the European Commission, DG Home Affairs, in particular Sebastiano Tiné, Mickaël Roudault, and Ingo Weustenfeld. The authors would furthermore like to thank all the many people who helped at the start of and during our research. Professor Henk Addink, Assistant Professor John Walker, Professor Frans van Waarden, Dr Madalina Busuioc, Mr André Tilleman, Professor François Kristen, Professor Erhard Blankenburg, Dr Steven Dawe, Dr Miguel Trindade Rocha and Assistant Professor Peter-Jan Engelen provided inspiring ideas and concepts at our regular research meetings in Utrecht during the study. The authors thank their project partner Wirtschaftsuniversität Wien (Vienna), in particular Professor Reinhard Pirker, for the organization of two regional workshops. We are particularly grateful to all the student-assistants and PhD students at Utrecht University School of Economics who supported us enthusiastically during the past four years: Bas van Marle, Melody Barlage, Jorrit Hendriksma, Daan van der Linde, Sofie Robbertsen and Maryam Imanpour.

Finally, the book would not be what it is without the help of participants in all the EU Member States. We are grateful to the many authorities and individuals who agreed to participate in the study between 2009 and 2012.We thank them for all their input, their hospitality in receiving us in their countries for interviews and their participation in our surveys and regional workshops.

The information contained in this study was current at 9 December 2012.

Acronyms and abbreviations

AML/CTF	Anti-money laundering and counter-terrorism financing
ARO	Asset recovery office
CARIN	Camden Asset Recovery Inter-agency Network
CCIB	Customs Criminal Investigations Bureau
CDD	Customer due diligence
CoE	Council of Europe
CTR	Currency transaction report
Deloitte study	Final Study on the Application of the Anti-Money Laundering Directive (ETD/2009/IM/F2/90)
DNFBPs	Designated non-financial businesses and professions
EC	European Commission
ECJ	European Court of Justice
ECOLEF	Economic and Legal Effectiveness of Anti-Money Laundering and Combating Terrorist Financing Policy (JLS/2009/ISEC/CFP/AG/)
EEA	European Economic Area
EU	European Union
EUROSTAT	The Community statistical authority designated by the Commission to develop, produce and disseminate European statistics (EC Regulation No. 223/2009, OJ L 87/164, 31.03.2009)
FATF-GAFI	Financial Action Task Force (Le Groupe d'Action Financière)
FI	Financial institutions
FIU	Financial intelligence unit
FTE	Full-time equivalent
GDP	Gross domestic product
HMRC	Her Majesty's Revenue and Customs
Implementing Directive	Commission Directive 2006/70/EC laying down implementing measures for Directive 2005/60/EC (OJ L 214/29, 4.8.2006)
IMF	International Monetary Fund
LEA	Law enforcement authority

LPP	Legal (professional) privilege
MER	Mutual evaluation report
ML	Money laundering
MLA	Mutual legal assistance
MLRO	Money Laundering Reporting Officer
MoF	Ministry of Finance
MoJ	Ministry of Justice
MoI	Ministry of Interior
MONEYVAL	Committee of Experts on the Evaluation on Anti-Money Laundering Measures and the Financing of Terrorism
MOU	Memorandum of understanding
MS	Member States
OCTA	Organized crime threat assessment
PEP	Politically exposed person
PPO	Public Prosecution's Office/Public Prosecutors' Office
RE	Reporting entities
SAR	Suspicious activity reports
SOCTA	Serious and organized crime threat assessment
STR	Suspicious transaction report
TSCP	Trust and company service providers
TF	Financing of terrorism
TFEU	Treaty on the Functioning of the European Union
Third Directive	Directive 2005/60/EC of the European Parliament and of the Council on the prevention of the use of the financial system for the purpose of money laundering and terrorist financing (OJ L 309/15, 25.11.2005)
UBO	Ultimate beneficial owner
UNODC	UN Office on Drugs and Crime
UTR	Unusual transaction report

1. Introduction and operationalization

Brigitte Unger

1.1 INTRODUCTION

How effective is anti-money laundering policy and is it worth the money spent? This book aims at giving an overview and evaluation of the economic and legal effectiveness of anti-money laundering policies in the 27 EU Member States.

It is based on the ECOLEF project, a more than 500-page study on the legal and economic effectiveness of anti-money laundering and combating terrorist financing policy in the 27 EU Member States. This EU Action Grant project was commissioned by the EU DG Home Affairs. The project has taken from December 2009 until December 2012. An interdisciplinary team of administrative and criminal law experts, economists, and criminologists, mostly located at Utrecht University, the Netherlands, guaranteed both diversity of disciplines and a homogeneous team of researchers to compare the countries in an identical way.

This book aims to give a compact overview of the major threats, hindrances, and positive examples of a successful anti-money laundering policy in the EU Member States from **both** a legal and an economic perspective. Given the still meagre results on combating terrorist financing (most countries still have had no convictions for terrorists and law enforcement takes place mainly in secret service-like organizations to which we did not have access), we do not treat terrorist financing in this book.

Member States differ in the degree to which they are threatened by money laundering – some with big financial centres like the UK or the Netherlands are gateways for laundering money, whereas others, like the Southern Member States, have a large cash economy and attract cash-intense forms of laundering.

Member States also differ in the way in which they respond to this threat. Policy responses to laundering activities can range from the implementation of the Third (and soon to be Fourth) EU Directive on anti-money laundering and combating terrorist financing to the criminalization of money laundering, the enforcement of preventive policy and prosecution and, ultimately, the conviction of launderers.

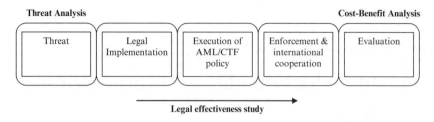

Figure 1.1   Building blocks of the ECOLEF Study

Our study comprises five steps of anti-money laundering policy, starting with the threat of laundering, followed by the implementation of the EU Directive, the execution of the Directive, enforcement and international cooperation up to the conviction of launderers. It ends with a cost-benefit analysis of the entire policy. Is anti-money laundering policy worth the effort and money?

1.2   EFFECTIVENESS STUDY

Many hindrances can appear in the long process between drafting the law and finally convicting launderers, potentially affecting the effectiveness of anti-money laundering policy.

Questions relevant for the legal effectiveness study are the following: how well does the EU Directive fit into the national legal system? Which authority in the Member State is responsible for implementing the Third Directive? (On implementation, see Chapter 4.) How and where is money laundering defined? What is the scope of predicate offences? (On criminalization, see Chapter 6.) Which customer due diligence measures are in place? How are the FIUs working? Which reporting obligations exist? (On the execution of preventive measures, see Chapter 3.) Which supervisors exist? What are their supervising and sanctioning powers? (On supervision, see Chapter 5.) What is the number of suspicious (or unusual) transaction (or activity) reports? What is the number of prosecutions and convictions? (On repressive enforcement, see Chapter 8.) How well does international cooperation work? Is money laundering an extraditable offence in the country? What possibilities exist for information exchange, how often is it used, how well does it work? What is the role of feedback in achieving compliance with law enforcement, the FIUs and the private sector? (For FIUs and international cooperation, see Chapters 7 and 9 respectively.)

In order to be able to identify best practices among Member States' policies in combating money laundering, we have gathered information as to how, from a legal, economic and practical perspective, this anti-money laundering and combating terrorist financing policy works in each Member State.

As a starting point we prepared a working document consisting of 201 questions to be answered for each Member State, covering the whole anti-money laundering policy process from facing a laundering threat and drafting laws against money laundering to the conviction of launderers.

In order to answer these 201 questions per country, as a first step we studied publicly available information from, inter alia, the Financial Action Task Force (FATF) and MONEYVAL Mutual Evaluation Reports, from the Annual Reports of FIUs and from national legislation for each country. This desk study was used to identify missing information which could only be obtained from the Member States themselves. Those questions that could not be answered with publicly available information were put into online surveys that were directed to relevant actors in combating money laundering at the national level. For this purpose, we created and circulated five online surveys, one for each type of institution important for AML/CTF policy: Ministry, FIU, Public Prosecutor, Supervisor and Obliged Entities (see ECOLEF Report, Annex 1.1). For further clarification we also travelled to the Member States and conducted over a hundred, mostly face-to-face, interviews with officials in these key agencies (see ECOLEF Report, Annex 1.2).

After carrying out desk studies, online surveys and face-to-face interviews in the countries, we organized four regional workshops. We chose, as far as possible, to focus on regional groupings of Member States, since the available evidence shows that most AML/CTF interaction – and indeed most money laundering – takes place between neighbouring countries. We invited financial intelligence units (FIUs), Ministry and Public Prosecution Office (PPO) representatives from all EU Member States. The results were presented at a final dissemination conference in December 2012 in Amsterdam where Member States had the opportunity to comment on our findings. This book includes their suggested revisions.

Some restrictions we faced concern the availability of data. In several parts of our study we criticize the lack of quality in the data and the fact that the data are not comparable across countries (e.g. the number of reports). We nevertheless use these data in the empirical part of the study, though we are aware of the fragile database. However, we make some suggestions for data improvement and managed to improve some of the EUROSTAT statistics on anti-money laundering policy.[1] We did not deal

---

[1] EUROSTAT (2010).

with matters of asset confiscation, an important part of fighting financial crime, since data collection is being carried out by the Asset Recovery Organization Working Group of the EU DG Home. A final restriction is that the last part of the anti-money laundering policy chain, namely judges and the courts, could not be studied. The link between public prosecution and judges would be worth investigating in a separate study, since even if the whole anti-money laundering policy chain fits perfectly but ends up reaching a judge who does not convict, all efforts would be deprived of success.

1.3   OPERATIONALIZATION OF LEGAL AND ECONOMIC EFFECTIVENESS IN THE ECOLEF STUDY

The AML/CTF policy responses of the Member States are studied from the perspective of the legal and economic effectiveness of the AML/CTF policies of the European Member States. Figure 1.2 shows how legal and

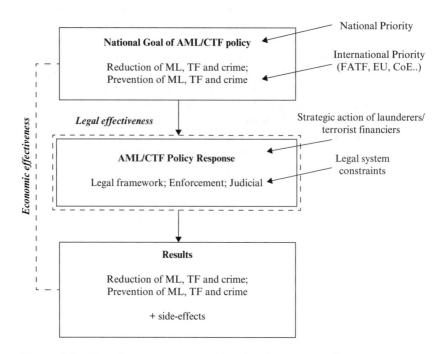

Figure 1.2   Visual representation of legal and economic effectiveness

economic effectiveness relate to each other. We then explain these concepts briefly and how we will operationalize the two.

1.4   ECONOMIC EFFECTIVENESS

In our study, the economic effectiveness of AML policy means that the goals of the AML policy – which can be the reduction and prevention of money laundering, or crime in general – are reached by producing results. Such results can be less money laundering or crime in general, as well as the prevention of money laundering or crime in general. The goals of AML policy may be more or less important in the Member States, depending on international and national priorities. Some countries might make money laundering policy a national goal because international organizations such as the FATF push it, for others it might be a domestic necessity in order to maintain the reputation of financial markets (see first box and arrows in Figure 1.2). In order to reach the goals, all kinds of policy responses are used. The legal framework, law enforcement, the judiciary all have to respond to the national anti-money laundering policy goal. This can be done more or less effectively (see section on legal effectiveness below, and the middle box in Figure 1.2). The results of this policy may be a reduction in laundering or crime, or the prevention of money laundering and future crime. Also side-effects can occur which have been unplanned (see the third box in Figure 1.2). Achieving the results of a policy goal we call economic effectiveness. When the goals are reached with the lowest costs possible, we speak of economic efficiency instead of effectiveness. Chapters 10 and 11 discuss different statistics which could indicate economic effectiveness as well as efficiency. In this study, we test for economic efficiency in Chapter 12. This chapter contains a cost-benefit analysis of Member States' AML/CTF policies using data concerning their AML/CTF policy responses.

1.5   LEGAL EFFECTIVENESS

In the present research, legal effectiveness is understood as follows. First, a policy is legally effective when the norms are applied and obeyed. Legal effectiveness is understood narrowly and as a functionality: if a rule is in force (and applied/obeyed), it functions and therefore a norm is effective.[2]

---

[2]   Navarro and Moreso (1997); Addink (2010); Addink et al. (2010), pp. 80–95.

An important element is the meaningfulness of the norms. Legal norms must be meaningful; they should contribute to the goals of the AML/CTF policy.

In general, the main goals[3] of the AML/CTF policy are:

- the prevention of money laundering and terrorist financing and crime in general – by developing systems that make it difficult for potential launderers and financiers of terrorism to actually launder or finance terrorism – and
- the reduction of money laundering, terrorist financing or crime in general.

If a particular norm is not considered meaningful by those who should comply with or enforce it, it is highly likely that the norm will not be applied (in full) or adhered to.

Second, a broader and more qualitative view of legal effectiveness allows us to go beyond the mere question of non-application of or non-adherence to the norms. On this view, a policy is legally effective when there are neither legal hindrances that make reaching the goal more difficult, nor other factors with legal consequences that negatively influence the application of the law.[4] Such legal hindrances might be that the norms conflict within a policy or that norms conflict with norms belonging to another policy at the same level ('horizontal' conflicts) or that the norms conflict with norms set at a different level, for example the international or European level ('vertical' conflicts). One can also think of gaps in legislation or where legislation provides insufficient powers to the authorities that should ultimately enforce the norms. Factors that negatively influence the application of the law include institutional factors; insufficient resources in obliged institutions, FIUs or supervisors in terms of capacity, money and organization to comply with or enforce the legal norms in place; insufficient awareness or support in obliged institutions to comply with the legal norms, and insufficient de facto cooperation between supervisors or between obliged institutions and supervisors. This framework of legal effectiveness allows us to look at Member States' law in the books, as well as whether the law is actually applied ('law in action').

---

[3]   Although, as is made clear in Section 1.4 the goals may be more or less important in the Member States, depending on international and national priorities.

[4]   Stouten (2012), pp. 22 et seq.

1.6 REMARKS CONCERNING THE OPERATIONALIZATION

In discussing the effectiveness of AML/CTF policies, we have focused on what we found to be interesting and relevant for this purpose. In this sense, we have built on what has been done before – sometimes by correcting other work, if it was fundamental to our research and otherwise by elaborating on the core message and expanding its field of application – and we have tried to refer to all other relevant research that we do not specifically target in this work. In this report, we have built on the substantive work of the FATF, MONEYVAL, and the reports of the EU-FIU Platform, the papers of the IMF, the reports of EUROSTAT and the reports of the Egmont Group. We have also made use of the annual reports of the EU FIUs and of the reports commissioned by the EU.

Next to this, there is a large body of literature upon which we have not built, which we have not discussed and yet which is, nevertheless, undoubtedly important in the AML/CTF context. There are several reasons why we have not done so. First of all, other research groups and professionals have already targeted the subject, and, in our view, have done consistent research which, given the time and resources we had available, we could not improve on. Just to name a few, in the matters of asset freezing and confiscation – the work of the national Asset Recovery Offices and of the CARIN group is substantive. We have also left aside matters of mutual legal assistance in judicial matters (including extradition) as the latter are taken up to a great extent by EuroJust and by the European Judicial Network.

1.7 CROSS-COUNTRY COMPARABILITY

The aim of the present study is to compare economic and legal effectiveness on a cross-country or cross-model basis in order to establish their levels of effectiveness. This is done with respect to various aspects from each of the building blocks shown in Figure 1.1, for example implementation delays, supervisory models, money laundering definitions (as applied in practice), models of information flows and types of FIUs.

However, sometimes a cross-country comparison cannot be made. This is particularly the case for the substantive norms in the preventive AML/CTF policy. The non-comparability of (legal) effectiveness in this area is the result of two important factors. First, there is a significant data asymmetry between the Member States. For some Member States there is a lot more information available than for other Member States. Additionally, the data sets available suffer from a time lapse. Some information on Member States is more outdated than for other Member States. This is especially the case for data obtained from FATF Third Mutual Evaluation Reports and MONEYVAL Reports on Fourth Assessment Visits. While some Member States were last assessed in full in 2006, other countries were assessed as recently as last year. Moreover, this study progressed in groups of countries. Therefore, interviews with Member States' representatives were held at different times over a period of 1.5 years. Second, comparability between Member States is made difficult due to the fact that the legal hindrances identified differ in importance – such that a mere quantitative calculation would not reflect reality – and that the importance that must be attached to it depends on the country-specific context. As to the weight that must be given to the legal hindrances identified, we believe, for example, that gaps in the scope of coverage of obliged institutions are more detrimental to the effectiveness than the fact that the requirement that third parties from third countries on which reliance is placed must be subject to a mandatory registration system and supervision is not implemented in legislation. Where cross-comparability appears impossible, we provide an overview of the state of affairs within the Member States.

In the following, the book includes a threat analysis (Chapter 2), a study on the implementation of AML policy (Chapters 3 and 4), the execution of this policy (Chapters 6 and 7) and its administrative and repressive enforcement (Chapters 5 and 8), including issues of international cooperation (Chapter 9). In addition, we have attempted to improve the statistics on anti-money laundering policy as initiated by EUROSTAT (Chapter 10) and to do initial calculations for the costs and benefits of anti-money laundering policy (Chapter 12). In Chapter 11 we measure the effectiveness of anti-money laundering policy in the 27 EU Member States. We draw all these together in a concluding chapter, where we also summarize the results (Chapter 13).

2. Threat of money laundering

Brigitte Unger and Joras Ferwerda

2.1 THREAT OF MONEY LAUNDERING

How much is a country threatened by launderers who aim to launder the proceeds of their crime? Which countries are particularly attractive to launderers? Evidently, if, theoretically speaking, a country was not threatened by launderers at all, it would not have to have an anti-money laundering policy. And if one country is threatened more than another country, it will have to make more anti-money laundering policy efforts than a country which is threatened less.

The threat can stem from different sources. First, there might be a significant amount of domestic crime which gives rise to proceeds of crime that criminals want to launder in the very same country. Second, there might be little crime in the country itself, but large amounts of proceeds of crime from other countries that this country attracts. These might be other EU countries or countries outside the EU. Third, the country might only be a through flow for illegal proceeds, so that neither the incoming nor the outgoing flows of money stem from the original crime country. Fourth, the threat might not stem from the financial side but from the fact that criminals permanently park their money by investing it in business and real estate. The threat might also stem from different types of crime. Some countries are more threatened by business and tax fraud, others by financial crime, others by drug smuggling, human trafficking or the proliferation of weapons and again others by corruption. The proceeds of these crimes might be laundered in different ways, using different channels and modes of laundering.

In order to assess the money laundering threat that countries face, one has to find a methodology for how to define and measure threat.

In this chapter, four methodologies will be presented. First, OCTA, the threat analysis of Europol's EU (Serious and) Organized Crime Threat Assessments (annual – most recently, April 2012). Since March 2013 the report has been called SOCTA (March 2013). Second, the International Monetary Fund (IMF) method, which was developed by Steve Dawe in parallel with our own methodology. Third, the threat analysis of Walker, which is a modification of the original Walker gravity model. Fourth, the threat analysis of Jakub Brettl, one of our students at Utrecht University, who developed independently another threat analysis in a seminar paper. In a final step, we will analyse how robust these methods are. How far will country threat assessments change if one applies a different method? How sensitive are the rankings of countries' money laundering threat to the chosen method?

2.2   OCTA AND SOCTA THREAT ASSESSMENT

Between 2006 and 2011, the EU Organized Crime Threat Assessment (OCTA) was carried out by Europol. It is the oldest threat assessment undertaken for the European Union. Academically, it was centred on Professor Michael Levi and the Cardiff School of Social Sciences, at Cardiff University in the UK. In 2013, Europol started a new cycle. The EU Serious and Organized Crime Threat Assessment (SOCTA 2012; see Europol SOCTA March 2013) developed in 2011 and 2012 using a new methodology. The SOCTA 2012 Report delivers a set of recommendations based on an in-depth analysis of the major crime threats facing the EU. The Council of Justice and Home Affairs Ministers will use these recommendations to define priorities for the coming four years. (See SOCTA 2012 Rob Wainwright, Director of Europol.)

The SOCTA Report for 2012 lists key threats on which European policy should focus. Money laundering is only one of them, the rest of the list comprising some predicate crimes for laundering: illegal immigration, human trafficking, counterfeiting goods with an impact on public health and safety, missing trader intra-community fraud, synthetic drugs and cybercrime. As emerging threats, the report lists illicit waste trafficking and energy fraud.

Annex 1 of the report lists the methodology used. The SOCTA is based on data from law enforcement agencies and open sources. Law enforcement data include data available within Europol, data obtained from Member States (MS) via questionnaires, and data obtained from third organizations and countries. The new methodology is developed by a multi-country team, including Dr Xavier Raufer (International Centre for the Study of Terrorism, Paris, France), Professor Dr Arndt Sinn (Zentrum für Europäische und Internationale Strafrechtsstudien (ZEIS)), University of Osnabrueck, Germany) and emeritus Professor Max Taylor, (Cork University, Ireland).

Both the OCTA and its follower SOCTA are qualitative assessments.

Experts developed criteria in order to classify threats into high, medium and low and in order to develop policy recommendations on which crimes policy should focus. The fact that the report lists money laundering as a crime, alongside a list of other sorts of predicate crimes for laundering, shows that this report focuses on the underlying crimes more than on the financial aspects of laundering. In order to assess money laundering threats, the proceeds of crime, the potential money involved and the threats that these amounts of money might pose to countries have to be evaluated. This requires a quantitative analysis, which OCTA and SOCTA – owing to their different purpose of making law enforcement alert to particular crimes – do not provide.

2.3 THE IMF THREAT ANALYSIS

The IMF report by Dawe and Fleming (2009) fills these gaps. It was developed especially to evaluate money laundering risks and also aims at quantitative analysis. It conducts a risk analysis and distinguishes between threat, vulnerability and consequence. Threat (T) is defined as the likelihood that money laundering will be attempted. Vulnerability (V) is the likelihood that money laundering will be successful. And consequence (C) is the likely impact that successful laundering will have on objectives.

The money laundering Risk = Threat times Vulnerability times Consequences.

For example if a drug dealer buys a crate of beer, the threat T is high (most likely the money stems from dealing with drugs), and vulnerability is also high, since the attempt will most likely be successful. So, as T times V is almost 100%, we can be sure that the drug dealer who buys a beer is successfully laundering unnoticed. However, the consequences – the impact – of this are very low, almost zero. So, in total, the risk, which is T times V times C, is almost zero and therefore negligible. In contrast, if a terrorist with a low chance of success launders money, and the consequences (a city being blown up) are very high, the risk can be very high. For this reason, the IMF emphasizes the interaction of three variables, threat, vulnerability and consequences, as being important for the money laundering risk. In addition, the IMF classifies three high-level risk events: first, that money laundering is attempted. Second, that, if attempted, the perpetrator is not caught. And third, that the perpetrator is caught, but not sanctioned adequately. The IMF attributes scores to the indicators and classifies risks between 1 and 7.

The IMF carried out threat assessments for different regions in the world, but not for the EU, so no rankings are available so far for the countries we are concerned with. However, it is not unlikely that this methodology will be used in the future for threat assessments in the whole world; the IMF's staff capacity would allow for the establishment, maintainance and updating of the large amount of data needed for such a worldwide assessment of threat on several hundred variables. This is why we have presented it here.

2.4   THE ECOLEF THREAT ASSESSMENT

While the IMF emphasized the importance of the consequences of a money laundering act (does it destabilize the economy or blow up a tunnel?), the ECOLEF study focused on anti-money laundering policy responses to the money laundering threat (do the authorities adequately monitor and prosecute laundering acts in order to scare off launderers?). The 'threat' posed by money laundering represents the demand for money laundering services, according to the IMF. For the ECOLEF project, we have chosen to interpret this as the amount of money that *could, or might*, be laundered in a country, if there were no barriers to laundering, and there was no 'more attractive' place for the launderer to launder the money.

For the threat assessment, John Walker – who was part of the ECOLEF team – first estimated the proceeds of crime generated in each country in the world in order to arrive at the total global proceeds of crime that form the potential for worldwide laundering. For the precise method, the percentage of criminal proceeds that are laundered per type of crime, and the types of crime taken into consideration, see Walker (1995), Walker and Unger (2010) and ECOLEF (2013, chapter 2). These calculations showed that there are considerable amounts of money generated from crime in EU countries that could pose a money laundering threat. Even greater amounts are generated in other regions of the world, which could, in principle, also be laundered in EU countries. But it is also unrealistic to say that the laundered part of the proceeds of crime could be laundered *anywhere* in the world. Money launderers are economic actors, and (even if they do not follow the criminal law) they follow the laws of economics, which dictate that they should maximize profits and minimize risks.

The Walker model assumes that it is the specific features of a country that make it attractive for money laundering. High gross domestic product (GDP), well-established financial markets and good financial services, and the absence of bank secrecy are important attraction factors. Trade relations, open opportunities for business but for launderers as well, distance from the home country, sharing the same language, historic bonds such as former colonialism, sharing the same religion are some more features which attract launderers.

These characteristics of countries are, as shown by Walker and Unger (2009), likely to be reflected in money laundering flows, and can be modelled using a 'gravity model' formulation. In the gravity model we used, 'distance' between countries was broadly defined, including both physical distance, which can act as a deterrent to trade, but also social or cultural factors that influence distance. Factors such as sharing a common language and colonial links can reduce 'distance'. 'Two countries that speak the same language will trade twice to three times as much as pairs that do not share a common language. Trade is about 65% higher if countries share the same border than if they do not have a common border'.[1] And money launderers may take into account that richer countries tend to trade more. Richer countries attract more money laundering funds from poorer countries.[2] Furthermore, countries with big financial centres which provide good financial service and advice will attract more legal and illegal funds than countries without this financial expertise.

Money launderers are therefore more likely to launder the money either domestically, where they are best placed to know the risks, or in a neighbouring country, or in a country with some shared characteristic such as trade or a common language or culture. We do not know, a priori, if the secrecy surrounding money laundering transactions results in factors such as common language or culture becoming even more important in determining where the transaction takes place, but it is a real possibility.

We used a modified Walker-style gravity-type model to express those factors, such as distance, trade, language etc., that make some countries more attractive for laundering activities than others, and produced estimates of the potential money that *might* be laundered in each EU country as an indicator for threat.

$$\text{Total Threat}_i = \sum_{ij} \frac{\text{Total Money Generated for Laundering}_j}{\text{Distance}_{ij}}$$

By setting distance equal to 1, all of the money generated for laundering in country *i* is part of the money laundering threat to country *i*. By setting distance equal to 1, for all countries, *j*, which share common borders with

---

[1]   Head (2003); Helliwell (2000).
[2]   Walker (1995).

country *i*, we also include the money generated for laundering in all neighbouring countries as part of the threat to country *i*.

The threat posed by other countries is determined by the distance D_{ij}, which, for all other countries, is calculated from the geographic distance between the countries' key financial centres, and may be reduced by some proportion if:

- a significant percentage of exports from country *i* goes to country *j*;
- countries *i* and *j* share a common language;
- countries *i* and *j* share a common religion (proxy for culture);
- the GDP per capita in country *j* exceeds that of country *i*,
- country *j*'s financial services exports, as a percentage of GDP, exceed those of country *i*.

For all other countries, *j*, the weights we used for distance reduction through economic, cultural and social factors can be seen in ECOLEF (2013, chapter 2).

Figures 2.1 and 2.2 show the estimates of threat obtained for the 27 EU countries. We distinguish between threat in absolute amounts, with large countries usually facing larger potential amounts of illegal money that might be laundered through them, and threat in relative terms. The latter shows the threat in relation to the size (GDP) of the country: a small country which faces a modest amount of laundering money but which exceeds its own (even more modest) GDP will feel (and be) more threatened than a large country which faces the same amount of illegal money. The 27 EU countries are ranked according to the threat they face – in terms of total monetary values in million Euros and in relative terms as a percentage of GDP.

With regard to absolute amounts, the most threatened countries that have to cope with and to protect themselves from large potential amounts of laundered money are the UK, which has to prevent 284 billion Euros of laundering money, followed by five founding members of the European Union: France, Belgium, Germany, Netherlands, and Luxembourg. It is rich countries with large financial centres that attract launderers most. The lowest threat is faced by Malta, amounting to 8 billion Euros. As the map in Figure 2.1 shows, it is the west of Europe which is threatened most in absolute terms of money for laundering. The figure makes sense in view of their relatively sophisticated financial markets, their relatively high GDP per capita levels, and their proximity and trade, language and cultural links to a wide range of proceeds from crime generating countries. Hot money will generally flow from the east to the west in search of safer havens for investment.

Rank	Country	Threat (€ Million)	Rank	Country	Threat (€ Million)
1	United Kingdom	282,004	15	Portugal	43,015
2	France	151,302	16	Latvia	42,639
3	Belgium	119,896	17	Estonia	40,074
4	Germany	108,872	18	Slovenia	35,106
5	Netherlands	94,121	19	Sweden	26,206
6	Luxembourg	93,765	20	Slovakia	23,557
7	Austria	88,810	21	Hungary	19,952
8	Italy	73,910	22	Cyprus	19,090
9	Denmark	59,177	23	Bulgaria	18,513
10	Spain	56,311	24	Greece	16,598
11	Ireland	54,439	25	Romania	14,075
12	Poland	53,923	26	Lithuania	12,870
13	Czech Republic	51,193	27	Malta	8,325
14	Finland	45,104			

Figure 2.1   EU countries by estimated threat in million Euros

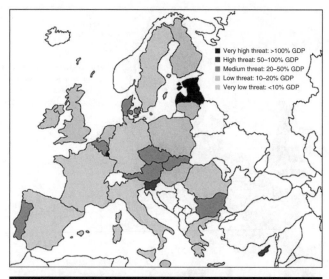

Rank	Country	Threat as % of GDP
1	Estonia	207.7%
2	Latvia	163.2%
3	Luxembourg	155.2%
4	Slovenia	75.3%
5	Cyprus	53.6%
6	Bulgaria	40.2%
7	Czech Republic	30.3%
8	Belgium	27.9%
9	Austria	24.6%
10	Portugal	21.2%
11	Slovakia	21.0%
12	Denmark	20.6%
13	Lithuania	19.5%
14	Finland	19.4%
15	Ireland	18.9%
16	Poland	14.5%
17	Netherlands	14.0%
18	United Kingdom	13.3%
19	Hungary	13.1%
20	Malta	11.0%
21	Romania	9.4%
22	France	7.3%
23	Greece	6.1%
24	Sweden	5.8%
25	Spain	5.4%
26	Italy	4.9%
27	Germany	4.7%

Figure 2.2   EU countries by estimated threat as a percentage of GDP

The picture changes dramatically, however, when corrected for country size and expressed as a percentage of each country's GDP. The threats can be very high – particularly for the smaller countries, such as Estonia, Latvia and Luxembourg. These countries, surrounded by much larger countries generating large amounts of money potentially available for laundering, face threats equivalent to a significant proportion of their total GDP, even – in the three countries mentioned – greater than their entire GDP. In a very real sense, these are the countries at most risk from money laundering, since 'money laundering has a corrosive effect on a country's economy, government, and social well-being', and 'the practice distorts business decisions, increases the risk of bank failures, takes control of economic policy away from the government, harms a country's reputation, and exposes its people to drug trafficking, smuggling, and other criminal activity'.[3]

2.5   THE BRETTL INDEX

Using threat factors from the existing criminological literature, Brettl and Usov (2010) compute a Threat Index that represents the degree of threat that a given country becomes a target for money launderers relative to other countries. Hence, threat here is not represented by the volume of criminal money that can potentially be laundered in a given country, but by the size of a computed threat index and a rank relative to other countries. Threat here is an index derived from a total of 35 different variables identified in the crime literature, ranging from criminal activities to economic and social variables. Brettl and Usov distinguish between opportunity factors such as economic factors (e.g. GDP per capita, trade) and government conditions (e.g. corruption), law enforcement and legal environment (e.g. rule of law, banking secrecy) the criminal environment (e.g. drug crime, theft, fraud) and special skills of access such as geographical proximity, language or historical experience such as colonialism (see ECOLEF (2013), annex 2.1 for a complete list).

The index is computed as follows:

$$Threat\ Index_i = \sum_{k=1}^{n} (TS_k * w_k)$$

Where the threat index equals the sum of (w) weighted Threat Scores (TS). The index assigns scores to identified variables (called threat variables)

---

[3]   McDowell and Novis (2001), at p. 6.

that contribute to threat and that are weighted according to their relative importance. Threat variables are then sorted into five different categories according to money laundering offences, as identified by Reuter and Truman (2004): drugs, bribery, blue- and white-collar crime and terrorism. Major drug traffickers, for example, face a unique problem, which is how to regularly and frequently manage large sums of money, much of it in small bills (Reuter and Truman, 2004). Clearly, such money launderers will, among others, be attracted to countries that allow for easy integration of large sums of cash into their economies. The majority of bribery and corruption occurs in poorer and undeveloped countries. The reason why corruption is distinct from white-collar crime is the fact that it mainly involves public officials. Hence, countries with, for instance, weak rule of law, banking secrecy and low GDP will be among those that are most threatened by this category of money launderers. The most significant contributors to demand for money laundering from blue-collar crime include gambling and people smuggling (Reuter and Truman, 2004). Such crimes, however, generate substantially smaller revenues than other markets (e.g. drugs). Nevertheless, a country that, for example, features a developed gambling sector will indeed be more vulnerable than others. White-collar crime is a category that includes a rather heterogeneous list of crimes such as embezzlement, fraud and tax evasion (Reuter and Truman, 2004). These offences are often closely tied to the financial sector and electronic transfers of money. Thus, countries with, for instance, developed financial systems and developed internet banking services are going to be relatively more threatened than countries without. Terrorism is distinctive owing to the fact that it takes mostly legally generated proceeds and converts them into money that is then used for illicit purposes (Reuter and Truman, 2004). Since terrorism financing usually involves somewhat smaller amounts of cash compared with other forms of money laundering, countries that have rather cash-heavy economies, with hawala or banking secrecy, will contribute to a higher threat to the given country coming from terrorist organizations.

Once the threat variables have been identified, each country is assigned a score for each variable (see ECOLEF (2013), chapter 2 for the exact scores).

Figure 2.3 shows the results of the two methods. If both rankings were identical, all countries would be on the 45 degree line. If a country is above the line, it is ranked as under more threat in the Walker assessment than in the Brettl index. If it is below the 45 degree line it is ranked higher in the Brettl index. Clearly there is a significant positive relationship between the two: countries ranked high according to one method tend to be ranked high by the other method, and vice versa. In other words, most rich Western economies are ranked by both methods as relatively the most

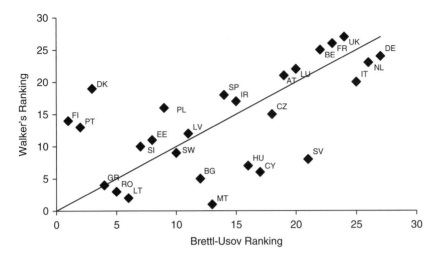

Figure 2.3 Comparing threat assessments

threatened, while the new EU Member States, with lower levels of GDP per capita, relatively small financial sectors and lower levels of trade, are ranked lower.

There are, however, also some differences. Nordic countries are ranked higher by Walker and Southern countries are ranked higher by Brettl and Usov. The reason is that Walker argues that Nordic countries have relatively high levels of crime, leading to high levels of generated proceeds of crime and thus a higher 'home-grown' threat. The reason behind low rankings in the Brettl-Usov index is that these countries feature rather small financial sectors and strong rule of law – characteristics that, in theory, should limit money laundering demand. The major difference between the two assessments is the importance of cash intensity in the economy. Brettl-Usov emphasizes cash intensity as a key driving force for threat while the Walker model emphasizes big financial centres. The larger the distance from the 45 degree line in Figure 2.3, the larger the two rankings differ. One can see that Malta is the most contested country. While it ranks lowest in the Walker model (number 27) with regard to volume of threat, it ranks number 11 in the Brettl-Usov ranking. Also countries such as Hungary, Slovakia and Cyprus appear more threatened in the Brettl index, while Denmark, Finland and Portugal appear more threatened in the Walker assessment. But apart from these minor differences, the ECOLEF threat assessment based on the Walker gravity model appears to be quite robust. It is rich Western countries that are mostly threatened by laundering, not poor or Eastern countries.

3. Harmonization of substantive norms in preventive AML policy

Melissa van den Broek*

3.1 INTRODUCTION

The preventive anti-money laundering (AML) policies of EU Member States are built on international, European and national norms. In particular, the Financial Action Task Force (FATF) Recommendations and the Third EU Directive[1] have played an important role in the harmonization of substantive norms in preventive anti-money laundering policy. Substantive norms are those norms comprising the obligations of obliged institutions and professionals in the prevention of money laundering. These are customer due diligence obligations, reporting obligations, record-keeping obligations and obligations regarding internal policies and controls.[2]

Earlier research has concluded that EU Member States have generally transposed the minimum requirements stemming from the Third EU Directive and the Implementing Directive.[3] This conclusion was confirmed by the ECOLEF study.[4] Notwithstanding the fact that Member States have implemented these substantive norms, there is considerable variation in the exact wording of these norms in the Member States.

---

* This chapter is an extended version of ECOLEF (2013), chapter 4.
[1] Directive 2005/60/EC of the European Parliament and of the Council of 26 October 2005 on the prevention of the use of the financial system for the purpose of money laundering and terrorist financing, OJ L 309/15 ('Third Directive'). The Directive is completed by Commission Directive 2006/70/EC, laying down implementing measures for Directive 2005/60/EC of the European Parliament and of the Council as regards the definition of 'politically exposed person' and the technical criteria for simplified customer due diligence procedures and for exemption on grounds of a financial activity conducted on an occasional or very limited basis, OJ L 214/29.
[2] For a short explanation, see Van den Broek and Addink (2013).
[3] Deloitte (2011), p. 285.
[4] ECOLEF (2013), pp. 62 et seq.

Section 3.2 of this chapter demonstrates this by focusing on some implementation aspects. It soon becomes clear that, although Member States have implemented the norms, these diverge considerably. The divergence also affects the legal effectiveness of Member States' preventive anti-money laundering policies. The third section of this chapter therefore deals with both general and country-specific factors that impact the legal effectiveness of Member States' preventive anti-money laundering policies.

It is important to observe the implementation aspects and the legal effectiveness of Member States' anti-money laundering policies in light of the high speed at which preventive anti-money laundering policy is currently developing. Therefore, Section 3.4 pays attention to the recent proposal for a Fourth EU Directive. This section summarizes a number of main changes that the new directive aims to bring about and relates these to some of the topics discussed in the earlier sections. Finally, the chapter ends with some concluding remarks in Section 3.5.

3.2 IMPLEMENTATION ASPECTS

This section deals with three aspects of implementation in a comparative way. These will show that EU Member States have implemented the various substantive norms, but at the same time will show the differences between the Member States. The first aspect we deal with concerns the scope of obliged institutions subject to the preventive AML/CTF obligations in the Member States. Secondly, we pay attention to the reporting obligation. Earlier studies have shown that the EU Member States have different types of reporting systems and that these are sometimes difficult to compare.[5] Thirdly, we discuss the matter of legal professional privilege in preventive anti-money laundering policy in the Member States. Although there exists quite some literature on this matter,[6] this section compares Member States regarding which professionals can apply for the legal-privilege exemption under the preventive anti-money laundering policy in the Member States, which types of exemption are in place in the Member States, and whether there is a crime-fraud exception in place.

---

[5] EUROSTAT (2010); Australian Institute of Criminology (2011), pp. 8–50 and executive summary.

[6] E.g. Komárek, J. (2008); Stouten and Tilleman (2013).

3.2.1   Extensions to the Scope of Obliged Institutions

All EU Member States have implemented the financial and credit institutions and types of designated non-financial businesses and professions (DNFBPs) as required by the Third EU Directive. However, the majority of Member States have opted for extensions to the scope of obliged institutions. These choices have been prompted for various reasons. Member States have chosen to extend the scope because of the existence of typical national financial institutions or professions or because the added categories of financial institutions or DNFBPs were considered to bear a certain risk of money laundering or terrorist financing. Sometimes the extensions were prompted by simplification purposes.

The Deloitte study showed that Bulgaria, in particular, appears to have extended the scope of application of its AML/CTF legislation to a considerable number of other institutions and professionals, among which are political parties, sports organizations, professional organizations, persons who organize public procurement orders assignments, and State and municipal authorities.[7] We analysed the most common extensions to the Third EU Directive and compiled a top ten of the most common extensions identified among EU Member States.

It appears that two extensions are most commonly made by Member States. For 11 Member States, we identified that institutions other than casinos that provide lottery, gaming and gambling activities were covered by national anti-money laundering legislation. The same number of Member States had opted for an extension to dealers of categories other than precious stones and metals, or had chosen a general extension to all dealers of goods when performing cash transactions of 15,000 Euros or more. Another extension was made by eight Member States and concerns the removal of limited activity-based scope for one or more types of legal professionals or an extension of grounds of the activity-based scope. The top ten was completed by the following extensions: postal service providers that accept or receive money or other valuables (6 MS[8]), auctioneers or specific auctioning activities (6 MS), pawnshops/pawnbrokers (6 MS), (private) bailiffs and/or court distrainers (4 MS), Foundations (4 MS), non-life insurance companies (3 Member States), and associations (3 Member States).

The reasons for the extensions are diverse. With regard to the extension of scope to institutions that provide lottery, gaming and gambling

---

[7]   Deloitte (2011), p. 31.
[8]   MS refers to 'Member States'.

activities, other than casinos – which already fall under the scope of the preventive anti-money laundering policy – the main reason was the fact that these institutions are considered to bear a certain risk of money laundering. The extensions to the category of dealers of precious stones and metals (FATF terminology) or dealers in high-value goods, such as precious stones or metals, or works of art, and auctioneers (preamble Third EU Directive terminology) were made via two methods. First, some Member States have opted to add other categories of dealers to the list. Categories that can be found explicitly in the Member States' preventive anti-money laundering legislation are gold, jewels, cars, works of art, tobacco, medicinal products, antiques, weapons, petroleum and oil (products), and items of cultural value or heritage. A second method identified is that Member States have decided to impose the preventive requirements on all dealers of goods when performing cash transactions of 15,000 Euros or more, notwithstanding the item sold. In this case, this was considered to be a strict requirement stemming from the Third EU Directive,[9] or Member States had done this for simplification purposes and not necessarily because there was a high(er) risk of money laundering or terrorist financing. With regard to the decision not to apply a limited activity-based scope for one or more types of legal professionals or where they have implemented more activity grounds for legal and fiscal service providers, a combination of arguments was present. Extensions to the grounds of the activity-based scope were often included due to a high(er) risk of money laundering and terrorist financing, while the choice not to apply a limited activity-based scope at all was often made either because of an increased risk of money laundering and terrorist financing or for simplification purposes.

3.2.2   Reporting Obligation

Regarding the reporting obligation, Article 22 of the Third EU Directive lays down the obligation to disclose suspicions of money laundering and terrorist financing to the competent authorities. All EU Member States have implemented this provision, albeit in various different ways. In order to be able to identify and capture the most important differences

---

[9]   The ECOLEF study identified interpretation differences between Member States as to whether the Third EU Directive requires to be included in the scope of *all* dealers of high-value goods, when accepting cash payments of 15,000 Euros or more, or whether the preamble provides an exhaustive list of dealers of high-value goods – albeit using the words 'such as'. Hence, Member States have implemented this category differently in their national legislation.

between the reporting systems of the Member States, we made an inventory on the basis of seven points of comparison. These points of comparison were:

- Type of report (CTR, STR, SAR, UTR, etc.);
- the substantive threshold for reporting (knowledge, suspicion, reasonable grounds for suspicion, unusualness, etc.);
- the moment of reporting (before or after the transaction, maximum time period);
- the objective threshold for reporting (amount of (cash) money involved, other objective factors);
- the definition of transaction (defined in national legislation or not);
- the coverage of attempt;
- the way in which the data is collected (one report is one transaction; one report can contain multiple transactions, etc.).

It appears that the first four points of comparison in particular provide a useful insight into the different reporting systems.[10] These are brought together for all EU Member States in Table 3.1. An analysis follows the table.

From the table it appears that, although all Member States have reporting systems in place, the extent and nature of these differs quite a lot. Regarding the types of report in place, it is interesting to observe that suspicious transaction (STRs) and currency transaction (CTRs) reports are the most commonly used types of report within the European Union. The Netherlands, Slovakia and Latvia have an unusual transaction reporting (UTR) system in place (in Latvia's case a partial system), while Cyprus, Finland, Poland, and the UK have a suspicious activity reporting (SAR) system in place (a partial system in Poland's case). Interesting also are Austria, which has a reporting obligation for credit institutions in relation to saving deposits, and Romania, which has a reporting obligation concerning cross-border transfers. This type of report is called an external transaction report (ETR).

Furthermore, one can observe that, although many Member States have STRs in place, the exact requirements differ a lot. Concerning the substantive threshold for reporting the following can be seen. For instance, while the German AML Act refers to 'knowledge', the substantive threshold is considerably lower in a large number of Member States which have

---

[10]   The full results of the comparison can be found in ECOLEF (2013), table 4.4 and online appendix 3.1.

Table 3.1   AML/CTF reporting systems in the EU

	Type of report	Substantive threshold for reporting: level of knowledge	Time of reporting	Objective threshold for reporting
AT	STR	Knowledge (insurance brokers only), suspicion or reasonable grounds to suspect	Immediately or promptly	N/A
	(C)TR	N/A	Immediately	Only for credit institutions: * the requests are submitted after 30 June 2002; * the customer's identity has not yet been ascertained for the savings deposit (i.e. savings accounts opened before 2002); * the payment is from a savings account which shows a balance of at least 1,000 Euros
BE	STR	Knowledge or suspicion, reasonable grounds to suspect	Before transaction takes place, or immediately thereafter	Only for casinos: purchase of chips amount to 10,000 Euros or more; or 2,500 Euros (when foreign currency)
BG	STR	Suspicion	Before transaction takes places, or immediately thereafter	N/A
	CTR	N/A	On a monthly basis not later than the 15th day of the month following the month of the information supplied	30,000 BGN (approx. 15,000 Euros) (cash transactions)

Table 3.1 (continued)

	Type of report	Substantive threshold for reporting: level of knowledge	Time of reporting	Objective threshold for reporting
CY	SAR	Knowledge and suspicion	Before transaction takes place, or immediately thereafter	N/A
CZ	STR	Suspicion	Without undue delay, but no later than five days after the transaction	N/A
DK	STR	Suspicion (but only reporting in case of suspicion of a criminal offence punishable by one year or more)	Immediately	N/A
EE	STR	Knowledge, suspicion or reasonable grounds to suspect	Immediately, but no later than two working days after the transaction	N/A
FI	CTR	N/A	No time frame indicated in AML Act	32,000 Euros (cash transactions)
	SAR	Suspicion. For pawnshops: 'if a transaction involves a pledge of a significant financial value'	Immediately	Customers related to a State whose AML/CTF system does not meet the international obligations in specific circumstances
	STR (suspicion)	Knowledge, suspicion or reasonable grounds to suspect	Prior to the transaction, otherwise without delay	N/A
FR	STR (system-matic)	N/A	As soon as one of the statutory criteria is established	Various objective grounds (see full table). One of which is the criterion that the identity of the customer or the beneficial owner (. . .) remains doubtful

DE	STR	Knowledge ('having established facts which permit the conclusion')	Immediately	N/A
GR	STR	Knowledge, suspicion, reasonable grounds	Promptly. However, in case of high-risk transactions, the FIU must be notified before the performance of the transactions or simultaneously	N/A
HU	STR	Suspicion, reasonable grounds to suspect	Without delay	N/A
IE	STR	Knowledge, suspicion, reasonable grounds	'As soon as practicable after acquiring that knowledge or forming that suspicion'	N/A
IT	STR	Knowledge, suspicion, reasonable grounds to suspect	Where possible before transaction, otherwise without delay	N/A
LV	UTR	N/A	In principle before the transaction, otherwise without delay	Depends on each category of obliged entities
	STR	Suspicion		N/A
LT	STR	Suspicion and unusual	Transactions must be suspended and a notification must be made to the FIU no later than within three working hours, irrespective of the amount involved	N/A
	CTR	N/A	Immediately and not later than within seven working days following its completion	15,000 Euros (cash transactions)

Table 3.1 (continued)

	Type of report	Substantive threshold for reporting: level of knowledge	Time of reporting	Objective threshold for reporting
LU	STR	Knowledge, suspicion, or reasonable grounds to suspect	Prior to the transaction; otherwise without delay	N/A
MT	STR	Knowledge, suspicion or reasonable grounds to suspect	As soon as is reasonably practicable, but not later than five working days from when the suspicion first arose	N/A
NL	UTR	Unusual	Within 14 days of establishing the unusual nature of the transaction	Depends on each category of obliged entities
PL	STR SAR	Suspicion, reasonable grounds to suspect	Immediately	N/A
	CTR	N/A	Within 14 days after the end of each calendar month	15,000 Euros (all transactions)
PT	STR	Knowledge, suspicion or reasonable grounds to suspect	Before transaction takes place, or promptly thereafter	In the case of transactions related to a jurisdiction subject to EU countermeasures, the supervisors may determine that transactions exceeding 5,000 Euros or more must be reported
RO	STR	Suspicion	Before the transaction or immediately thereafter, but no later than 24 hours after the transaction	N/A

	CTR	N/A	Within ten working days from the performing of the transactions subject to the reporting obligation	15,000 Euros (cash transactions)
	ETR	N/A	Within ten working days from the performing of the transactions subject to the reporting obligation	15,000 Euros (not limited to cash; coming from or going to accounts outside Romania)
SK	UTR	Unusual	Before the transaction takes place, otherwise without undue delay	N/A
	STR	Suspicion	Before the transaction takes place, or as soon as is practicable thereafter or immediately when the suspicion raises	N/A
SI	CTR	N/A	Immediately after the transaction is completed and not later than within three working days following its completion	30,000 Euros (cash transactions)
ES	STR	Knowledge, suspicion, reasonable grounds to suspect	Before the transaction takes place, otherwise without delay	N/A
	CTR	N/A	On a monthly basis	Depends on each category of obliged entities
SE	STR	Suspicion, reasonable grounds to suspect	Before the transaction takes place, otherwise without delay	N/A
UK	SAR (S. 327–9 POCA 2002)	Knowledge, suspicion or reasonable grounds to suspect	Before any action is taken; as appropriate consent is required	N/A

Table 3.1 (continued)

Type of report	Substantive threshold for reporting: level of knowledge	Time of reporting	Objective threshold for reporting
SAR (S. 330 POCA 2002)	Knowledge, suspicion or reasonable grounds to suspect	As soon as is practicable after the information or other matter comes to him	N/A

Notes:
AT – Austria; BE – Belgium; BG – Bulgaria; CY – Cyprus; CZ – Czech Republic; DK – Denmark; EE – Estonia; FI – Finland; FR – France; DE – Germany; GR – Greece; HU – Hungary; IE – Ireland; IT – Italy; LV – Latvia; LT – Lithuania; LU – Luxembourg; MT – Malta; NL – Netherlands; PL – Poland; PT – Portugal; RO – Romania; SK – Slovakia; SI – Slovenia; ES – Spain; SE – Sweden; UK – United Kingdom.
N/A indicates 'not applicable', e.g. in relation to the objective threshold for reporting this means that there is no threshold for reporting established by law.

As to the other points of comparison:

• Data collection with regard to transactions. A report contains one transaction in AT (CTR), BG (CTR), EE (CTR), LT (CTR), PL (STR) and RO (CTR + ETR). One report may contain several individual transactions in all other cases.
• Definition of transaction in AML Act was missing for: AT, BE, BG, CY, DK, EE, FI, FR, GR, HU, LV, LT, LU, MT, PT, RO, SK, ES, SE, UK. Definition of transaction in AML was present for: CZ, DE, IT, NL, PL, SI. Ireland uses specific definitions of transactions for professional and legal service providers, casinos and private members' clubs.
• Attempted transactions are not required to be reported in HU.

'knowledge, suspicion or reasonable grounds to suspect' as the standard. A deviating standard can be found, for example, in the Netherlands where transactions must be reported when they are to be considered 'unusual'. Some Member States also stipulate in their legislation that information that raises suspicion should come to that person's attention in the course of that person's trade, profession, business or employment. This is, for example, the case in Cyprus and Ireland.

The objective threshold of reports, usually CTRs, also varies considerably. The highest identified threshold is 32,000 Euros for cash transactions in Estonia. Poland is also worth mentioning in this respect, as it requires that all transactions, and not only cash transactions, which exceed (an equivalent of) 15,000 Euros must be reported to the FIU. Latvia, the Netherlands and Spain have a mixed approach to the reporting of cash transactions as the amount differs for each category of obliged institution. Finally, some Member States appear to have reporting systems on the basis of other objective factors. For instance, Finland has an enhanced reporting obligation for transactions with customers related to a State whose AML/CTF system does not meet the international obligations in specific circumstances. A similar possibility exists in Portuguese legislation: in the case of transactions relating to a specific jurisdiction subject to countermeasures decided by the Council of the European Union, the competent supervisors may determine that transactions exceeding 5,000 Euros must be reported. There is no evidence that use has been made of this possibility. Also French legislation contains various subjective grounds for reporting.

Finally, the moment of reporting also varies between the Member States. In various Member States obliged institutions must report before performing a transaction and, where this is not possible, immediately after the performance of the transaction. A stronger requirement applies to Consent SARs in the UK where the FIU needs to provide consent to obliged institutions performing specified future activities. In that case, reporting can only take place before the performance of the transaction. Some other Member States only require that the information is disclosed to the FIU as soon as becomes practicable after performing the transaction. Terms most commonly used are 'promptly', 'as soon as possible', 'immediately after', 'without (undue) delay', and so on. It is not common, but where Member States impose a maximum period for disclosing reports, this timescale also varies. For example, Romania has a maximum reporting time of 24 hours after the transaction took place and Estonia requires a maximum of two working days after the transaction took place.

3.2.3   Legal-Privilege Exemption

Following the case law of the European Court of Justice and subsequent Constitutional Court decisions,[11] legal professional privilege in relation to the prevention of money laundering and terrorist financing has been a heavily debated topic both among practitioners and academia.[12] The Third EU Directive sets out that Member States may decide not to apply the reporting obligation 'to notaries, independent legal professionals, auditors, external accountants and tax advisors with regard to information they receive from or obtain on one of their clients, in the course of ascertaining the legal position for their client or performing their task of defending or representing that client in, or concerning judicial proceedings, including advice on instituting or avoiding proceedings, whether such information is received or obtained before, during or after such proceedings'. In order to gain insight into the different ways of implementing this provision, one study compared Member States on the basis of the scope of professionals that can apply for the legal-privilege exemption, as well as the type of activities that fall under the legal-privilege exemption. Finally, the study verified whether there is a crime-fraud exception in the national AML/CTF legislation. The results were as follows.[13]

With regard to the scope of the application, the analysis shows that the legal-privilege exemption from the preventive anti-money laundering applies to lawyers in all Member States. Some Member States such as Bulgaria, Finland, and Spain have limited this legal-privilege exemption to lawyers only. In contrast other Member States allow the full range of legal and fiscal service providers to rely on the legal-privilege exemption. This is the case in Denmark, Greece, Italy, Malta, and Romania. Other Member States take a more nuanced approach.

As to the type of legal privilege, a distinction has to be made between the procedural exemption and the legal-advice exemption. The proce-

---

[11]   ECJ, Case C-305/05, *Ordre des barreaux francophones et germanophones and Others v Conseil des ministres*, [2007] I-5305; French Conseil d'Etat, Lecture du 10 avril 2008, Nos. 296845, 296907 (Conseil National des Barreaux et autres); Belgian Constitutional Court, 23 January 2008, No. 10/2008 (case nos. 3064 and 3065); Trybunał Konstytucyjny (Polish Constitutional Court), 2 July 2007, Judgment, 72/7/A/2007.
[12]   A small selection: Luchtman and van der Hoeven (2009); Hermelinski (2005); Komárek (2008); Stouten (2012).
[13]   The full results of the comparison can be found in ECOLEF (2013), table 4.5 and online appendix 3.2.

dural exemption means that the exemption applies to a situation where information is obtained during confidential communications made for the purpose of providing or obtaining legal advice about proposed or contemplated litigation. The legal-advice exemption concerns the situation where information is obtained during communications concerning advice matters outside the context of criminal or other court proceedings. The Third EU Directive here speaks about ascertaining the legal position of a client. There are various Member States, for example, Cyprus, Finland, Hungary, Latvia, and Poland, that have not implemented one of the two exemption grounds (explicitly) in their national AML/CTF legislation. Moreover, the ECOLEF study identified different interpretations on the procedural and legal-advice exemption grounds. One of the differences in interpretation concerns the notion of judicial proceedings. While in Spain it is stated explicitly that judicial proceedings do not include administrative proceedings, in Poland, the Netherlands, and Sweden administrative proceedings are included or there are at least discussions as to whether or not this should be included. Mediation proceedings are also a point of debate. A second example concerns the legal-advice exemption. For example, in Denmark there is a general understanding of legal advice that it includes the provision of business advice as well, while in the United Kingdom advice from a lawyer on a purely financial, operational, public relations or strategic business issue – i.e. not in the context of obtaining legal advice on related matters – is normally not privileged. Furthermore we observed that in the Netherlands the legal-advice exemption only applies to the first meeting between the professional and the client.[14] In comparison with the other Member States that have implemented the legal-advice exemption this seems a strict(er) interpretation.

The last point of comparison is the crime-fraud exception. This is essentially an 'exemption to the exemption' and it means that under normal circumstances a particular situation falls under the legal-privilege exemption, but because the professional knows or has reasons to believe that the client is abusing confidentiality for the purpose of money laundering or terrorist financing, the legal-privilege exemption no longer applies and the reporting obligation is revived. In ten Member States there is (some form of) a crime-fraud exception present in national anti-money laundering legislation: namely, Austria, Belgium, Cyprus, Czech Republic, Denmark, France, Germany, Greece, Ireland, and the United Kingdom.

Altogether the implementation of the legal-privilege exemption in the

---

[14]   See online appendix 3.2 at http://goo.gl/VZgJb3 for the full table in which this information is specified.

preventive anti-money laundering legislation of the EU Member States shows a highly diversified picture.

3.3   LEGAL EFFECTIVENESS OF MEMBER STATES' PREVENTIVE AML/CTF LEGISLATION

The divergences in the implementation of international and European anti-money laundering norms could affect the legal effectiveness of Member States' preventive anti-money laundering legislation.[15] A distinction can be made between general and country-specific factors.

We identified two general factors that negatively impact the legal effectiveness of Member States' preventive anti-money laundering policies. First, there is a divergence between the international FATF Recommendations and the EU Directive concerning the notion of equivalence as well as the (non)-allowance of full exemptions applicable in case of simplified due diligence. Second, there is the widespread presence of open norms, vague definitions and, as a result thereof, application and interpretation difficulties. Subsections 3.3.1 and 3.3.2 deal with these general factors. As regards the country-specific factors, these were mostly the result of a lack of implementation or other factual problems that hampered the application of the law. Subsection 3.3.3 provides some examples.

3.3.1   General Factor I: Divergence of FATF and EU Norms

The divergence between FATF and EU norms concerns the notion of equivalence and is best illustrated with respect to the aspects of simplified due diligence and third-party reliance.[16] With respect to simplified due diligence there is a second point of discussion, which concerns the full exemption of simplified due diligence as allowed by the Third EU Directive. This full exemption is criticized by the FATF.

Simplified Customer Due Diligence

Under the simplified due diligence regime, there are possibilities both under the FATF Recommendations and the Third EU Directive for obliged institutions to perform simplified customer due diligence (CDD)

---

[15]   Chapter 1 of this book explains how legal effectiveness has been operationalized.

[16]   Van den Broek (2011); EBA, ESMA and EIOPA (2012).

measures. One of the situations for which simplified CDD is allowed is when clients are institutions which themselves are subject to the anti-money laundering policy of another country that has an 'equivalent' standard. The fact that an institution comes from an 'equivalent third country', however, only constitutes a refutable presumption that simplified CDD suffices. This does not override the need for obliged institutions to continue to operate the risk-based approach.

Within the European Union, the equivalence is interpreted such that all Member States' anti-money laundering policies are considered equivalent automatically. This stems from the mutual recognition that all Member States apply the same minimum norms, namely those stemming from the Third EU Directive. As regards third countries, being countries that do not belong to the European Union, EU Member States have jointly concluded a Common Understanding in which they list equivalent third countries. Since June 2012 the list includes Australia, Brazil, Canada, Hong Kong, India, Japan, South Korea, Mexico, Singapore, Switzerland, South Africa, and the United States of America.[17] Third countries are considered equivalent, because they are a Member of the FATF and they have obtained a good rating score in the last country evaluations by the FATF or FATF-style bodies.[18] The Common Understanding is drafted by Member States' representatives themselves and is formally non-binding in nature. However, in practice the national equivalence lists are a copy and paste of the Common Understanding.

Although the FATF Recommendations do not contain substantive requirements on the notion of equivalence, it seems that the FATF opposes the approach taken by the Member States. With respect to the automatic acknowledgement of equivalence between EU Member States through *de jure* mutual recognition, the FATF considered that 'there is no presumption by the FATF that the treatment of all EU Member States as being equivalent is appropriate in terms of a country fulfilling the requirements of the FATF Recommendations'.[19] Regarding the fact that Member States jointly decide on which third countries can be

---

[17]   Common Understanding between Member States on third country equivalence under the Anti-Money Laundering Directive (Directive 2005/60/EC), June 2012, available at: http://ec.europa.eu/internal_market/company/docs/financial-crime/3rd-country-equivalence-list_en.pdf.

[18]   FATF (2011b), pp. 128–9: 'According to the understanding, any FATF member that receives a Partially Compliant (PC) or above on FATF Recommendations 1, 4, 5, 10, 13, 17, 23, 29, 30 and 40 and Special Recommendations II and IV is considered "equivalent"'.

[19]   FATF (2011b), p. 128.

considered equivalent, the FATF takes the position that such an approach is not consistent with the FATF Recommendations. First, the fact that countries fulfil the Recommendations cannot lead to a presumption of equivalence.[20] Second, the FATF Recommendations presume that each of the Member States has individual responsibility to assess which other countries can be considered equivalent to their own national AML/CTF policy, taking into account specific national risks on money laundering and terrorist financing. In its Mutual Evaluation on the Netherlands the FATF considered that '[t]he Dutch authorities have not undertaken an independent and autonomous risk assessment of the countries on the list, although they have participated in the joint assessment of such countries undertaken at the EU-level'.[21] The FATF came to similar conclusions in its evaluation of Germany and in follow-up reports on France, Sweden and the United Kingdom.[22] Similar considerations can also be found in the MONEYVAL Fourth Assessment Visit Report on Cyprus.[23]

In addition to the discussion concerning equivalence and simplified due diligence, the FATF also disagrees with the fact that the Third EU Directive allows a full exemption from the scope of due diligence where a customer or a certain product meets the requirements for simplified due diligence. Various Member States have implemented this provision directly into their national legislation. As various FATF and MONEYVAL reports show, the FATF considers that a full exemption to customer due diligence does not mean that obliged institutions apply reduced or simplified CDD measures as suggested by the FATF Recommendations, although some form of CDD has been performed by obliged institutions in order to establish whether the customer or product qualifies for simplified due diligence.[24]

Third-party reliance

The diverging views on equivalence also appear in the context of third-party reliance. The FATF evaluated the Netherlands as non-compliant on this point. One of the reasons for the negative evaluation is that the Dutch anti-money laundering legislation (automatically) presupposes that all EU and EEA Member States have an equivalent AML/CTF policy

---

[20]   FATF (2010e), p. 132.
[21]   FATF (2011b), p. 129.
[22]   FATF (2010e), pp. 133, 139–41; FATF (2011a), pp. 276–7; FATF (2010c), p. 10; FATF (2009a), p. 9.
[23]   MONEYVAL (2011d), p. 72.
[24]   E.g. FATF (2011b), p. 129; FATF (2007b), p. 97; FATF (2006c), p. 78; FATF (2007c), p. 88; MONEYVAL (2011a), p. 88; MONEYVAL (2012), p. 88.

and, consequently, that institutions from these countries can act as a third party.[25] Again, the FATF seems to be of the view that Member States should decide, taking into account the specific national risks, which other countries can be considered equivalent to their own national AML/CTF policy. A general presumption that EU/EEA Member States have an equivalent policy conflicts with this individual responsibility. The FATF came to similar conclusions in its follow-up reports on Denmark and the United Kingdom.[26]

Altogether, at the heart of the moot points between the EU Member States and the FATF one can find the automatic acknowledgement of equivalence between EU and EEA Member States and the allowability of a joint European approach in deciding which third countries have an equivalent AML/CTF policy compared to the 'European' policy. As the Mutual Evaluation on the Netherlands shows, a strict implementation of the Third EU Directive can lead to a (partial) negative FATF evaluation. The difference in approach by the FATF and the EU obviously lowers the legal effectiveness of Member States' AML/CTF policies, as Member States have to make a choice between the conflicting standards set at international and European level. There is a risk that EU Member States make different choices or interpret or apply norms in a different way. The ECOLEF study, therefore, concluded that it is advisable that the FATF and EU work together to solve this discrepancy and ensure that there are no tensions between the standards set at international and European level.

3.3.2 General Factor II: Open Norms, Application and Interpretation Difficulties

A second element that we identified as lowering the legal effectiveness of Member States' AML/CTF policies concerns the open definitions of ultimate beneficial ownership, politically exposed persons, trust and company service providers, and the different interpretations regarding the notion of tipping-off. The open definitions on the one hand ensure that Member States can implement the elements in their national legislation, thereby using their national terminology and systems, but on the other hand this can result in diverging interpretations and differences in the application of the norms.

With respect to diverging interpretations and difficulties in the application of norms it is important from the perspective of legal effectiveness

---

[25] FATF (2011b), pp. 152–3.
[26] FATF (2010d), p. 23; FATF (2009a), p. 10.

that the differences and difficulties do not undermine the AML/CTF policies of the Member States by creating legal gaps or loopholes or by causing hindrances in the application of the norms. There is also a risk that due to the open nature, interpretation and application difficulties, norms cannot be said to contribute to the overall objectives of the AML/CTF policy. The risk that norms are no longer applied or applied wrongly should be prevented.

UBO, PEP, TSCP

With respect to the implementation of the definitions and application difficulties that Member States face in relation to the concepts of ultimate beneficial ownership (UBO), politically exposed persons (PEP) and trust and company service providers (TSCP), we refer to studies devoted to these topics.[27] The Deloitte study points out differences in definitions, and to the lack of public reference databases in the application of norms on UBOs and PEPs. Regarding UBOs, the Joint Committee of the European Supervisory Authorities' Sub-Committee on Anti Money Laundering has expressed its concern that differences in the ways in which Member States have implemented obligations for obliged institutions to identify ultimate beneficial owners may create gaps or loopholes in the European AML/CTF policy.[28] It noted that the difference seems mostly to be the result of lack of clarity as to the minimum requirements in relation to beneficial owners.[29]

Simplified customer due diligence

There is a high risk of variations in the way in which Member States have implemented the concept of simplified customer due diligence in their respective national anti-money laundering policies. A recent report from the Joint Committee of the European Supervisory Authorities' Sub-Committee on Anti Money Laundering concluded that Member States have adopted different approaches with regard to the matter of simplified due diligence. The differences concern both the scope of simplified due diligence, meaning the extent to which institutions are exempt from the application of the full CDD elements, and the degree of freedom of judgement for the institutions in assessing whether simplified customer due

---

[27] Deloitte (2011), pp. 35, 50–70 (UBO), 35, 86–95 (PEP), and 219–20 (TCSP); Greenberg et al. (2010), in particular chapters 2 and 4; EBA, ESMA and EIOPA (2012).
[28] EBA, ESMA and EIOPA (2012), pp. 5–6.
[29] EBA, ESMA and EIOPA (2012), p. 6.

diligence can be applied in individual circumstances.[30] There are clearly implementation and interpretation differences, which could potentially negatively affect the Member States' AML/CTF policies.

We obtained anecdotal information from which it appeared that in order to avoid liability issues or for cost-related reasons, obliged institutions in the Member States avoid making use of simplified due diligence measures. This seems a more general issue in the Member States.[31] The key rationale of the risk-based approach is that efforts should be proportionate to the risks involved and that stakeholders need to respond to money laundering threats in ways that are proportionate to the risks involved. In other words: resources must be devoted to those areas where risks are highest. Simplified due diligence was incorporated as a means to 'ease the lives' of the obliged institutions by allowing them to devote most of their resources to high-risk situations in order to prevent money laundering and terrorist financing more effectively. The fact that there is evidence which suggests that the simplified due diligence regime is not or not fully applied because it actually adds a layer of complexity and additional costs for obliged institutions could lead to the conclusion that this is a factor which lowers the legal effectiveness of all Member States' anti-money laundering policies.

Prohibition of tipping-off
The prohibition of disclosure, or tipping-off, is a norm that aims to prevent obliged institutions from informing their clients or third parties about the fact that they have disclosed a suspicion report or any information in relation to the report to the competent authorities or that an investigation is being, or will be, performed on the client and the transaction. The rationale is simple: if a client becomes aware of the fact that he is suspected by the institution of money laundering or terrorist financing, the client could potentially flee or act to frustrate any further action taken by the obliged institution or competent authorities. It has been said that in practice the tipping-off prohibition interferes with the ordinary conduct of obliged institutions and that it potentially harms relationships with clients and customers. To mitigate these potential consequences, the FATF Recommendations and Article 28 of the Third EU Directive allow a number of detailed exceptions to this prohibition. At the same time, these exceptions are accompanied by some guarantees.

We discovered practices in some Member States where obliged

---

[30]   EBA, ESMA and EIOPA (2012), p. 4.
[31]   See also: Deloitte (2011), p. 84.

institutions inform each other of suspicious persons – not necessarily clients – or the possibility of suspicious transactions on a rather frequent basis. It appeared that paragraphs 4 and 5 of Article 28, in particular, are interpreted differently in the Member States. Article 28, fourth paragraph, of the Third EU Directive regulates that auditors, external accountants, tax advisors, notaries and other independent legal professionals are allowed to disclose information about suspected clients or transactions as long as they belong to the same network[32] or work within the same legal person. Therefore, in principle it is not allowed to disclose information to similar institutions or professionals outside the scope of the network. There is one exception provided by Article 28, fifth paragraph, of the Directive. This provision states that the financial institutions and professionals are allowed to disclose information to their counterparts not belonging to a conglomerate or network only in cases related to the *same customer* and the *same transaction*. Thereby, institutions or professionals must be from the same professional category and subject to equivalent obligations as regards professional secrecy and personal data protection. Furthermore the information may only be used for the purpose of the prevention of money laundering and terrorist financing.[33]

The difference in interpretation is best demonstrated by a hypothetical case.[34] The case concerns Mr X who goes to a tax advisor in a Member State. He asks for advice about a certain financial construction that he wants to use in the future. The tax advisor has reasonable grounds to suspect that this construction may be part of a larger money laundering scheme. The laundering as such has not yet taken place. The tax advisor therefore refuses to start a business relationship with this person. The tax advisor is worried that Mr X might go to other tax advisors in the region in order to obtain advice and he wants to warn them (prevent 'shopping'). It appears that in most Member States this is allowed. In some of the Member States the name of the refused client can be mentioned, while in others the name of the refused client cannot be mentioned as this would be considered tipping-off. In that situation, the person must be described by his characteristics, the advice requested and other relevant information.

---

[32] Network means the larger structure to which the person belongs and which shares common ownership, management or compliance control.

[33] EU FIU Platform (2008a), p. 14.

[34] Throughout the ECOLEF study the matter of tipping-off has been the focus of attention in individual meetings with Member States' representatives. Representatives at the Third Regional Workshop have discussed this hypothetical case in full. At the Fourth Regional Workshop representatives answered questions relating to the hypothetical case, but these have not been discussed with them.

However, a small group of Member States' representatives argued that in the underlying hypothetical case the requirements of paragraph five of Article 28 of the Directive were not fulfilled. After all, there was no client, as the tax advisor had refused to accept Mr X as his client in the first place. And in the second place, no transaction had taken place. Due to this interpretation of paragraph 5 of the Third EU Directive – as implemented in the national AML/CTF legislation, the tax advisor would not be allowed to warn his colleagues outside the network in some Member States. Theoretically the situation could become even more complicated in cases where more than one type of professional can provide the same type of service: can these professionals be considered counterparts or not? This means that, for example, Mr X could not only go to tax advisors to ask for advice about a certain financial construction, but also to accountants or lawyers.

What appears to be the case is that in one Member State the financial and fiscal service providers are more restricted than in other Member States when it comes to 'warning' other professionals about potential money launderers or suspicious transactions. Most likely this is the result of a balancing difference between, on the one hand, the objective of fighting launderers and terrorist financiers and preventing money laundering and terrorist financing in a most effective way, and on the other hand the right to privacy of the clients or persons involved. The fact that there are interpretation differences and different practices of application between the Member States concerning the prohibition of tipping-off should be considered a legal hindrance that lowers the legal effectiveness of the overall European AML/CTF policy and, hence, that of the Member States.

3.3.3 Country-specific Factors

Country-specific factors that have a negative impact on the legal effectiveness of Member States' preventive AML/CTF policies are mostly the result of a legal gap or practical hindrances to the application of the law. Almost every EU Member State faces some of these factors. We identified a wide variety of types of legal hindrance. Sometimes these are of a mere technical nature, while other legal hindrances are of a more fundamental nature. Technical hindrances are deficiencies that can be resolved relatively easily by implementing a specific provision in the AML/CTF Act legislation or secondary regulations.

Examples of identified hindrances include the fact that in Austria trust and company service providers were not fully covered under the preventive anti-money laundering policy, while in Germany the Anti-money

Laundering Act does not oblige financial institutions to provide anti-money laundering training to staff. And in the Netherlands the preventive AML/CTF Act does not contain provisions on internal controls, compliance or audit and only limited provisions on training as required by the Third EU Directive, and other legislation does not apply uniformly to all obliged institutions. Slovakia has not implemented the record-keeping obligation adequately, as the anti-money laundering legislation does not require obliged institutions to maintain records of the account files and business correspondence. Some legal issues arise in more than one Member State. One fundamental legal hindrance identified concerns the legal-privilege exemption. We found six situations where the legal-privilege exemptions went beyond what is allowed by the Third EU Directive. This is the case in Finland, France, Hungary, Latvia, Luxembourg and the Netherlands. In these Member States the applicable anti-money laundering legislation states that when lawyers (FI, FR, HU, LV, LU, NL), notaries (FR, HU, LV, NL) and other legal and fiscal service providers (LV, NL) fall under the legal-privilege exemption, 'the obligations prescribed in this (part of the) Act shall not apply' or that the 'Act does not apply'. In some situations this comes down to a full exemption of application of the AML/CTF Act to these professionals, including an exemption to perform customer due diligence and to keep records. In other situations this means an exemption from fulfilling (elements of) customer due diligence requirements. This goes beyond an exemption from the reporting obligation as allowed by the Third EU Directive. Unless there is other professional legislation that contains similar customer due diligence and record-keeping obligations, the exemptions in the AML/CTF legislation of these Member States are too broadly formulated. Finally, practical issues, such as a low level of application of CDD requirements or low reporting levels, have also been presented in a considerable group of Member States.

3.4   LOOKING TOWARDS THE FUTURE: THE FOURTH EU DIRECTIVE

On 5 February 2013 a proposal for a new directive on the prevention of the use of the financial system for the purpose of money laundering and terrorist financing was published by the European Commission.[35] The proposal was broadly steered by changes to the FATF Recommendations

---

[35]   European Commission (2013).

in February 2012 and various reports and assessments conducted by or on behalf of the European Commission. At the time of writing, the proposal is being discussed in the European Parliament. The text of the proposal may therefore change; it is important to bear this in mind.

The proposal makes changes to a wide range of aspects, including – inter alia – the risk-based approach, the inclusion of tax crimes as a predicate offence to money laundering, the definitions and obligations concerning politically exposed persons and ultimate beneficial ownership, simplified due diligence, record-keeping, internal policies and procedures. With respect to the risk-based approach, for example, the proposal shows greater focus on the use of the risk-based approach as a way to identify and mitigate money laundering risks. Article 7 of the proposal obliges Member States to conduct national risk assessments and to keep these up to date. On the matter of the prohibition of disclosure the proposal does not include any changes. In light of what has been discussed in Sections 3.2 and 3.3 of this chapter, we now turn to three selected issues: clarification with respect to obligations concerning UBOs, extensions to the scope of the Directive and the matter of simplified due diligence.

In the first place, the proposal shows that the European Commission has taken into consideration the practical difficulties in applying the PEP and UBO definitions and obligations. Section 3.3 outlined this as a general factor negatively impacting Member States' anti-money laundering policy. With respect to UBOs, the proposal now requires that the trustees of any express trust governed by their law are required to hold adequate, accurate and current information on beneficial ownership regarding the trust.[36] The information must at least include information on the identity of the settlor, of the trustee(s), of the protector (if relevant), of the beneficiaries or class of beneficiaries, and of any other natural person exercising effective control over the trust. Upon establishing a business relationship or the carrying out of a transaction, trustees are required to disclose the information to the obliged institution. With this requirement it is hoped that it provides more clarity regarding beneficial ownership information and that this takes away some practical difficulties for obliged institutions in verifying the identity of the ultimate beneficial owner. At the same time, however, it is argued that it is not clear how this will make a significant difference to the fight against financial crime and that in practice this is likely to impose significant administrative burdens on legitimate companies.[37]

---

[36] Article 30 of the proposal.
[37] Law Society of England and Wales (2013).

The second aspect concerns the scope of obliged institutions. Section 3.2.1 dealt with this matter. The proposal shows that the numbers one and two of the top ten extensions to the scope made by Member States have now been incorporated in the proposal. Article 2, first paragraph, under f of the proposal stipulates that the Directive applies to providers of gambling services. This means that institutions other than casinos, which provide gambling services, have now been brought under the scope. The voluntary convergence between Member States on this point has thus been picked up by the European Commission. The proposal also extends the application of the Directive in relation to traders of goods as it lowers the threshold to 7,500 Euros. The proposal states that the Directive shall apply to traders in goods, 'only to the extent that payments are made or received in cash in an amount of EUR 7,500 or more, whether the transaction is executed in a single operation or in several operations which appear to be linked'. In this last respect, however, the EU Directive deviates from the revised FATF Recommendations, which still uphold a threshold of 15,000 Euros for dealers in precious metals and dealers in precious stones.[38] This may (again) lead Member States to pose the question: will we opt for the standards of the FATF Recommendations or the EU Directive? As we have seen before in this chapter, from a legal effectiveness perspective this is an inconvenient situation.

In contrast, the proposal does align the revised the FATF Recommendations and the Directive in one respect. On the matter of simplified due diligence, the proposal now clearly states in Article 13 that in case of simplified due diligence no exemption applies. As shown in Section 3.3.2, the FATF found such exemption overly permissive. The re-alignment between the FATF and EU standards on this point is very welcome from a legal effectiveness perspective.

3.5   CONCLUDING REMARKS

The substantive norms in the preventive anti-money laundering policy are to a large extent harmonized within the European Union. National variations do exist but in all Member States' AML/CTF legislation the basic obligations of customer due diligence, reporting, record-keeping and internal policy are present. The differences in wording between Member States were demonstrated by the implementation aspects of extensions to

---

[38]   Recommendation 23 FATF Recommendation and the Interpretative Note thereto.

the scope of obliged institutions, the reporting obligation and the legal-privilege exemption. These aspects once again showed that Member States have generally implemented the substantive norms, although with considerable differences in the exact wording.

As a result, the preventive anti-money laundering policies of the Member States suffer from general and country-specific factors that impact the legal effectiveness of the policies in a negative way. The general factors concern the diverging norms from the FATF Recommendations and the EU Directive, as well as the existence of very general definitions, open norms and interpretation difficulties. Examples are the notions of ultimate beneficial owner, politically exposed persons, trust and company service providers and tipping-off. Furthermore, Section 3.3.3 indicated that virtually all Member States to some extent face legal hindrances, sometimes specific to a country and at other times specific to a group of countries. Sometimes the hindrances are of a mere technical nature, while other legal hindrances are of a more fundamental nature. One example concerns an overly broad legal-privilege exemption identified in six Member States. There is also evidence to suggest the existence of practical hindrances, such as a low level of awareness or application of anti-money laundering obligations by one or more types of obliged institutions in various Member States.

The proposal for a Fourth EU Directive shows that the European Commission intends a wide range of improvements to the current legal framework. It has taken on board some of the implementation aspects dealt with in Section 3.2 of this chapter. For example, while the scope of the anti-money laundering legislation has already been extended in 11 Member States to institutions, other than casinos, that provide lottery, gaming and gambling services, the proposal now also includes providers of gambling services. In terms of the diverging standards between the FATF and the EU Directive, the Directive removes the discrepancy on the matter of simplified due diligence. The proposal demonstrates that simplified due diligence is no longer a full exemption in line with the FATF Recommendations. In contrast, the proposal diverges on the inclusion of traders in goods under the scope of the Directive as it lowers the threshold for this group. From a legal effectiveness perspective this can result in an inconvenient situation for Member States.

4. Implementing international conventions and the Third EU Directive

Brigitte Unger and Melissa van den Broek

4.1 INTRODUCTION

The anti-money laundering policy of European Member States is a policy that comprises many international norms, stemming from different international organizations and the European Union. All of these international norms have to be implemented in national legislation.

This chapter deals with the implementation of international conventions in the sphere of anti-money laundering and counter-terrorist financing (AML/CTF) policies (Section 4.2), and with the implementation of the Third EU Directive (Sections 4.3–4.6). These sections will demonstrate that the implementation of international conventions and the Third EU Directive will not always be complete, adequate or on time. Section 4.7 contains some concluding remarks.

4.2 IMPLEMENTATION OF INTERNATIONAL CONVENTIONS

Especially in the light of international cooperation, the fact that Member States have not signed, ratified, or fully implemented the relevant international Conventions can be considered a factor that negatively impacts the legal effectiveness of Member States' AML/CTF policies. Relevant international conventions are the main international conventions addressing money laundering and terrorist financing besides the FATF Recommendations and the Third EU Directive, and referred to in the evaluations of the FATF and MONEYVAL. These are:

- UN Convention against Illicit Traffic in Narcotic Drugs and Psychotropic Substances 1988 (Vienna);

46

- UN Terrorist Financing Convention 1999;
- UN Convention on Transnational Organized Crime 2000 (Palermo);
- UN Convention against Corruption 2005 (Merida);
- Council of Europe (CoE) Convention on Laundering, Search, Seizure and Confiscation of the Proceeds from Crime 1990; and
- Council of Europe Convention on Laundering, Search, Seizure and Confiscation of the Proceeds from Crime 2005 (Warsaw).

Table 4.1 indicates for each Member State whether the relevant international Conventions have been signed, ratified, and fully implemented. The question of full implementation is addressed only in relation to the UN Conventions of Vienna and Palermo, and the UN Terrorist Financing Convention.

In terms of signature, Table 4.1 shows that a sizable group of Member States has yet to sign and/or ratify the Council of Europe Convention on Laundering, Search, Seizure, and Confiscation of Proceeds from Crime and on the Financing of Terrorism 2005 (Warsaw Convention). Only 12 Member States have signed and ratified the Convention. Apart from this Convention, it seems that with regard to the international Conventions there are no ratification problems in the Member States. An exception is the Czech Republic, which is reported still not to have ratified the Palermo Convention and the Merida Convention.[1] A second exception is Germany, which is reported not to have ratified the Merida Convention. The table also shows that the international Conventions have not been fully implemented in law in the majority of the Member States, with the exception of Belgium, Estonia, Ireland, Portugal, Spain and the United Kingdom. The types of implementation failures differ, varying – inter alia – from the absence of self-laundering to the fact that the financing of terrorism constitutes an incomplete predicate offence for money laundering, the lack of a strong confiscation regime, and so on.

Because they have signed and ratified all relevant international conventions and there are no deficiencies in their implementation, Belgium, Portugal and Spain are most legally effective when it comes to signing, ratifying and implementing international conventions in the field of AML/CTF policy. In order to identify the Member States that are least legally effective on this point, we applied a simple scoring

---

[1] Czech representatives have indicated that, at the time of finalizing this book, the Czech Republic is in the process of ratifying the Palermo Convention, the Merida Convention and several other Conventions. Because the ratification procedures have not yet been finalized, these developments have not been taken into account in the analysis.

Table 4.1 Principal international conventions

	UN Vienna Convention 1988			CoE Convention 1990		UN Terrorist Financing Convention 1999			UN Palermo Convention 2000			UN Merida Convention 2005		CoE Convention 2005 (Warsaw)	
	S	R	FI	S	R	S	R	FI	S	R	FI	S	R	S	R
AT	X	X		X	X	X	X		X	X	X	X	X	X	
BE	X	X	X	X	X	X	X	X	X	X	X	X	X	X	X
BG	X	X	X	X	X	X	X		X	X		X	X	X	
CY	X	X		X	X	X	X		X	X		X	X	X	X
CZ		X*		X	X	X	X		X			X			
DK	X	X	X	X	X	X	X		X	X		X	X		
EE		X**	X	X	X	X	X	X	X	X	X		X**	X	
FI	X	X		X	X	X	X		X	X		X	X	X	
FR	X	X		X	X	X	X	X	X	X		X	X	X	
DE	X	X	X	X	X	X	X	X	X	X		X			
EL	X	X	X	X	X	X	X		X	X		X	X	X	
HU	X	X		X	X	X	X		X	X		X	X	X	X
IE	X	X	X	X	X	X	X	X	X	X	X	X	X		
IT	X	X	X	X	X	X	X		X	X	X	X	X	X	

	C1	C2	C3	C4	C5	C6	C7	C8	C9	C10	C11	C12
LV		X**	▦	X	X	X	X	X	▦	X	X	■
LT		X**	▦	X	X		X**	▦	X	X	■	■
LU	X	X	▦	X	X	X	X	▦	X	X	X	X
MT		X**	X	X	X	X	X	X	▦	X	X	X
NL	X	X	X	X	X	X	X	▦	▦	X	X	X
PL	X	X	X	X	X	X	X	▦	X	X	X	X
PT	X	X	X	X	X	X	X	X	▦	X	X	X
RO		X**	▦	X	X	X	X	X	▦	X	X	X
SK		X*	▦	X	X	X	X	X	▦	X	X	X
SI		X*	▦	X	X	X	X	X	▦	X**	X	X
ES	X	X	X	X	X	X	X	X	▦	X	X	X
SE	X	X	X	X	X	X	X	X	▦	X	X	■
UK	X	X	X	X	X	X	X	X	X	X	■	■

Notes:

Black indicates that an international convention has not been signed, ratified or fully implemented. Grey indicates that there are deficiencies.

Please see online appendix 4.1 at http://goo.gl/VZgJb3.

* = through succession; ** = through accession. References can be requested from the authors. Declar just put see xxxxxations, reservations, and territorial restrictions have not been incorporated in this table. These can be found on the websites of the UN and CoE.

system.[2] The Member States that were identified as least effective were Denmark, Lithuania, Germany and the Czech Republic.[3]

4.3   LITERATURE ON THE IMPLEMENTATION OF EU DIRECTIVES

Several studies in the social sciences have analysed ways of implementing EU Directives in the EU Member States and problems that may arise. Prominent studies are by Falkner et al. (2008), Versluis (2007), Haveland and Romeijn (2007), and Boerzel (2001). Several hundred EU Directives have been studied in order to find out under which conditions Directives can be implemented smoothly (in the social sciences, these are described as being 'transposed' as opposed to 'implementation', the term used by lawyers).

These studies see several deficits in implementing EU Directives and in particular stress the difference between complying in the books and complying in practice. One important issue is the level of acceptance of Directives by the Member countries. Areas studied are food regulation, transport regulation and social policy regulation – areas in which there are a lot of conflicting interests and, therefore, potential resistance in implementation. According to these studies, an important variable for measuring 'resistance' is time delay. Opposing forces in a country will resist implementation and this will lead to delays in implementing the Directive, runs the argument.

Kaeding (2007), who studied regulation in transport, lists the following reasons for delay in implementation: the time constraints set for the implementation, whether it is a Commission or legislative Directive (the latter taking more time), problems of discretion, number of recitals, level of inter-institutional agreement and whether it is an amending or a new Directive. Apart from these more technical areas, a wide range of constitutional, legal and political factors play a role.

Variables affecting the implementation process are numerous and may

---

[2]   The ECOLEF study applied the following scoring system: signature (S) of Conventions is awarded 3 points. Ratification (R) of Conventions is awarded 2 points. Full implementation (FI) of Conventions is awarded 1 point. Full implementation is analysed only for the Vienna, the Terrorist Financing and Palermo Conventions. This means that the following scores could be given: Vienna Convention (6), CoE 1990 (5), UN Terrorist Financing Convention (6), Palermo Convention (6), Merida Convention (5) and CoE 2005 (5). The maximum score is 33 points.

[3]   BE (33), PT (33), ES (33), MT (32), NL (32), LV (31), PL (31), CY (30), HU (30), IT (30), RO (30), SK (30), SI (30), SE (30), AU (29), BG (29), FR (29), EL (29), EE (28), FI (28), IE (28), LU (28), UK (28), DK (25), LT (25), DE (24), CZ (21).

be country-based, sector-wide or policy-specific.[4] The delays are never caused by a single factor but rather by combinations of 'several constitutional, legal, political and factual factors', which should be considered in relation to the national system concerned.[5]

Berglund, Gange and van Waarden (2005) did a meta study on transposition studies and tried to filter out the most important variables for time delays presented in a large variety of such transposition studies. According to their findings, it is above all the effectiveness of governments and the rules of law which explain the timeliness of transposition of EU Directives in a variety of policy areas such as utilities and food regulation.

4.4   TIME DELAYS IN IMPLEMENTING THE THIRD EU DIRECTIVE

Anti-money laundering policy is a policy area which depends on the compliance of very many actors (governments, the executive, the judiciary, the private sector), but has no direct lobby. While the regulation of ingredients that are allowed in beer clearly affects beer brewers and helps beer drinkers, and regulation of health warnings on cigarettes clearly affects the tobacco industry and helps non-smokers, anti-money laundering regulations do not directly affect anybody. AML policy only indirectly affects the private sector, since it increases costs in the process of establishing a reporting system, in particular for the financial sector. Second, it indirectly affects notaries and lawyers, who have a reporting duty and might fear for their legal privilege, possibly leading to some resistance. AML policy does not have promoters from the private sector who push *in favour* of it. It is governments who have to implement the Directive mostly due to international pressure. It is governments who have to balance the international need for cooperation and the national pressure for low costs of reporting and other duties related to anti-money laundering policy. Anti-money laundering policy helps to prevent the abuse of the financial sector by criminals and therefore helps to maintain the reputation of banks. This in turn lowers resistance to the Directive from this group. Overall, resistance will be weaker towards anti-money laundering policy regulation compared with areas that affect health and safety or income distribution, which have clear groups within the private sector competing over regulation.

---

[4]   For a useful inventory of factors and description of theories, see Steunenberg (2004).
[5]   Steunenberg and Voermans (2006).

Nevertheless, when one looks at the process of implementation of the Third Money Laundering Directive, one notices quite substantial time delays. As Figure 4.1 shows, only Denmark, Hungary, Italy, Slovenia and the United Kingdom formally managed to implement the Directive on time, before the deadline of 15 December 2007.

As the above-mentioned studies on implementing EU Directives show, the UK is special in that it frequently implements Directives on time. Berglund et al. (2005, p. 21) explain this in terms of the political process in the UK:

> Typical for the British procedure is the early involvement of both Houses of Parliament, still during the negotiations in Brussels. Both the House of Commons and the House of Lords have committees (the Select Committee on European Legislation in the Commons and the European Union Committee in the House of Lords) that consider any EU-document still in the drafting stage, such as draft proposals submitted to the European Council of the Council of Ministers, or a draft text for a Commission directive, and form an opinion about its consequences for British policy and law. They can forward it for further investigation to one of three European Standing Committees. These can draft a resolution regarding the European document, which then are voted on the House floor. Furthermore, the Commons in 1990 and the Lords in 1999 issued resolutions forbidding the government to agree on any proposal in the Council in Brussels before their European Committees had been able to form an opinion on the issue.[6] Thus Parliament de facto binds the hands of the negotiating British minister in the Council, limiting his room for maneuver considerably. This can be seen as an expression of the great distrust of the Brits as against Brussels and its legislative activity, and as an attempt to maintain the British supremacy of parliament. The counter side is that once a directive has been enacted in Brussels, the British parliament is not only well informed about the directive and its consequences for British law and policy, but has been also committed to the result, thus facilitating swift transposition even more.

Furthermore, the British Parliament has given itself a constraint to ensure speedy decision-making. A Bill – the draft text for a law – has to get accepted and acquire 'Royal Assent' (the signature of the Queen, elevating a Bill to an Act of Parliament) in the same Parliamentary session in which it got its first reading. That is, Parliament has less than a year to discuss, modify, and accept a draft. Otherwise it has to start all over again.[7] This is a general legislative institution of the country, but it applies also to transposition, when that has to be done through an Act of Parliament.[8]

Apart from the five Member States which implemented the EU Directive

---

[6] Vervloet (2000), pp. 16–17.
[7] Vervloet (2000), p. 16.
[8] Berglund et al. (2005); Vervloet (2000), p. 16.

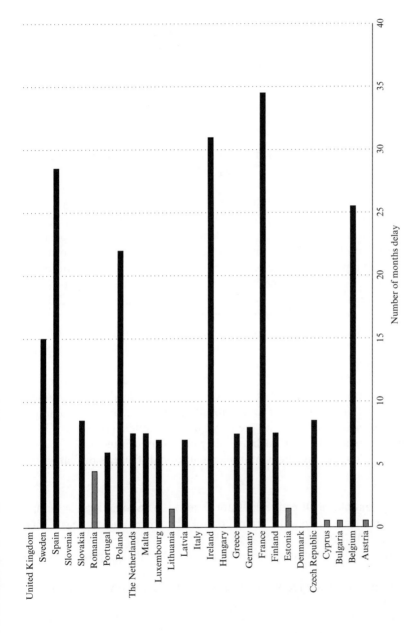

Figure 4.1   Implementation delays

on anti-money laundering policy and combating terrorism financing on time, there is quite some variation in the delays among the Member States. Countries like Austria had a minor two weeks' delay, whereas France is the last Member State to fully implement the Directive, almost three years later, with a delay of 34.5 months. In Figure 4.1, the Member States indicated in black have an implementation delay of more than one year. Member States indicated in dark grey have an implementation delay of between half a year and a year. Member States indicated in grey have an implementation delay of less than half a year.

4.5 REASONS FOR DELAY IN IMPLEMENTATION OF THE THIRD EU DIRECTIVE

Reasons given by Member States for delays in implementation were mostly domestic and varied form country to country. Kaeding (2007) classifies the following reasons for delay: the number of transposition packages, number of actors involved, number of implementation measures, political priorities and election time. We opted for a slightly different classification and grouped the reasons countries gave us for delay into four categories, namely into legal, social, political and administrative difficulties. One example of a legal difficulty mentioned was that the system of the Directive did not fit the national legal system of common law (Ireland). The UK, though also having a common law system, did not face this problem, because while the Irish constitution contemplates the law being civil or criminal in nature, the British system does accommodate administrative sanctions. Among the social difficulties mentioned was the opposition of legal professions (Belgium, France, and Poland). An example of political difficulties mentioned was that there was no government (Belgium). Other difficulties included a long parliamentary procedure (France).

There follows an inventory of implementation difficulties per category. Legal difficulties

- System of the Directive does not fit into the national legal system;
- Some legal definitions are open and, therefore, unclear (e.g. UBO, PEP, TCSP);
- Appointment of supervisory authorities for the purpose of AML/CTF policy;
- Implementation required amendments to very many different pieces of legislation;
- Opposition of legal professionals to aspects of AML/CTF policy due to legal privilege.

Social difficulties

- Role of secrecy in a Member State;
- Opposition of legal professionals to aspects of AML/CTF policy due to legal privilege;
- Low trust in supervisors to actually enforce AML/CTF policy.

Political difficulties

- Change in government (combined with constitutional law principle of discontinuance);
- Ongoing unstable political situation;
- Federal structure (competences);
- Formal responsibility of more than one authority for the implementation (division of responsibilities).

Administrative difficulties

- Extensive consultation procedures;
- Lengthy parliamentary procedures;
- Limited resources available at the authority/ies responsible for the implementation;
- Relatively high costs of compliance for small firms and one-person practices.

4.6 STATISTICAL TESTS FOR REASONS OF DELAYS IN IMPLEMENTATION OF THE THIRD EU DIRECTIVE

Apart from collecting the explanations Member States gave for implementation delays, we also tried to test whether there was a relationship between the implementation delays and the authorities formally and de facto responsible for the implementation of the Directive. Earlier research on implementation delays has shown that the need for interministerial coordination is a factor strongly associated with implementation delays.[9] Also, where responsibility for the implementation of Directives is ambiguous and not transparent, this affects the duration of implementation in

---

[9]   Bekkers et al. (1993); Haverland and Romeijn (2007); Mastenbroek (2003), at p. 378; Steunenberg (2006).

a negative way.[10] Table 4.2 illustrates for all EU Member States which authorities have been formally and de facto responsible for the implementation of the Third Money Laundering Directive.

From Table 4.2 one can see that there are many authorities in the Member States involved in the implementation processes. In 20 Member States the Ministry of Finance (MoF) is the authority with *formal* implementation responsibility, whether or not jointly with the Ministry of Justice (MoJ). In some Member States the Ministry of the Interior (MoI) (also) has full or shared responsibility. Italy seems an outlier in that its representatives have indicated that there are at least ten authorities with formal responsibility for the implementation of the Third Money Laundering Directive. With regard to the de facto involvement of authorities in the implementation process, just over half of the Member States have indicated close involvement of the Financial Intelligence Unit (FIU) in the drafting process. There is anecdotal evidence however that the extent to which the FIUs played a role in the implementation process has been different. In some Member States the FIU has been the authority that actually drafted the AML/CTF legislation, while in other Member States the FIU was only involved because it was part of or subordinate to the authority formally responsible for the implementation of the Directive. On the basis of statistical analyses, it appears that no relationship can be identified between the number and type of implementation authorities and implementation delays.[11]

We also tried to relate the implementation delays to the methods applied when implementing the Directive.[12] Two ways have been identified in which the Third Money Laundering Directive has been

---

[10]   Steunenberg and Voermans (2006), pp. 59–60.

[11]   The statistical calculations have been done using 'pairwise correlations' between implementation delays and the type and number of authorities involved in the implementation process. None of the correlations were significantly different from 0 with a 95% confidence interval. All calculation results can be requested by contacting the ECOLEF research team.

[12]   It should be pointed out that there are very many ways to implement EU Directives in national law, and that both scholars and practitioners tend to use many different terms and points of comparison to indicate the methods of implementation. Commonly heard terms are integration, segregation, reference, copy-paste, elaboration, executive implementation, implementation by primary legislation, and so on. See for an inventory of variables that play a role in the implementation method: European Parliament – DG Internal Policies of the Union (2007). See also Prechal and Van den Brink (2010). In the present research the decisive criterion is whether Member States have opted to draft entirely new legislation or have decided to build on previous legislation.

Table 4.2   Implementation authorities

	FORMAL RESPONSIBILITY				DE FACTO IMPLEMENTATION	
	MoF	MoJ	MoI	Other	FIU	Other
Austria	Yes	Yes	No	Ministry of Economy, Family and Youth	No	MoI, supervisors and more
Belgium	Yes	Yes	No	No	Yes	No
Bulgaria	Yes	No	No	No	Yes	Public Prosecutor's Office
Cyprus	No	No	No	Council of Ministers	Yes	Central Bank of Cyprus, MoF, MoFA, other supervisors and more via Advisory Authority
Czech Republic	Yes	No	No	No	Yes	No
Denmark	No	No	No	Danish Financial Services Authority	No	Danish Commerce and Companies Agency
Estonia	Yes	No	No	No	No	No
Finland	No	No	Yes	No	No	MoF, MoJ, MoFA
France	No	No	No	Ministry of Economy	No	Other Ministries through interministerial project
Germany	No	No	Yes	No	No	FMoJ, FMoF, Federal Ministry of Economy and Technology, and BaFin
Greece	Yes	Yes	No	No	No	Other Ministries, supervisors, professional associations, and judiciary
Hungary	Yes	Yes	No	No	Yes	Prosecution Service, judiciary, FIU, supervisors through Interministerial Committee
Ireland	Yes	Yes	No	Garda Síochána and Central Bank of Ireland	No	No

Table 4.2 (continued)

	FORMAL RESPONSIBILITY				DE FACTO IMPLEMENTATION	
	MoF	MoJ	MoI	Other	FIU	Other
Italy	Yes	Yes	Yes	MoFA, FIU, Law enforcement authorities, Bank of Italy, ISVAB, CONSOB and Anti-Mafia Investigation Body	Yes	No
Latvia	Yes	No	No	No	Yes	Financial and Capital Market Commission, FIU supervisors and others via Working Group
Lithuania	No	No	Yes	No	Yes	MoF, MoJ and supervisors
Luxembourg	Yes	Yes	No	No	No	No
Malta	Yes	No	No	No	Yes	No
The Netherlands	Yes	Yes	No	DNB and other supervisors	No	No
Poland	Yes	No	No	No	Yes	No
Portugal	Yes	Yes	No	No	Yes	Supervisors, MoJ, FIU and more through Interministerial Working Group
Romania	No	Yes	No	No	Yes	No
Slovakia	Yes	Yes	Yes	No	Yes	Prosecutor General's Office
Slovenia	Yes	No	No	No	Yes	No
Spain	Yes	No	No	No	Yes	MoI, Supervisors, Prosecution Service and more through Commission for the Prevention of Money Laundering and Monetary Offences
Sweden	Yes	No	No	No	No	MoJ, MoFA
United Kingdom	Yes	No	No	No	No	Home Office

implemented in national laws. The method applied by the majority of the Member States (19 out of 27) is the repeal of previous legislation and adoption of a single new AML/CTF Act to implement the provisions stemming from the Directive. Eight Member States have applied another implementation method, namely implementing the provisions of the Directive through amendments to existing legislation: Austria, Belgium, Bulgaria, France, Lithuania, Luxembourg, Poland, and Romania.[13] The method of implementation by reference, which means that the national implementation legislation makes reference to the Directive without reproducing its content in any further provision in national legislation and regulations, is not identified in any of the Member States. On the basis of a statistical analysis, it appears that no relationship can be identified between the method of implementation and the implementation delays.[14]

Since neither of these two important factors could explain implementation delays, the question remains which other factor or factors have influenced the non-timeliness of Member States in their implementation of the Third Money Laundering Directive. We have statistically analysed the implementation delays against various country characteristics – more than 30 variables in total. Variables that have been included are, for example, the population of a country, the GDP of a country, the GDP per capita, the Transparency International perception on Corruption (2010), and years of EU Membership.[15] We were able to relate the implementation delays to two variables. It appears that years of EU Membership are significantly related to the implementation delays: the longer a country has been an EU Member State, the more delay a Member State has experienced in implementing the Third Money Laundering Directive.[16] The other significant relation we found relates to the supervisory architectures[17] of Member States: Member States that can be categorized under the 'Internal model'

---

[13] See table on implementation methods at http://goo.gl/VZgJb3.

[14] The statistical analysis has been done using 'pairwise correlations' between implementation delays and the type method of implementation (new Act or amendments to existing legislation). The correlation was not significantly different from 0 with a 95% confidence interval. All calculation results can be requested by contacting the ECOLEF research team.

[15] All variables included in the statistical analysis can be requested by contacting the ECOLEF research team.

[16] The correlation value between implementation delay and year of EU Membership is -0.3963, with a P-value of 0.0407.

[17] See e.g. Lumpkin (2002); Goodhart et al. (1998); De Bos and Slagter (2008); Group of Thirty (G30) (2008). In the field of AML/CTF policy, modelling has been carried out in relation to FIUs: IMF (2004); Thony (1996).

appear to have more implementation delays than Member States that have other supervisory architectures.[18]

The fact that older Member States on average took longer to implement the EU Directive than younger Member States could be explained by path dependency. Many older Member States already had some sort of anti-money laundering policy implemented, even if it was named differently. Questions of how to deal with proceeds from stolen goods and how to deal with financial fraud were already regulated, as were the processes of enforcement and prosecution. This path dependency makes it more difficult for older than for younger member states to change laws and implement the Directive. Younger Member States might also have a greater need for anti-money laundering regulation in the absence of already existing regulation.

Apart from the statistically significant relation between age of membership and time delay of implementation, we found a second statistical explanation for time delay: the way in which Member States regulate the supervision in anti-money laundering policy. Countries with internal supervision, which means that supervision is partly delegated to professional organizations, have a longer delay than countries with other forms of supervision. One explanation might be that countries with established professional institutions to which some of the State's responsibilities have been delegated (some being a thousand years old and stemming from the medieval guilds) need more consultation before a Directive can pass. It might also indicate some resistance from certain groups, like the Bar Association of Lawyers or Notaries, who saw problems with regard to legal privilege. More empirical research is needed in order to find a statistical relationship here.

4.7   CONCLUDING REMARKS

With respect to the implementation of international conventions, it can be observed that, overall, most relevant international conventions have been signed and ratified, with the exception of the Council of Europe Convention on Laundering, Search, Seizure and Confiscation of the Proceeds from Crime 2005 (Warsaw). A considerable number of Member States have not signed and/or ratified this Convention. As regards the Vienna, Palermo and Terrorist Financing Conventions, most Member

---

[18]   The correlation value between implementation delay and the internal supervisory model is 0.4983, with a P-value of 0.0082.

States have not yet fully implemented these Conventions. Belgium, Portugal and Spain are most legally effective when it comes to signing, ratifying and implementing international conventions in the field of the AML/CTF policy.

Compared with other EU Directives, the Third EU Directive could well be transposed smoothly. The Member States considered the Directive as well prepared and expected. There were some minor problems, such as how to interpret ultimate beneficial ownership, but altogether the Third EU Directive can be seen as a smoothly implementable (transposable) Directive.

Time delays in implementation seem mainly due to domestic factors and not to external factors or factors related to the quality of the Directive itself. The number and type of implementation authorities and methods of implementation applied have not appeared to be significant in explaining the non-timeliness of some Member States. Among more than 30 explanatory variables tested, only two turned out to be significant.

- Old Member States show statistically significantly more delay than new Member States;
- Member States with internal supervisory architecture (professional associations) show statistically significantly more delay.

5. Supervisory architectures in the preventive AML policy

Melissa van den Broek*

5.1 INTRODUCTION

While it appears that the substantive norms under the preventive anti-money laundering policy have to a large extent become harmonized within the European Union, the contrary can be observed with respect to the procedural norms. On the points of supervision and sanctioning of obliged institutions, the Third EU Directive only requires Member States to ensure that obliged institutions and professionals are subject to adequate regulation and supervision. For this reason, supervisors must be provided with some minimum powers, such as compelling the production of any information that is relevant to monitoring compliance and the possibility of imposing 'effective, proportionate and dissuasive' sanctions for failure of compliance.[1]

The limited influence on procedural matters in preventive anti-money laundering policy is not surprising. European Union law is implemented, applied and enforced within the framework of the national laws of the Member States, which means that national rules of procedure apply. The power of Member States to determine the competent authorities and the procedural norms is referred to as the principle of national procedural autonomy.[2] The principle has the effect of causing differences between the Member States, because their procedures concerning the application and enforcement of European substantive norms are different.[3] In turn, these

---

* This chapter is an elaborated version of ECOLEF (2013), chapter 6.
[1] Articles 36, 37 and 39 Third EU Directive.
[2] Jans et al. (2007), pp. 40–42.
[3] The principle of procedural autonomy is limited by two preconditions, however, namely the principle of equivalence that requires that rules that govern a dispute with an EU law dimension may not be less favourable than those governing similar domestic disputes and the principle of effectiveness. This principle implies that the exercise of rights conferred by the Union legal

differences potentially create difficulties in supervision and enforcement in cross-border situations, where businesses and professionals operate in more than one Member State.[4] There are, however, changes expected with respect to norms on sanctioning. The proposal for the Fourth EU Directive contains provisions strengthening the administrative sanctioning regime. It contains a range of sanctions which Member States must make available for breaches of obligations such as customer due diligence, record-keeping, reporting and internal controls.[5] This would mean a step towards more harmonization of the sanctioning regime in preventive anti-money laundering policy.

While procedural norms have not been harmonized, EU Member States' preventive policies diverge on the matter of supervision and enforcement. None of the Member States regulates this in exactly the same manner as these systems are fashioned through a process influenced by factors like politics, culture, legal tradition, economy and finances. A patchwork of AML/CTF supervisory architectures exists in the European Union.[6] Therefore, we need to gain more insight into these different supervisory architectures.

This chapter aims to model the supervisory structures under the preventive anti-money laundering policy. The objective is to draw a more systematic approach to the different AML/CTF supervisory architectures than has been done before and to show in an abstract fashion the main commonalities and differences throughout the European Union. This helps to illuminate differences in the supervisory architectures for those stakeholders working in the AML/CTF area and contributes to a dialogue on the key matters of the prevention of money laundering and terrorist financing. Section 5.2 shows how the models are built and presents the models that can be identified on that basis. Section 5.3 shows which EU Member States belong to which model. Section 5.4 identifies potential

---

order may not be rendered virtually impossible or excessively difficult by rules of national procedural law: ECJ, Case 33/76, *Rewe* [1976] ECR-1989; ECJ, Case 45/76, *Comet* [1976] ECR-2043 and subsequent case law of the European Court of Justice.

[4] See, on the matter of allocation of supervisory responsibilities in cross-border situations, Commission Staff Working Paper on Anti-money laundering supervision of and reporting by payment institutions in various cross-border situations, SEC(2011) 1178 Final, 4 October 2011.

[5] See Section IV of the proposal on the Fourth EU Directive: European Commission (2013).

[6] Van den Broek (2010). The notion of 'supervisory architecture' used in this chapter refers to the legal norms that regulate the supervision of obliged institutions and sanctioning in case of non-compliance (enforcement).

strengths and weaknesses of the models.[7] These strengths and weaknesses are primarily based on interviews held in the context of the ECOLEF study and discussions with representatives that have taken place at various regional workshops. Where possible, other data are used as a means of illustration. Finally, Section 5.5 contains some concluding remarks.

5.2   MODELS OF AML/CTF SUPERVISORY ARCHITECTURES

The starting point for the building of the models has been the formal legislative texts of the EU Member States in the field of the prevention of money laundering and terrorist financing.[8]

Two criteria were used for the comparison.[9] The first concerns the level of concentration of AML/CTF supervision in a particular Member State. For this the total number of supervisory authorities involved in supervision of the preventive AML/CTF policy is relevant. This number is related to the end-responsibility for AML/CTF supervision, which means that this criterion concerns the question of whether end-responsibility for AML/CTF supervision is given to one supervisory authority or is shared among the total number of supervisory authorities. The second criterion concerns the nature of the supervisory authorities. The criterion is whether supervision is performed by external supervisors or by internal supervisors seen from the perspective of obliged institutions and professionals. External supervisors can be defined as those authorities that perform AML/CTF supervision but which have no direct, professional relationship with their supervisees. Often these are public administrative or government authorities. This is in contrast to internal supervisors, which are often professional associations that have a strong professional relationship with the members that they oversee. This criterion is of particular relevance to AML/CTF supervision in relation to many designated non-financial businesses and professions that fall within the ambit of the preventive AML/CTF policy.

On the basis of these two criteria, the ECOLEF study identified four

---

[7]   Dealing with 'potential' strengths and weaknesses has the consequence that these are not necessarily present.

[8]   Legislative changes that have taken place after August 2012 have not been included.

[9]   Inspiration for this modelling was drawn from financial law and regulation literature. Cf. Lumpkin (2002); Goodhart et al. (1998); De Bos and Slagter (2008); Group of Thirty (G30) (2008).

models of AML/CTF supervisory architectures: the FIU (financial intelligence unit) model, the external model, the internal model and the hybrid model.[10] The institutional models are presented and described in the following subsections.

5.2.1 The FIU Model

The first supervisory model is the FIU model. Its main characteristic is that the Financial Intelligence Unit is the national authority with end-responsibility for AML/CTF supervision. In principle FIUs are (part of) national authorities that have responsibility for receiving, analysing and disseminating financial intelligence submitted through suspicion reports by obliged institutions or persons. The institutional embedding of FIUs differs country by country.[11] Supervisory end-responsibility for verifying compliance with the preventive AML/CTF obligations is here centralized with one supervisor, namely the FIU. Where an FIU has end-responsibility for verifying compliance with AML/CTF requirements, this does not necessarily mean that no other supervisory authorities are involved at all. In practice, the involvement of other supervisors is based on legislation or secondary regulations, or occurs on the basis of agreements concluded between the FIU and other authorities. It is decisive, however, that the end-responsibility for the proper carrying out of supervision by other supervisory authorities in respect of the preventive AML/CTF policy remains with the FIU. Because of the original functions of an FIU, it does not have direct, professional relationships with any of the obliged institutions or persons. Therefore, the FIU is an external supervisor.

5.2.2 The External Model

The second model is the external model. The term external is used to indicate that there is no direct, professional relationship between the supervisory authority and the supervisees. External supervisors are

---

[10]   The names of the models are indicative only; the models themselves are wider in their content. Therefore, one needs to read the description of the models to fully understand the models.

[11]   Generally four models of FIUs can be distinguished: administrative FIU, law enforcement FIU, judicial FIU and hybrid FIU. The most important comparative elements are the institutional embedding of the FIU and of lesser importance are the functions of the FIU and the staff that works at the FIU. See Egmont (2004); IMF (2004); Thony (1996).

public administrative or government authorities. Under this model end-responsibility for AML/CTF supervision is shared among a number of external supervisors. The AML/CTF Act or regulations drafted pursuant to the legislation appoint the supervisory authorities. The main characteristic is that, in general, existing supervisory structures are used and that the authorities designated as responsible for AML/CTF supervision usually already had some supervisory tasks, possibly, but not necessarily, for this policy. Because of the nature of external supervisors there is a certain distance between the supervisors and supervisees, by which we mean that there is no direct, professional relationship.

This general outline of the model does not disregard the fact that in practice supervision and/or the sanctioning of legal or fiscal service providers can also be (partially) performed by professional associations. This is either on the basis of legislation or supervision agreements between the external supervisors and the professional associations. These agreements concern the situation that professional associations take over supervisory and/or sanctioning tasks from the external supervisor, and perform anti-money laundering supervision or sanctioning on behalf of the external supervisor or do so on a complementary basis. Under supervision agreements external supervisors can mostly perform some kind of oversight supervision on the internal supervisors, but they continue to have the right to perform supervision themselves.

5.2.3   The Internal Model

The third model is the internal model. Apart from supervision of financial and credit institutions and casinos, AML/CTF supervision is mainly performed by professional associations. The principle of this model is that where supervision can be performed by internal supervisors, these will be the designated anti-money laundering supervisors. This principle is usually prompted by national legislators' belief that professional associations are better able to perform AML/CTF supervision. Only where these associations have no jurisdiction, for example for unregistered professionals or dealers in goods, may other (external) authorities have supervisory competences. A characteristic of this model is that there are comparatively many supervisors, while each category of professionals has its own professional body. Sometimes this is even further subdivided due to specializations within the profession or because of territorial competences. Under this model, all external and internal supervisors share end-responsibility for AML/CTF supervision.

In practice this means that it will never be the case that an AML/CTF supervisory architecture is solely composed of internal supervisors.

Decisive in order to be placed under this model, however, is the extent of the presence of internal supervisors in a particular architecture. This is expressed either in scope, for the type of professionals, or in the factual number of internal supervisors.

Professional associations have close links to the professionals, because the professionals are members. In general terms professional associations have as their main objectives to further a particular profession as a whole, to protect individual professionals, as well as to protect the public interest. There is a tension in the relationship between professions and society, which has been called the 'society-profession nexus':[12] the professions' pursuit of autonomy versus society's demand for accountability. Professional ethical norms play an important role in reconciling the three objectives and are often embodied in professions' codes of ethics. Where professional associations perform anti-money laundering supervision, the AML/CTF obligations for the professionals are often (implicitly) incorporated in the professional norms or these obligations are at least referred to in these professions' codes. Also, anti-money laundering supervision mostly becomes part of broader supervision programs that concern the quality of the profession and the integrity of the professional.

5.2.4 The Hybrid Model

This model combines elements of the three models mentioned earlier. The exact combination of the models differs from country to country, but in general there seem to be two variations within the hybrid model.[13]

The first variation concerns a combination of both internal and external supervisory authorities. In relation to the internal model, the difference is the extent to which internal supervisory authorities are involved in AML/CTF supervision of designated non-financial businesses and professions. Under the hybrid model there is generally only one professional association involved in AML/CTF supervision, although many legal and fiscal service providers are members of a professional association. In Member States that apply this model, the professional association that is competent to perform AML/CTF supervision is the bar association for

---

[12] Frankel (1989).
[13] Of course, this is not to deny that in the future other forms of the hybrid model may appear.

lawyers. Other professionals are supervised by external supervisors. End-responsibility is shared among all the supervisors involved.

The second variation concerns a mixture of the three models mentioned above. Here end-responsibility for anti-money laundering supervision is shared between external and internal supervisors, and the FIU. Characteristic of this variation is the position of the FIU. It either serves as a 'default' supervisor for those professions or businesses that originally have no or a very weak supervisor or it performs anti-money laundering supervision on the entire range of obliged institutions and professions but with limitations on the scope of its supervisory activities. By this we mean that the FIU can perform AML/CTF supervision of a particular obligation only, for example the reporting obligation, and that the obliged institutions also deal with supervisors that verify compliance with the other AML/CTF obligations.

5.3   CATEGORIZATION OF MEMBER STATES

As explained, the legislative texts of the EU Member States in the field of the prevention of money laundering and terrorist financing are used to categorize the Member States.

The Member States that can be categorized in the FIU model are: Bulgaria, Czech Republic, Lithuania, Malta, Poland, Slovakia and Spain. Greece and the Netherlands are countries that belong to the external model. The Member States that can be brought under the internal model are: Austria, Belgium, France, Germany, Ireland, Latvia, Luxembourg, Portugal and the United Kingdom. As explained, there are two variations on the hybrid model. The first variation is hybrid I, for those Member States that have designated internal and external supervisors as AML/CTF supervisors. The Scandinavian Member States – Denmark, Finland and Sweden – follow this pattern. The second variation is hybrid II in which all types of supervisors are mixed: external, internal and the FIU. Member States that belong to this group are Cyprus, Estonia, Hungary, Italy, Romania, and Slovenia.

The formal supervisory architectures of the Member States look as shown in Figure 5.1.

From the figure one can observe that generally all the Eastern and Southern EU Member States include the FIU in the AML/CTF supervisory architecture, either as the authority with end-responsibility for AML/CTF supervision or as a default supervisor under the hybrid model. Exceptions to this observation are Latvia, Portugal (both internal model) and Greece (external model). By contrast, Northern and Western Member

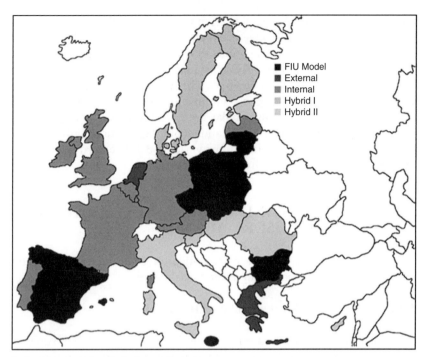

*note, colors used do not refer to a scaling value.

FIU model:	BG, CZ, ES, LT, MT, PL, SK
External:	EL, NL
Internal:	AT, BE, DE, FR, IE, LU, LV, PT, UK
Hybrid 1:	DK, FI, SE
Hybrid 2:	CY, EE, HU, IT, RO, SL

Figure 5.1   AML/CTF Supervisory Architectures in the EU

States are inclined to use existing institutions as anti-money laundering supervisors – either public administrative or government authorities alone or in combination with professional associations.

We identified three explanations for the involvement of FIUs in supervision and enforcement. A first explanation is that the FIU became involved in supervision of those obliged entities that did not have any existing supervisory authorities. This is often the case for unregulated professions in a country. A second explanation concerns the fact that in some Member States there is a low level of trust in the existing supervisors or professional associations. Therefore, these were not considered suitable by the legislator to perform AML/CTF supervision. A third explanation is the fact that the FIU, being the central authority in the fight against money laundering and terrorist financing, is considered most knowledgeable about the preventive anti-money laundering system and is therefore better able to verify non-compliance with the obligations than external (sectorial) supervisors or professional associations. This was a decisive factor in some Member States' decision to provide the FIU with end-responsibility for AML/CTF supervision or for designing a joint supervisory system with external supervisors – which can also make use of information obtained from sectorial supervision. Both the first and second explanations only apply to the involvement of the FIU under the hybrid model. The third explanation applies to both the FIU and hybrid models.

5.4 STRENGTHS AND WEAKNESSES OF THE AML/CTF SUPERVISORY MODELS

This section attempts to give a more in-depth insight into the models by presenting their potential strengths and weaknesses.

5.4.1 Strengths and Weakness of the FIU Model

As explained, the FIU has end-responsibility for AML/CTF supervision in the FIU model. It is generally competent to perform anti-money laundering supervision on all obliged institutions and professions, but it may, on the basis of legislation or supervisory agreements, such as memoranda of understanding, allow for supervision to be performed by other authorities (as well).

5.4.1.1 Strengths

Focus One of the strengths is that when the FIU is the single authority with end-responsibility for AML/CTF supervision there is a clear focus on anti-money laundering supervision. As FIUs are generally considered to exercise their tasks at the heart of the AML/CTF policy there is a significant accumulation of specific money laundering and terrorist financing knowledge in terms of trends, typologies and risks. In this way, verification of compliance with the preventive obligations receives full attention throughout the supervisory process. The situation may be different where financial regulators are competent at performing AML/CTF supervision alongside their other supervisory tasks. In that case, anti-money laundering supervision is to a large extent included in general prudential or conduct-of-business supervision programs. Professional associations also tend to include AML/CTF compliance in their broader disciplinary standards and controls. The AML/CTF obligations are in these circumstances not always (sufficiently) included in supervision.[14]

Cross-over analytical and supervisory functions of the FIU A second strong aspect is that information that FIUs gather from disclosed suspicions can help in the supervisory process. The information contained in a disclosure of suspicion of money laundering or terrorist financing can indicate the level of internal measures adopted by an obliged institution. There is a clear link between the function of the FIU as a central receiving authority of suspicions of money laundering and terrorist financing and the tasks related to supervision. Supervision can benefit from information available in the suspicious transaction report (STR) databases of FIUs. Delays in reporting, lack of cooperation with the FIU or a lack of adequate supporting documentation in the reporting process can trigger a compliance visit.[15] Various FIUs have praised the possibility of cross-checking names and data from the STR databases for supervisory purposes. The general idea is that this is allowed, unless legislation prohibits it. There is no evidence that in any Member State an FIU is prohibited from using data obtained under its analytical functions for its own supervisory purposes.

Comprehensive overview of compliance A third strong point from the model follows from the two foregoing strengths. When end-responsibility of AML/CTF supervision is centralized with an FIU there is a good and complete overview of compliance by the obliged institutions and professionals. The FIU has end-responsibility for supervision and should thus be aware of the compliance level for all obliged institutions. The compliance information is not fragmented between (too) many authorities.

5.4.1.2 Weaknesses

Resource issues A weakness is that the supervisory tasks distract FIUs from their core tasks, which are the receiving, analysing and disseminating of report suspicions on money laundering and terrorist financing.[16] As many FIUs already have quite a broad range of tasks[17] and often have

---

[14] Compare for example, FATF (2010d), pp. 14–15 and FATF (2011b), p. 211.
[15] ECOLEF (2013), p. 112.
[16] For the exact description, see Article 21, second paragraph, Third EU Directive.
[17] See Chapter 7 in this book.

limited resources available, there is also a likelihood of staff capacity
and resources problems in relation to supervision. The ECOLEF study
showed that this was mentioned in various FATF and MONEYVAL
evaluations.[18] In some Member States supervision for certain categories
of professionals was only deemed theoretical or particular categories of
professionals had never received any supervisory controls.

The tension between FIU resources devoted to supervision in terms of
number of staff and population to be (partially) supervised by FIUs can
be illustrated by a handful of examples. The Spanish FIU had ten full-time
equivalents (FTE) available for supervision in 2011, while in 2010 it had to
supervise 19,322 institutions and professionals. In Malta three FTE were
available for supervision in 2011, who were responsible for the supervision
of 900 institutions and professionals. A last example concerns the Czech
FIU, which had five FTE available for supervision in 2011, but which had
a supervisory population of 141,346 in 2012.

In order to diminish resource tensions, FIUs and legislators have been
seeking additional supervisory tools, for example by entering into supervisory agreements with financial regulators and other supervisory authorities to exercise anti-money laundering supervision on their behalf. For
Malta, MONEYVAL considered that '(. . .) in view of the arrangements
entered into by the FIAU with other supervisory authorities for on-site
visits to be carried out on its behalf by officers of the supervisory authorities, compliance monitoring for AML/CFT purposes is being conducted
by a sufficient number of officers working within the FIAU, the MFSA
and the LGA'.[19] Similar considerations can be found in the MONEYVAL
report for the Czech Republic and were also mentioned in the FATF
evaluation on Spain.[20] In Slovakia, AML/CTF supervision can also be
performed by the National Bank of Slovakia and the Ministry of Finance
and in the Czech Republic by the Czech National Bank, the Czech Trade
Inspection and some professional associations. In Bulgaria the financial
regulators should include anti-money laundering supervision in their
wider supervisory responsibilities. Resource tensions for the Polish FIU
are mitigated by the anti-money laundering legislation, which states that
supervision may also be performed by a number of other authorities.[21]
That these structures are very important is demonstrated by the annual
reports of the FIU that show that the inspections performed by other

---

[18] ECOLEF (2013), p. 112. This was reported for Bulgaria, Spain, Malta, the
Czech Republic, Poland and Slovakia.
[19] MONEYVAL (2012), p. 122.
[20] MONEYVAL (2011c), pp. 190–92; FATF (2010b), pp. 15–16.
[21] Article 21(3) of the Polish Anti-money Laundering Act.

supervisory authorities on behalf of the FIU outweigh by far the number of FIU inspections.[22]

A second supervisory tool concerns the obligation to submit annual compliance reports to the FIU. In Spain, considering that the Spanish FIU has sole end-responsibility for AML/CTF supervision but cannot perform supervision on all obliged institutions and professionals in practice, legislation requires that in principle all obliged institutions and professionals must have their internal policies assessed annually by a so-called external expert. Pursuant to Article 26 of the Spanish AML Act and secondary regulations,[23] these external experts must notify the Spanish FIU and make available their annual assessments. The board of directors or the director of the obliged institutions is obliged to adopt the necessary measures to solve identified deficiencies. The Spanish FIU may decide, on the basis of the external report, to perform an on-site inspection or to require corrective measures.[24] In Malta a similar system applies, though annual compliance reports have to be reported by the money launder-ing reporting officers (MLRO) of the obliged institutions themselves.[25] The implementing procedures introduced this obligation for MLROs.[26] These annual compliance reports assist the Maltese FIU in deciding on its supervisory activities.[27]

Lack of sectorial knowledge Another weakness the ECOLEF study identified is the fact that some sectors or professions require specialized knowledge or expertise about the sector or profession as such. For various Member States this has been the reason for establishing the bar associa-tion as the competent supervisory authority for lawyers. The argument is that bar associations are better able to balance the professional legal privilege with the reporting obligation. An FIU, which is precisely the authority to which reports must be submitted,[28] may be more biased in this respect and will not have sufficient knowledge to determine whether

---

[22]   Polish FIU (2012), pp. 25–6.
[23]   Order EHA/2444/2007.
[24]   FATF (2010b), p. 18.
[25]   MONEYVAL (2012), p. 122.
[26]   Regulation 17 Maltese AML/CTF Regulations. The Implementing Procedures are guidance drafted by the Maltese FIU pursuant to the Prevention of Money Laundering and Funding of Terrorism Regulations. The Implementing Procedures of the FIU are legally binding and sanctionable where an obliged institution does not comply with it.
[27]   See FIU Malta website: www.fiumalta.org.
[28]   If Member States have not decided to make use of indirect reporting through self-regulatory organizations (SROs): Deloitte (2011), pp. 245–6.

a particular situation is privileged or not. More importantly, privilege is already breached if the information is submitted to the FIU in the first place. For this reason, supervisory cooperation may be found with other sectorial supervisory authorities who can provide the FIU with the necessary expertise.

5.4.2 Strengths and Weaknesses of the External Model

Under the external model, responsibility for AML/CTF supervision is formally shared between public administrative and government authorities. In practice, however, internal supervisors may play an indirect role in supervising and enforcing AML/CTF obligations.

5.4.2.1 Strengths

Sectorial knowledge   Because of the fact that external supervisors often, though not necessarily, have supervisory experience with group institutions or professionals, they are knowledgeable on the specifics of the sector, the latest developments, the risks, vulnerabilities and so on. The ECOLEF study reported that this potential strength had been mentioned several times.

In the Netherlands financial regulators already had knowledge about the respective sectors and Bureau Financial Supervision too had been competent for a long time in the sphere of financial supervision of notaries and bailiffs. The Tax and Customs Authority clearly has powers in the field of taxation and revenue, although functionally the Dutch Tax and Customs Administration and Bureau Supervision Wwft (Wet ter voorkoming van Witwassen en Financiering Terrorisme) are separate. The Tax and Customs Authority, Bureau Supervision Wwft, operates independently and receives information from other divisions of the Tax and Customs Authority, but does not forward information to the other divisions. In Greece, the three financial regulators all have previous supervisory experience with their supervisees. Furthermore, the Accounting and Auditing Supervisory Commission was established in 2003. Since 2008 the Commission has had the task of performing public oversight over the accounting profession.[29] The Gambling Control Commission has also had years of supervisory experience. The General Directorate for Tax Audits of the Ministry of Economy and Finance has transferred supervisory responsibilities to local tax offices that have supervisory experience in the

---

[29]   Law 3148/2003 as amended by Law 3693/2008.

field of taxation and revenue. The Ministries of Justice and Development were also reported to have previous supervisory experience.

External supervisors more suitable for AML/CTF supervision A characteristic of this model is the fact that external supervisors do not have any direct, professional relationship with the supervisees. This leads to a certain distance between the two. Because there is no professional relationship to be maintained, the supervisor does not need to 'satisfy' the wishes of its members. As a result, a supervisory authority has a more independent position in relation to the supervisees and it can act more strictly in case of non-compliance. Another argument for reasoning that external supervision is more suitable in the fight against money laundering and terrorist financing is that fighting money laundering is a prerogative of the State. It is the State which has the primary interest in combating these phenomena. Anti-money laundering policy is, after all, pursued for the protection of the public interest. While external supervisors act either directly or indirectly on behalf of the State, they can be said to provide a more adequate type of supervision necessary for the AML/CTF policy. In contrast, professional associations have as their principal task to maintain a high level of integrity for the profession as a whole, for which a workable and continuous relationship between the two is required.

5.4.2.2 Weaknesses

Lack of supervisory powers or difficulties in applying those powers The risk of problems with the use of supervisory powers is comparatively higher than for internal supervisors. Internal supervisors can generally rely on their internal norms, disciplinary powers and procedures. Due to fundamental rights' protection in particular, it may be that an external supervisor encounters more difficulties than would an internal supervisor in performing an on-site inspection. This is the case in the Netherlands, where Bureau Financial Supervision (BFT) does not have access to lawyers' and – up until 1 January 2013[30] – to notaries' records and can thus not perform adequate on-site inspections. For lawyers this problem still exists. BFT used to have a supervisory agreement with the Bar Association, the *Nederlandse Orde van Advocaten*, which included

---

[30] On this date amendments to the Dutch Notaries Act (*Wet op het Notarisambt*, WNA) and AML Act entered into force. Section 111a, third paragraph, of the WNA provided BFT with the power to access notaries' records, including client files. Legal privilege vis-à-vis the Bureau has therefore been set aside explicitly. Before this time, BFT was able to access notaries' records indirectly. See Faure et al. (2009), p. 81.

provision that the Bar Association would perform a number of AML/CTF inspections annually. BFT would still have its own supervisory authority, but would oversee this supervision on a systematic basis. However, this supervisory agreement was terminated due to the impression on the part of BFT that the audits performed by the Bar Association did not include sufficient investigation into compliance with anti-money laundering obligations. The fact that BFT cannot perform supervision itself clearly diminishes the effectiveness of its supervision of lawyers. The Dutch legislator currently intends to move anti-money laundering supervision of lawyers to an independent division within the Dutch Bar Association, although there is quite some criticism of this plan.[31]

A matter that also gave rise to attention during the FATF evaluation of the Netherlands in 2010 is the fact that the Dutch financial regulators explained that, in conducting verification of compliance with anti-money laundering obligations, they mostly rely on their powers under the Act on Financial Supervision (*Wet financieel toezicht*). The reasons brought forward were the fact that obligations regarding internal controls are lacking in the Dutch AML/CTF Act and that supervisors have more extensive and more wide-ranging supervisory and sanctioning powers under this Act than under the Dutch AML/CTF Act.[32] FATF assessors were willing to accept this interpretation at the time of the evaluation, but provided various reasons on the basis of which this interpretation could be challenged in the courts and stated that this interpretation is not robust.[33]

Knowledge of the supervisees   A second potential weakness relates to the supervisors' knowledge regarding whom they should supervise. In contrast to internal supervisors who generally supervise their members, and thus know who they are, external supervisors may encounter difficulties in discovering whom they should supervise. Especially where a profession is not regulated and thus no or limited licensing or registration systems apply, it is difficult for the supervisor to know whom it should supervise exactly. As a consequence, they will also have more difficulties in understanding and recognizing the risks in the sector and understanding the general level of compliance with the norms in place on the part of institutions or professionals. Where a sector or profession is entirely unregulated, this weakness

---

[31]   www.rijksoverheid.nl/documenten-en-publicaties/persberichten/2012/07/06/herziening-toez icht-advocatuur.html, last visited 16 May 2013. Already in May 2012 the Dutch Council of State was very critical of the proposal: Staatscourant 2012, 15879.

[32]   FATF (2011b), pp. 184 et seq.

[33]   Ibid., pp. 185–7.

can be limited if there are registration requirements in place for these institutions or professionals. If there is no (central) register, then even more effort must be made by the supervisor to find out which institutions or professionals fall under its supervision and, subsequently, to formulate a proper risk-based supervision program.

Our study observed that a problem existed for the Netherlands and Greece in relation to supervisors of dealers in (high-value) goods and real estate agents. In the Netherlands, there are strategies in place to enable the supervisor to focus on the most risky institutions or professionals. Bureau Supervision Wwft has also sought cooperation with professional associations, where possible. In Greece, real estate agents and dealers in high-value goods are required to register with the tax authorities.[34] In practical terms, however, it seems that this obligation is not strictly enforced. The FATF mentioned in relation to real estate agents that 'more than half are not registered and are not members of the national association of real estate agents (OMASE)' and that 'real estate agents are generally not subject to any supervision or oversight (. . .)'.[35]

In some Member States, anti-money laundering legislation has specifically designed a registration system for the purpose of AML/CTF supervision of unregulated professions and institutions. This is the case in the United Kingdom. Under the Money Laundering Regulations 2007, Her Majesty's Revenue and Customs (HMRC) is assigned the duty of maintaining registers.[36] HRMC may keep the register in any form it thinks fit and may publish or make available for public inspection all or part of the register maintained under Regulation 25.[37] Regulation 26 obliges institutions and persons, such as dealers in high-value goods and trust or company service providers, to be registered. If they do not register, they are not allowed to act in such a capacity.[38] The Financial Services Authority and the Office of Fair Trading have also been given the power to maintain an AML register under Regulation 32 MLR 2007 in relation to the institutions and professionals that they supervise. Another example

---

[34] FATF (2007c), p. 23.
[35] Ibid., p. 23.
[36] HMRC is a default supervisor because it supervises all businesses and persons that fall outside the scope of any of the other ML Supervisory bodies. It supervises high-value dealers, money services businesses, trust and company service providers, but also, for example, accountants who are not a member of any of the professional associations. See: Regulation 21(1)(d) Money Laundering Regulation (MLR) 2007 and insertion of subparagraphs, inserted by SE 2009/209, Regulation 126, Schedule 6, point 2, paragraph 6(e).
[37] Regulations 25(2) and 25(3) MLR 2007.
[38] Regulation 26(1) MLR 2007.

of a registration system is Sweden. Here, dealers in precious metals and stones and other professional traders in goods, providers of other book-keeping or auditing services other than those subject to supervision by the Supervisory Board of Public Auditors and other independent legal professionals and trust and company service providers, are supervised by County Administrative Boards. Pursuant to Chapter 6, section 16, of the Swedish AML/CTF Act these institutions and professionals are required to notify the Swedish Companies Registration Office (*Bolagsverket*) that keeps a register of companies subject to supervision. County Administrative Boards have access to this register and can find out who they should supervise.

AML registration systems may appear very helpful for those institutions and professionals that are not regulated elsewhere and thus enable supervisory authorities to devote their time and resources to actually performing anti-money laundering supervision. In this way, a potential weakness of appointing external supervisors as AML/CTF supervisors can be overcome.

AML/CTF supervision entirely integrated in general supervision   A third potential weakness might be that anti-money laundering supervision becomes completely integrated in the overall supervision performed by the external supervisor, with the risk that insufficient attention is paid to AML/CTF matters or that specific money laundering or terrorist financing risks are not recognized. This was, for example, reported for the Dutch Authority Financial Markets, where the FATF stated: '[t]he mission was concerned that this approach may result in too low a priority being given to AML/CFT matters'.[39] It has also been reported for some external supervisors in other Member States, for example for the ISA in Finland and the FSA in Denmark, which are external supervisors but which both fall under the hybrid model.[40]

5.4.3   Strengths and Weaknesses of the Internal Model

The internal model is characterized by a large presence of internal supervisors. As explained, the principle is that, where possible, professional associations are responsible for AML/CTF supervision in relation to their members.

---

[39]   FATF (2011b), p. 217.
[40]   FATF (2007b), pp. 137–8; FATF (2006a), pp. 127, 132 and 143. See also: FATF (2010d), pp. 14–15.

5.4.3.1 Strengths

Dialogue with obliged institutions to stimulate compliance   The internal model can be found in a considerable number of EU Member States, although its exact form varies from country to country. A strength of anti-money laundering supervision performed by internal supervisors is that professional associations have close relationships with their supervisees and that a culture of dialogue could potentially stimulate compliance within the professional sector. In regulatory literature this style of enforcement is known as a conciliatory or cooperative style. It is concerned with the prevention of violations, remedying underlying problems, and interaction with the private sector through advice, negotiations, meetings, or seminars.[41] Under this style, supervisors tend to turn to informal processes in striving for compliance. The imposition of sanctions is useful as a threat, but is only used as a last resort.[42] This fits with the close relationship that professional associations wish to maintain with their members. A prerequisite for the success of the internal model and this potential strength in particular is, however, that both the professional associations and the professionals must be convinced of the need to combat money laundering, that they find this policy important and that they are willing to apply the norms.

Internal supervisors generally expend considerable efforts in creating awareness by means of guidance and training, and often give members a chance to correct behaviour before imposing a sanction. The UK Treasury noted that: '[s]upervisors seek to promote compliant behaviour, which generally means that members who are found to be non-compliant are given an opportunity to correct their behaviour before sanctions are imposed'.[43] The previously mentioned strength of external supervisors, that they can impose more severe sanctions because they are at a distance from their supervisees, may not even be necessary or may be less applicable under this model.[44] However, this strength continues to be of a theoretical nature for the most part.

---

[41]   Hawkins and Thomas (1984), p. 13.
[42]   Ibid., p. 13.
[43]   HM Treasury (2011), p. 11.
[44]   Cf. ibid.: '(. . .) There is, however, evidence that some Supervisors have taken robust action where necessary. For example, Supervisors have struck businesses off their membership list for breaching their AML /CTF obligations. Others have taken decisions to suspend members for up to five years.'

Professional knowledge   Another potential strength is that professional associations in some Member States already have experience with supervision and monitoring, though not specifically with anti-money laundering obligations.[45] Owing to their experience with quality assurance and the fact that professional associations have as their main objective to further the profession as a whole and to represent the interests of individual professionals, there is expert knowledge on the part of professional organizations about the nature of the profession, the risks and vulnerabilities present, and about ongoing developments.[46] It goes without saying that this does not necessarily mean that the professional associations have expertise in AML/CTF matters in relation to their professionals. This strong point is more concerned with knowledge of the profession as a whole.

Sufficient resources   Another point is that professional associations are unlikely to have resource problems. In a considerable number of Member States, external supervisors are often funded through the State budget. Professional associations, however, are funded through fees paid by their members. Professional associations can raise their fees according to the tasks they perform.

In the UK, for example, members of accountancy professional associations must generally apply for anti-money laundering supervision. Members pay an additional fee to be supervised for compliance with the Money Laundering Regulations 2007. One example is the ICAEW, the professional association for chartered accountants in England and Wales, which indicates on its website that 'a sole practitioner should expect to pay no less than £300 (plus VAT) per year. Fees for larger firms will depend on the information provided at the time of application, including the firm's size, complexity and risk-profile'.[47] Another example comes from the Association of Accounting Technicians, which applies a 'money laundering supervision fee of £80 and a reduced fee of £20, payable by each sole trader and principal of a firm (except principals providing only administrative support) regulated by AAT'.[48] In other Member States the

---

45   This was also mentioned under the external model for those supervisors that already had other supervisory competences with respect to their supervisees before becoming an AML/CTF supervisor as well.

46   Cf. HM Treasury (2011), p. 6.

47   Institute of Chartered Accountants in England and Wales (ICAEW, UK), http://www.icaew.com/en/technical/legal-and-regulatory/money-laundering/anti-money-laundering-supervision/applying-for-anti-money-laundering-supervision.

48   Association of Accounting Technicians (UK), http://www.aat.org.uk/sites/default/files/assets/Money_Laundering_Supervision_Factsheet.pdf.

professional associations are also independent of government in terms of funding. We were able to report this for Germany, Latvia, Denmark, Finland and Hungary, but could not provide more insight into how fees for anti-money laundering supervision are calculated, and whether and how this is integrated in the annual contributions of members.

5.4.3.2 Weaknesses

Conflict of interests   In the literature it has been said that, despite the fact that professional associations often have supervisory experience and professional knowledge, the nature of such supervision is different from what is needed to verify compliance with the anti-money laundering obligations.[49] Professional associations tend to base their supervision on quality checks of professional standards, thereby verifying the quality of professional conduct in order to maintain the quality and reputation of the profession as a whole. The cooperative supervisory style is thereby important in order to maintain a good professional relationship between the professional organization and the members. This, however, may not always be in line with the type of supervision needed for compliance supervision under preventive anti-money laundering policy. In fact, sometimes the two may be incompatible with each other. In the wider setting of professional self-regulation, Frankel summarizes the conflict of interests as follows: '[s]hielding members from outside knowledge of their deviance also shields the profession from embarrassment, with its potential for precipitating a decline in public trust'.[50] We can illustrate this conflict of interest by means of an example: while non-compliance with AML/CTF obligations sometimes requires robust action due to the severity of the breaches and to show other professionals that the professional association is taking the matter seriously, a high number of sanctions imposed by the professional association could lead to the impression that the professionals do not maintain a high quality standard. This, in turn, may lead to a decreased level of trust in the profession as a whole. Obviously this goes against what the professional associations stand for, which is to further the quality of the profession. It may therefore not always be favourable for the professional associations themselves to actively verify compliance with AML/CTF obligations and impose sanctions.

---

[49]   Cf. Stouten (2012), who is of the opinion that internal supervision in the AML/CTF policy is only possible when it is backed by a form of external supervision.

[50]   Frankel (1989), at p. 113.

This matter becomes especially problematic where the professional associations are not convinced of the need and importance of combating money laundering and terrorist financing. Dutch research on the involvement of professional associations in enforcing AML/CTF obligations through disciplinary law has shown that in the Netherlands professional associations rarely impose sanctions or refer cases to disciplinary courts for the imposition of sanctions in relation to AML/CTF norms, and that the disciplinary sanctions ultimately imposed are often very mild compared to the administrative sanctions.[51] In addition, disciplinary procedures for non-compliance of AML/CTF obligations also tend to last a long time.[52]

Independence of the supervisor   There may be doubt about the actual independence of internal supervisors and about the potential for them to be truly critical vis-à-vis their members. Independence requires that supervisors' day-to-day activities should not be subject to external direction or influence in any way, whether by government, Parliament, or the private sector.[53] In the literature, the independence of the supervisor is seen as a precondition for effective supervision and enforcement.[54] In some Member States supervisors working for professional associations are generally also professionals. Generally, they tend to be less critical of their colleagues than would an external supervisor. Hence, while the close relationship between professional associations and professionals was above considered a potential strength, a downside might be that professional associations are influenced too much by the wishes of their members and are not, or not sufficiently, in a position to take their own decisions in relation to their supervisory activities.

Cooperation and consistency of supervisory practice   A special point of attention in the internal model is cooperation and consistency of supervisory practice. In some Member States there are many professional associations due to the fact that one profession has various professional associations or because of a territorial limitation on professional associations. This is sometimes further complicated because actual supervision is performed by the regional associations, which, in turn, fall under the umbrella of the national professional association.[55] The two outliers

---

[51]   Stouten (2012), at pp. 467–9; Faure et al. (2009), at pp. 152–53.
[52]   Faure et al. (2009), at pp. 152–3.
[53]   Political independence and market independence.
[54]   Cf. Ottow (2006).
[55]   This is, for instance, the case in Germany and was also reported by the Hungarian Bar Association (though Hungary falls under the hybrid model).

in the European Union are the United Kingdom, with 22 professional associations, and Ireland, with 11 professional associations supervising anti-money laundering compliance.

As an aside, it must be stressed that cooperation between anti-money laundering supervisors is very important notwithstanding the supervisory architecture that is in place. We found forms of cooperation between supervisors in all Member States, although the extent and intensity of the cooperation differs. In all Member States cooperation between supervisors takes place through informal means, and in the large majority of Member States this occurs through a combination of informal and formal means. Informal cooperation is very important and takes place through ad hoc meetings, telephone calls, the exchange of supervisory information and the publication of information. The most commonly identified formal tool for cooperation is the conclusion of Memoranda of Understanding between two or more supervisory authorities.[56] In some Member States there are also more formalized cooperation platforms, either exclusively for anti-money laundering supervisors or with a broader range of institutions. Examples of specialized AML/CTF supervisors' platforms can be found in the UK with the Anti-Money Laundering Supervisors' Forum and in Sweden with the Coordination Body. Wider cooperation platforms in which AML/CTF supervisors participate or in which anti-money laundering supervision is considered a part are – inter alia – reported in Cyprus (Advisory Authority), Denmark (*Hvidvaskforum*), the Netherlands (*Toezichthoudersoverleg*), and Portugal (*Conselho Nacional de Supervisores Financeiros*).

We found that, under the internal model, however, cooperation is even more important because the professional category must be supervised in a consistent and equivalent way, notwithstanding the professional association. Hence, cooperation efforts cannot solely focus on general legal or policy issues and general supervisory issues, but must focus on the day-to-day practice of professional associations to ensure that professionals are supervised in an equivalent manner throughout the same professional category. It must be ensured that the methodology of supervision and the level of sanctions imposed are more or less the same. This, in combination with the presence of a large(r) number of internal supervisors designated as AML/CTF supervisor, makes it more challenging to ensure proper coordination and coherence of supervisory practice.

---

[56]   The ECOLEF study found this to be the case for Cyprus, Estonia, Ireland, Italy, Lithuania, Luxembourg, Malta, Spain, and the United Kingdom.

AML/CTF supervision entirely integrated in general supervision   As with external supervisors, a potential weakness of the internal model might be that AML/CTF supervision is entirely integrated within the overall supervision performed by the internal supervisor, with the risk that insufficient attention is paid to AML/CTF matters or that the specific AML/CTF risks are insufficiently recognized. Various professional associations from different Member States include the verification of compliance with AML/CTF obligations in wider supervisory programs, such as quality assurance programs. Professional associations can regard compliance with AML/CTF requirements as a professional duty. The integration of AML/CTF supervision in general supervision may lead to situations where professional associations perform insufficient AML/CTF supervision. We found some indications of this potential weakness in Member States.

5.4.4   Strengths and Weaknesses of the Hybrid Model

It goes without saying that the strengths and weaknesses of the three models described above can be found in the hybrid model. Some examples follow hereafter.

With regard to the hybrid I model, some weaknesses of the external model are present. The possible weakness of a lack of supervisory powers has been identified in Denmark, Finland[57] and Sweden. In Denmark it has been stated that there are no powers for the Danish FSA to revoke a licence or registration for non-compliance with the AML/CTF Act, and that it has no on-site inspection powers in relation to insurance brokers. In Sweden there are some legal problems concerning the power to perform on-site inspections for the Estate Agents Inspectorate. The AML Act refers to the Estate Agents Act and the supervisor thus obtains its supervisory powers from that Act. However, due to the terminology used, the supervisor cannot perform on-site inspections. Obviously this hinders the Inspectorate in performing its task effectively, because with off-site AML inspections the Inspectorate must always rely on the information provided by the supervisees. The potential weakness that supervision may be too integrated in the sectorial supervisory activities of external supervisors is also present in this variant on the hybrid model. As has been explained, in both Finland and Denmark remarks have been made about the integration of AML/CTF supervision in broader supervisory programs, which has resulted in too low a priority being accorded to AML/CTF in inspections.

---

[57]   FATF (2007b), p. 136.

Regarding the second variation it is self-evident that the strengths named in the context of the FIU model apply here as well. FIUs have a special anti-money laundering focus. Obviously, under the hybrid model this strength is limited to the institutions or professionals for which they have supervisory responsibilities. Also, with respect to its supervisees, the FIU can use data present in the 'STR database' in the process of supervision and for designing the risk-based supervisory program. This is why Hungary included the FIU as the default supervisor. In Romania too there is a clear link between the analytical functions of the FIU and supervisory activities.[58] In Italy the FIU supervises all obliged institutions with respect to the reporting obligation, alongside their regular AML supervisors. In particular, access to the STR database plays a role in providing the FIU with this power. As regards the strength of sectorial knowledge mentioned earlier in respect of both the external and internal models, the FATF mentioned that for Italy the current supervisory authorities already had supervisory responsibilities over their supervisees under different legislation.[59] In Hungary too the experience of supervisory authorities, both internal and external, was praised.[60]

The above-mentioned weaknesses of resource problems also apply to this second variation on the hybrid model. For example, in Slovenia the FIU lacks the power to perform on-site inspections.[61] This gap in the FIU's supervisory powers negatively affects the effectiveness of AML/CTF supervision. Resource problems for the FIU were also present in Cyprus, where this had resulted in there being no on-site inspections of real estate agents or dealers in high-value goods,[62] as well as in Slovenia and Romania.[63] This weakness, however, is again limited because the FIUs have a more limited supervisory role than under the FIU Model.

5.5 CONCLUDING REMARKS

Unlike substantive norms, procedural norms are only minimally harmonized. As a result there exists a patchwork of supervisory architectures within the European Union. This chapter's aim has been to present four different models of anti-money laundering supervisory architectures:

---

[58]   MONEYVAL (2011e), p. 21.
[59]   FATF (2009b), 13.
[60]   MONEYVAL (2010b), p. 138.
[61]   MONEYVAL (2011b), p. 113.
[62]   MONEYVAL (2011d), p. 144.
[63]   MONEYVAL (2011e), p. 16.

the FIU model, external model, internal model and the hybrid model. This shows the diversity present in the European Union. Discussion of the potential strengths and weaknesses of the models gives a first insight into the institutional differences between the Member States. Generally Eastern and Southern European Member States include the FIU in their AML/CTF supervisory architecture.

6. Definitions of money laundering in practice

Joras Ferwerda

6.1 INTRODUCTION

Our research revealed that, although the FATF 40 Recommendations, the EU Directive and various international conventions[1] require various essential elements of money laundering to be criminalized, there remains considerable divergence between the actual practices across Member States.

During regional workshops, participants were asked to work on a case study, containing various situations that potentially involved money laundering. For each situation, they were asked to stipulate whether it would be considered money laundering in their countries. Analysis of their responses follows presentation of these hypothetical cases below. It should be stressed that the answers are based on the practical experience of participants and that they are not official statements of policy of the countries represented.

6.2 MONEY LAUNDERING

Participants were asked: would this be considered money laundering?

- Mr X robs a bank and gets caught red-handed with the proceeds in his bag.
- Mr X robs a bank and hides the proceeds at home.
- Mr X robs a bank and puts the proceeds bit by bit into his own bank account.

---

[1] E.g. the 1988 United Nations Convention against Illicit Traffic in Narcotic Drugs and Psychotropic Substances (the Vienna Convention), the 2000 United Nations Convention Against Transnational Organized Crime (the Palermo Convention), the 1990 and 2005 Council of Europe Conventions on Laundering, Search, Seizure and Confiscation of the Proceeds from Crime.

- Mr X robs a bank and starts a business with the proceeds.
- Mr X robs a bank and buys a car for Ms Y. Money laundering for Mr X and/or Ms Y?
- Mr X robs a bank and travels from country A to country B without declaring the money.
- Mr X abuses inside business information and sells his securities at a very convenient moment ('insider trading'). He uses his proceeds to buy a house.

6.2.1   Analysis of the Answers

There is a clear pattern in the answers when one distinguishes the countries that have not criminalized self-laundering (DE, DK, FI, IT and SE).[2] All these countries clearly indicated that all our examples are not considered money laundering, because it is done by the same person who acquired the proceeds by committing a crime. All Member States indicated that third-party laundering, the situation where Ms. Y enjoys the proceeds of the crime committed by Mr. X, would be considered money laundering. Because there is such a uniformity of the answers of these countries, they will not be mentioned in the analysis below.

In practice, we could add Ireland to the list of countries that have not criminalized self-laundering.[3] Although Ireland has criminalized self-laundering in law, in practice it is hardly ever prosecuted. The reason for this lies in the pragmatic approach of the prosecutors. The goal of prosecution is to secure (as high as possible) a penalty for the offender; for which crime the offender gets this penalty is not so important. In Ireland it is quite hard to prove money laundering; basically the predicate offence has to be proven and if money laundering is also proven (along with the predicate offence), this would not increase the penalty. So, in practice, it is only necessary to prove the predicate offence, because adding a prosecution for money laundering only complicates the case needlessly. It is therefore the case that, in practice, self-laundering is hardly ever prosecuted in Ireland.

The cases are designed to range from a very wide definition of money laundering to a narrower definition where certain standards of proof are being met. With a very wide definition we mean that the money laundering

---

[2]   Sweden will amend their law to criminalize self-laundering. At the time of writing, these amendments (see http://www.regeringen.se/sb/d/16005/a/188405) had not yet come into force and are therefore not taken into account.

[3]   Please note that this conclusion is based on the case study results presented in Table 6.1 and that it is not based on analysis of the law, jurisprudence and/or case law in the different countries.

Table 6.1 *Results case study 1 – Money laundering*

	Robber gets caught red-handed	Robber hides proceeds at home	Smurfing (small amounts on own bank account)	Starts a business with proceeds	Buys car for Ms Y, ML for Mr X?	Buys car for Ms Y, ML for Ms Y? (knowledge of origin)	Cross-border without declaring	Insider trading
AT	No	No	Yes	Yes	Yes	Yes	Yes	Yes
BE	No	No	Yes	Yes	Yes	Yes	Yes	Yes
BG	No	Yes	Yes	Yes	Yes	Yes	Yes	No=
CY	Yes	Yes	Yes	Yes	Yes	Yes	Yes	Yes
CZ	No	No	Yes	Yes	Yes	Yes	Yes*	No
DE	No	No	No	No	No	Yes	No	No
DK	No	No	No	No	No	Yes	No	No
EE	No	No	No	Yes	Yes	Yes	No	No+
EL	No	No	Yes	Yes	Yes	Yes	Yes	Yes
ES	No	No	Yes	Yes	Yes	Yes	Yes	Yes
FR	?	?	?	?	?	?	?	?
FI	No	No	No	No	No	Yes	No	No
HU	No	No	Yes	Yes	Yes	Yes	No	Yes
IE	No	No	No#	No#	No#	Yes	No#	No#

Table 6.1 (continued)

	Robber gets caught red-handed	Robber hides proceeds at home	Smurfing (small amounts on own bank account)	Starts a business with proceeds	Buys car for Ms Y, ML for Mr X?	Buys car for Ms Y, ML for Ms Y? (knowledge of origin)	Cross-border without declaring	Insider trading
IT	No	No	No	No	No	Yes	No	No
LV	No	No	Yes	Yes	Yes	Yes	Yes	Yes
LT	No	No	No	Yes	Yes	Yes	No	Yes
LU	Yes	Yes	Yes	Yes	Yes	Yes	Yes	Yes
MT	No	No	Yes	Yes	Yes	Yes	Yes	Yes
NL	Yes	Yes	Yes	Yes	Yes	Yes	Yes	Yes
PL	No	No	Yes	Yes	Yes	Yes	Yes	Yes
PT	No	No	Yes	Yes	Yes	Yes	No⁻	No
RO	No	No	Yes	Yes	Yes	Yes	Yes*	Yes
SK	No	No	Yes	Yes	Yes	Yes	No	Yes
SI	No	No	Yes	Yes	Yes	Yes	Yes	No
SE	No	No	No	No	No	Yes	No	No
UK	No	Yes	Yes	Yes	Yes	Yes	Yes	Yes

Notes:

AT – Austria; BE – Belgium; BG – Bulgaria; CY – Cyprus; CZ – Czech Republic; DE – Germany; DK – Denmark; EE – Estonia; ES – Spain; FI – Finland; FR – France; GR – Greece; HU – Hungary; IE – Ireland; IT – Italy; LV – Latvia; LT – Lithuania; LU – Luxembourg; MT – Malta; NL – Netherlands; PL – Poland; PT – Portugal; RO – Romania; SK – Slovakia; SI – Slovenia; SE – Sweden; UK – United Kingdom.

* Remark made by representatives: only if Mr X had the intention of concealing the illicit origin of the money abroad.

+ There was no consensus among Estonian representatives. In general, insider trading is a predicate offence to money laundering. However, according to most representatives, by buying a house for himself, Mr X is not actually hiding the money – which is a prerequisite for money laundering.

– If Mr X stays within the EU.

= In Bulgaria there is a provision similar to, but not exactly the same as, insider trading. MONEYVAL evaluated this provision and advised that this legislation be changed, because it was found not to be in line with the FATF Recommendations. That is why in this example the Bulgarian answer is no.

Although it is possible to prosecute such conduct for money laundering in Ireland, in practice this will not be done, because it is easier to prove only the robbery (since that has to be proven also for money laundering) and adding money laundering to the case does not increase the penalty.

France was not able to attend our regional workshop and we therefore have no answers from them on this case study. We emailed the case study to them and asked them to fill it in, but we did not receive an answer.

Source: The authors, based on case study 1 discussed at regional workshops 2, 3 and 4. The same case study was sent to the countries of regional workshop 1. Answers in the affirmative are marked in light grey.

definition is very broadly interpreted so that it includes many acts that might not constitute money laundering in other countries, and vice versa for a narrower definition. The analysis will follow this line of questioning.

First, being caught with the unused proceeds does not constitute money laundering in most Member States. The minimum requirement is that the origin of the illegally obtained goods is concealed. Therefore, when caught red-handed after robbing a bank, the person will be prosecuted for robbery and not for (attempted) money laundering. Even in countries that have criminalized self-laundering it is doubtful whether this is a true form of concealment. Representatives of the Member States have explained that in their countries the mere possession of the proceeds of crime (at home) is not considered as 'hiding the proceeds'. Rather, it is seen as a by-product of being in possession of the proceeds after committing a robbery. What is furthermore mentioned as a missing element is the intention of the principal offender to launder the proceeds. In Belgium there is a saying, which takes away any confusion over which crime should be prosecuted in a case such as we have presented: 'de steler is geen heler'. Although this is of course not legally binding, it does reflect the prosecutor's idea in practice. 'De steler is geen heler' basically means that the thief is not the one trading criminal goods; so long as the offender is seen as only a thief, one should not consider him or her a money launderer. Exceptions to the analysis above are the Netherlands and Luxembourg. These two countries have indicated that even when a robber gets caught red-handed, this can be considered money laundering as well. Representatives from Luxembourg indicated that their main reason would be the extraterritorial application of the money laundering offence. When the robbery took place outside Luxembourg, the prosecution service could still prosecute the principal offender for money laundering in Luxembourg.[4] In the Netherlands the wide definition of money laundering is applied in court; the mere possession of money from a crime is considered money laundering. Because this makes it relatively easy to prove money laundering in court, it is often easier to prosecute for money laundering than for the predicate offence.[5]

---

[4]   Although we did not indicate in our case study that any international aspect was relevant, Luxembourg is often faced with the international dimension when prosecuting money laundering and therefore seems to respond in this light.

[5]   The Dutch representatives said that when a robber gets caught red-handed the predicate offence (robbery) is also very easy to prove, so in this case the prosecutor might just as easily prosecute for the robbery, but as soon as there is any doubt as to whether the robbery can be proven, money laundering would be the crime for which the robber would be prosecuted. It should be reported that established case law of the Supreme Court of the Netherlands contradicts this approach,

This makes the Netherlands the opposite of Ireland, where the predicate offence is in practice easier to prove than money laundering.

As a small side-step from the case study, we would like to point out that there are differences within the European Union with respect to the criminalization of negligent money laundering. The following countries have criminalized negligent money laundering: Cyprus, Czech Republic, Finland, Germany, Latvia, the Netherlands,[6] Slovakia, Slovenia, Spain and Sweden, while the following countries have not: Austria, Bulgaria, Belgium,[7] Estonia, France,[8] Greece, Italy, Lithuania, Luxembourg,[9] Malta, Portugal, United Kingdom[10] and Romania.[11] Ireland has not

---

because it indicates that in certain circumstances the mere possession of the proceeds from a crime could not be considered money laundering (e.g. HR (April 2012): http://zoeken.rechtspraak.nl/detailpage.aspx?ljn=BW1481. To quote from the case, which is unfortunately only available in Dutch: '3.2.2 – In een geval als het onderhavige, waarin het gaat om een verdachte die geldbedragen voorhanden heeft als bedoeld in art. 420bis Sr en waarvan vaststaat dat die afkomstig zijn uit een (mede) door hemzelf begaan misdrijf, kan het enkele voorhanden hebben van die geldbedragen niet worden aangemerkt als witwassen indien die gedraging niet kan hebben bijgedragen aan het verbergen of verhullen van de criminele herkomst van die geldbedragen (vgl. HR 26 oktober 2010, LJN BM4440, NJ 2010/655, rov. 2.4.2).')

[6] Article 420quater Dutch Penal Code refers to 'should have known'.

[7] FATF (2005), p. 38.

[8] There are some discussions in France as to whether or not negligent money laundering is criminalized, but during the parliamentary discussions on the original passing of the Act in 1996, it was made clear that money laundering is an intentional crime, or at least a crime committed knowingly. See: FATF (2011a), p. 102.

[9] Article 506–1 of the Luxembourg Penal Code refers to 'knowingly engage'.

[10] FATF (2007d), p. 135: 'The three money laundering offences of sections 327–329 of POCA are all offences for which intent is required. Hence these offences apply to persons who knowingly engaged in the conduct in question.' A UK representative indicated that this statement by the FATF is not legally correct.

[11] In Finland, chapter 32 contains provisions about negligent receiving (section 5) and negligent money laundering (section 9). In Germany there is a similar provision in Article 261, fifth paragraph, of the Criminal Code, which provides for 'criminal liability of negligent ML if the perpetrator – recklessly did not know that the objects in question stem from the commission of a predicate offence' (FATF (2010e), p. 55). In the Czech Republic, negligent money laundering is criminalized via Article 252 of the Criminal Code (MONEYVAL (2007b), pp. 63–4). Sweden also has forms of negligent money laundering in its criminal legislation (sections 7(2), 7(3) and 7a(2) Swedish Criminal Code; see FATF (2006d), p. 30). Negligent money laundering is furthermore criminalized in Article 245, fifth paragraph, of the Slovenian Criminal Code (MONEYVAL (2011b), p. 26). In Latvia too, prosecutors can prosecute for negligent money laundering. The 2009 progress report states: 'Prosecutors do not have to prove intent or willful blindness to prosecute money laundering, i.e. unintentional (negligent) money laundering

criminalized negligent money laundering, but refers in its legislation to the standard of 'recklessness'.[12]

Smurfing on the other hand can constitute sufficient grounds for concealment.[13] The fact that it is not considered money laundering in Estonia is due to a recent Supreme Court decision.[14] In this case, a person had committed theft and had built a summer cottage from the proceeds. The Supreme Court decided that this could not be considered money laundering. Estonian stakeholders indicated that a similar line of reasoning should be followed regarding the placing of the money in one's own bank account: placing the money in one's own account cannot be considered 'concealment'.

Starting a business with the proceeds constitutes money laundering in practice in all the countries that have criminalized self-laundering (except Ireland, as explained above). This means that it is also considered money laundering in the countries that did not consider the deposit of the money to be money laundering: Lithuania and Estonia. In Lithuania, according

---

also can be prosecuted' (MONEYVAL (2009a), p. 6). Cyprus has criminalized negligent money laundering (MONEYVAL (2006), p. 47). Slovakia has criminalized negligent money laundering in Article 232 of the Criminal Code. Spain has a form of negligent money laundering. Chapter XIV of the Spanish Criminal Code on Money Laundering contains, after amendments made by Organic Law 5/2010 of 22 June 2010, in paragraph 3 the provision that '[i]f the events can be classed as criminal negligence, the punishment will be a prison term of six months to two years and a fine of three times the amount involved' (FATF (2010b), p. 38). Lithuania, Estonia, Austria, Romania and Italy have not criminalized negligent money laundering; in these countries the offence is applicable only to persons who knowingly engage in money laundering. It seems that Bulgaria and Greece have also not criminalized negligent money laundering. (MONEYVAL (2008a), p. 50 stipulates '[t]he mental element for natural persons is knowledge or assumption that property is acquired through crime or another act that is dangerous for the public. "Assumption" is equated with subjective suspicion.' Furthermore Article 2, paragraph 2, of the Greek AML Law does not give any indication regarding the criminalization of negligent money laundering.) Also in Malta and Portugal, negligent money laundering is not explicitly covered. However, in both countries there exist concepts such as 'wilful blindness' or 'dolus eventual' that may interpreted – in theory – in such a way that they cover money laundering by negligence. So far, in both countries this has not happened in practice. (Information on the basis of interviews held with representatives.)

[12]   Section 7 Irish AML Act. This seems to be in line with the concepts of 'wilful blindness' and 'dolus eventual' as outlined for Malta and Portugal; see previous footnote.

[13]   This is mentioned explicitly by the Czech, Latvian and Slovenian representatives.

[14]   The case of this Supreme Court decision has to be confirmed.

to Article 216(1), the money is being used in a commercial activity for the purpose of concealing the proceeds; hence it is considered money laundering.

When Mr X buys a car for Ms Y there is a transfer of property between a party that has committed the predicate offence and another party not involved in the criminal act. Mr X can still not be prosecuted for ML in countries that do not criminalize self-laundering. With respect to the question as to whether Ms Y has committed money laundering, all representatives stated that it is considered money laundering as long as it is possible to prove her intent to conceal, and knowledge, reasonable grounds or suspicion (or, for countries that have negligent money laundering, (gross) negligence) that the car was bought with stolen money.

The situation where a person robs a bank and travels from country A to country B without declaring the money yielded quite different answers for different reasons. The majority of countries consider this money laundering, although some (Czech Republic and Romania) note that it can only be considered money laundering when the intent can be proven. Six countries would not consider this money laundering: Estonia, Hungary, Ireland, Latvia, Portugal and Slovakia. Portugal indicated that this would not be considered money laundering as long as countries A and B are both Members of the EU. Estonia mentioned that here too considering Supreme Court case (as discussed above in relation to smurfing) leads them to conclude that travelling with proceeds without declaring them would not be considered money laundering. The representatives explained that in Hungary it is only when the act endangers another subject (e.g. the due course of business) that self-laundering is criminally punishable; therefore the mere transportation of one's own proceeds would not be considered money laundering. It should be mentioned that we only asked whether or not declaring the transportation of proceeds would be considered money laundering. Representatives indicated to us that even when it is not considered money laundering, non-declaration of the money could still be a criminal or administrative offence.

Apparently, insider trading is not a predicate offence in all the EU Member States. In Bulgaria there is a provision similar to insider trading, but not exactly. MONEYVAL has not accepted this provision and advised Bulgaria to change this piece of legislation. That is why in this example the Bulgarian representatives had to answer that insider trading is not considered a predicate offence for money laundering. In Portugal the following approach to predicate offences exists: some crimes are described exhaustively as predicate offences and then there is a general 'catch-all' clause, with a rule that all crimes that are punished with more than five years of imprisonment are predicate offences for money laundering. Stock market crimes in Portugal are sanctioned very lightly, which means that an offence as insider trading is not considered a predicate offence for money laundering. Representatives of some countries indicated that this act would not be considered money laundering because in our case the money derived from insider trading was only used to buy a house. According to the Estonian representatives, this would not be considered money laundering due to the aforementioned decision of the Supreme Court. According to the Czech representatives, the concealment of the origin of the illicit funds is a precondition for money laundering. Buying a house does not seem a reasonable proof of concealment. The Slovenian representatives indicated that their answer would be different if the person had bought a house for somebody else.

All in all, the following factors seem most influential in the different outcomes:

- Where self-laundering is not criminalized, almost all questions are answered negatively.
- Where self-laundering is criminalized, the mere possession of criminal proceeds is not considered money laundering in most Member States, with Luxembourg and the Netherlands (in certain cases) as exceptions.
- There are large interpretation variations in what should be considered 'concealment' (hiding the proceeds).
- The intention to hide and the knowledge, and/or reasonable grounds (and (gross) negligence), of the fact that the proceeds come from criminal activity in case of third-party money laundering is required in all Member States.
- Insider trading is not a predicate offence for money laundering in all Member States.

We can, based on the answers given in our regional workshops, classify the 27 EU Member States on how broad their money laundering definition in practice is: Germany, Denmark, Finland, Ireland, Italy and Sweden interpret the definition of money laundering very narrowly, mostly because they do not criminalize self-laundering. Estonia and Lithuania interpret the money laundering definition narrowly. Most countries can be classified in the group with normal/average interpretation of money laundering (AT, BE, CZ, EL, ES, HU, LV, MT, PL, PT, RO, SK, SL). One could say that Bulgaria and the UK have a rather broad interpretation and that Cyprus, Luxembourg and the Netherlands interpret money laundering very broadly.

7. FIUs in the European Union – facts and figures, functions and facilities

Ioana Deleanu

7.1 INTRODUCTION AND HYPOTHESES

In this chapter we investigate some of the hypotheses surrounding FIUs that are put forward by the economic and institutional literature as well as by anecdotal evidence gathered from anti-money laundering specialists.[1] As our main investigative tools we use the facts and figures put forward by the IMF (2004), ECOLEF (2013), the FATF and MONEYVAL country evaluation reports or by the FIUs themselves.

Article 21 of the Third EU AML/CTF Directive[2] establishes FIUs as '[. . .] a central national unit [. . .] responsible for receiving (and to the extent permitted, requesting), analyzing and disseminating to the competent authorities, disclosures of information which concern potential money laundering [. . .]', but a closer look reveals a large diversity among the FIUs of the European Union. This diversity – which was documented as early as 2004 by the International Monetary Fund and by the World Bank – originates from the various national arrangements made when establishing the first FIUs in the 1990s. Trying to distinguish similarities between these arrangements, the IMF (2004) report presents four FIU typologies – administrative, law enforcement, judicial and hybrid – on the basis of the institutional position and investigative capacity of the FIUs. Each of these typologies presents some generic advantages and disadvantages. The administrative type is thus more likely to be a buffer between the reporting entities and the law enforcement agencies, thereby supporting the obliged entities in reporting, while missing the legal powers to investigate suspicion reports. The law enforcement type can better investigate the criminal suspicion identified in a report but may not give

---

[1]   Hypotheses appear in italics.
[2]   The text of the Directive is available at:http://eur-lex.europa.eu/LexUriServ/site/en/oj/2005/l_309/l_30920051125en00150036.pdf.

sufficient confidence to the obliged entities to report on their customers. The judicial type is assumed to be politically independent and able to investigate suspicion reports very fast and thoroughly, but it is not considered to be a natural interlocutor for the obliged entities. Finally, the hybrid FIU attempts to combine the advantages of each type of FIU. We thus investigate whether the EU FIUs have converged to a single type or whether these types are equally observed.

Are all FIUs equally financially independent? According to the Egmont Group, when establishing an FIU, a country is asked to ensure that the FIU has operational autonomy and adequate resources (staff and budget) to be able to independently and efficiently handle the incoming flow of reports. Some EU FIUs have their own budget that is allocated directly from the State budget and that is negotiated every year. The advantage of such an arrangement is that the FIU has a clear overview of its budget for the entire year and that it can plan ahead its expenditures and its cuts. Other FIUs are paid from the overall budget of a larger institution, which might be the police, the secret services, the Public Prosecutor's office, the Ministry of Finance or the Ministry of Justice. In the face of fiscal shocks (i.e. budget cuts during mid-year budget recalculations), one could argue that FIUs with an independent budget are less vulnerable.

Are FIUs in rich countries allocated higher budgets? This hypothesis also originated from anecdotal evidence, namely that rich countries have more money to spend on fighting crime. If this hypothesis is confirmed, we would expect that FIUs belonging to older EU Member States would also have higher budgets, on average.

Do administrative FIUs employ more staff and are more bureaucratic than others? This hypothesis was introduced by means of anecdotal evidence. With too few means of measuring the level of FIU bureaucracy, one could only test whether administrative FIUs do indeed have more staff than the others. The size of staff, however, can be influenced by many factors. First of all, some FIUs may have more additional duties or more duties that are human capital intensive. This in itself would explain why those FIUs in particular need more staff. Besides this, given the overall level of capital intensity in a country, capital might also be replaced by human labour. In other words, when labour is cheap relative to capital, it is more efficient to employ more staff in order to analyse more reports than to install a more sophisticated IT system. Finally, more staff are needed when the FIU has its own premises, simply because the externalities can no longer be shared among departments.

Are there large differences in staff background across different types of FIUs? In some law enforcement type FIUs, most, if not all, employees are trained police officers, while the administrative type of FIU seems to have primarily employees with a background in academia, especially law and economics. *Does staff background motivate or discourage financial entities from reporting?* This hypothesis was brought forward through the institutional literature, where staff background is believed to have important implications for the ultimate focus and goals of the FIU. This means that law enforcement FIUs may focus more on fighting crime, while administrative FIUs may focus more on the analysis of financial data necessary to identify unusual patterns of behaviour. Finally, anecdotal evidence suggests that *staff background could induce certain expectations among the reporting entities over the goals of the FIU.* These expectations could, in turn, motivate or discourage reporting entities with respect to the provision of information to the FIU.

Having looked at the most frequently stated hypotheses on FIU organization, we turn to hypotheses related to the effective functioning of the FIUs. According to the Egmont Group, when setting up an FIU, a country is asked to give consideration to, among other things, the core duties and additional duties of the FIUs and to allocate enough resources for it to be able to perform all these tasks. *FIUs with more additional tasks should therefore have (on average) more resources (both staff and budget) in order to be able to address them.* The first hypothesis was born out of the numerous pieces of anecdotal evidence we were presented with.

The institutional literature argues that institutions that have changed organization retain some characteristics from their old organizational setting. This persistence led us to hypothesize that *FIUs that had originally been placed under another structure have retained some of their old tasks and have therefore more additional tasks on average.* Finally, FIUs are a relatively new addition to the crime prevention systems of the EU Member States. We see that they take different shapes and roles and are assigned diverse tasks in order to better fit the national institutional culture. For this reason we hypothesize that *older EU FIUs have more additional tasks, than the new EU Member States* that have only had to implement the Third EU Directive.

Reporting entities are vital sources of information for all FIUs. Following the behavioural economics literature, we expect that motivating the obliged entities will improve reporting. *We take stock of the ways FIUs communicate their knowledge to the obliged entities (generic feedback, through annual reports, or on a case-by-case basis)* and of *the extent to which the FIU positions itself as a trusting cooperative partner* in the fight against money laundering or as a coercive superior agent that will ultimately constrain obliged institutions to report according to the law, or both. *We further hypothesize the larger the country the more difficult it is for the FIU to give feedback.*[3] These hypotheses follow from the EU FIU (2008) report and from further anecdotal evidence provided by some FIU representatives.

The FIUs have been assigned primarily a filtering task by the Third EU Directive. We examine to what extent the FIUs are prepared to undertake this assignment in an effective way. We therefore look at which databases the FIUs have access to – and to what extent – in a direct and speedy way. *We expect to see that administrative FIUs do not have access to police and other law enforcement databases.* This hypothesis comes from the IMF (2004) report.

Finally, we also examine the ways in which FIUs receive information from the obliged entities. We further ask to what extent the FIUs have made use of data-mining systems to conduct preliminary analyses on the suspicious reports received. We test whether *reporting is done manually in small countries*, since implementing an electronic reporting system would be too costly and not needed due to small country size. Another hypothesis is that *large countries have installed data-mining systems* to process the comparatively large numbers of incoming reports more efficiently. Finally, our third hypothesis is *that online reporting and electronic reporting takes place predominantly in countries with a high IT intensity.* This means that, when most reporting entities are not prepared to safely use the internet, FIUs will receive a large proportion of their reports manually.

7.2   TYPES OF FIUs PRESENT IN THE EUROPEAN UNION

The IMF (2004) recognized the wide diversity of FIUs as early as 2004. The report pointed to the fact that, despite all FIUs sharing the same core duties, these institutions were substantially different. As a result, the IMF (2004) classified the FIUs into quasi-strict typologies – administrative, law enforcement, judicial and hybrid. When setting up an FIU, countries were advised on the pros and cons of each typology of FIU, and on the type of FIU that would best suit their national legal and institutional framework. This classification has therefore been actively used since 2004 in setting up new FIUs across the world and has been primarily enforced by the Egmont Committee.[4]

The Egmont Committee serves as a worldwide consultation and coor-

---

[3]   EU FIU Platform (2008b).
[4]   Egmont classification at http://www.egmontgroup.org/about/what-is-an-fiu.

dination mechanism among FIUs. Its primary functions include assisting the Egmont Group in a range of activities, from internal coordination and administration, to representation at other international forums. All EU FIUs belong to the Egmont Group. The Egmont Group had 94 members in 2004 and by 2012 it had over 130 members, an expansion that has been documented in the 2011 Egmont Census.[5] Using this census, research was done into the typologies to which each FIU considers itself to belong. The results were not made publicly available and could not be compared with the ECOLEF (2013) overview.

This chapter sets out to update the IMF (2004) list of classified FIUs.[6] Based on the Egmont/IMF categorization, we arranged the remaining FIUs according to their typology. Figure 7.1 shows that, in the EU, the predominant types of FIU are the administrative (12 FIUs) and the law enforcement (11 FIUs) types. They account for two-thirds of EU FIUs. Further, there are only two judicial (Luxembourg and Cyprus) and two hybrid FIUs (Hungary and the Netherlands).

7.3 EU FIUs – INSTITUTIONAL AND ORGANIZATIONAL FACTS AND FIGURES

The budget independence of the FIUs is a hot topic. All Member States' representatives have argued that their FIUs have autonomous budgets. This means that FIUs can decide autonomously on how to spend their budget. This additional certainty over an FIU's planned expenses is higher when its budget is also independent. However, when FIU budgets are part of the budget of a larger institution, aspects of redistribution can significantly impact this budgetary autonomy. When the budget of the FIU belongs to that of the 'parent institution', decisions such as adding new staff, acquiring new IT support, increasing operational expenditures, need to be approved/countersigned by the hierarchy of the 'parent institution'. In times of fiscal fitness this may cause no problems, but in times of fiscal contraction, when there are budget cuts or during mid-year budget recalculations, budgetary dependence can impact the budgetary autonomy of the FIUs.

---

[5] Egmont (2011).
[6] Missing from the IMF (2004) classification were the Belgian, Finnish, Greek, Italian, Latvian, Lithuanian and Portuguese FIUs. Only three of the EU FIUs that were classified in the IMF (2004) report no longer agreed with their classification – the Danish, the Dutch and the Hungarian FIUs. This was mostly due to institutional reorganizations that had taken place in the meantime.

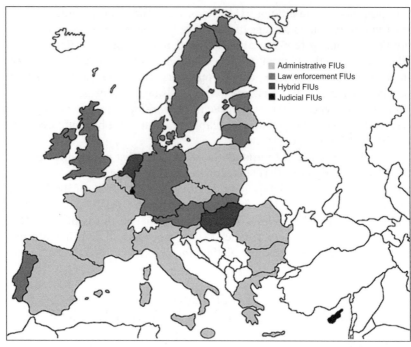

*note, colors used do not refer to a scaling value.

Administrative FIUs:	BE, BG, CZ, EL, ES, FR, IT, LV, MT, PL, RO, SL
Law enforcement FIUs:	DK, DE, EE, IE, LT, AT, PT, SK, FI, SE, UK
Hybrid FIUs:	HU, NL
Judicial FIUs:	CY, LU

Source: ECOLEF (2012).

Figure 7.1   EU FIU classification

The third column of Table 7.1 illustrates the position of non-independent FIUs within the hierarchy of the budget-providing institution. In case of budget restructuring, the impact on the FIU budget depends on the priority this department has in the larger 'parent institution' and on its capacity to negotiate its position. We see that in four Member States (Austria, Ireland, Sweden and the United Kingdom) the FIU holds a low position in the overall hierarchy of the budget-providing institution. Having regard to this line of argument, we have classified the budgets of FIUs according to their potential vulnerability to fiscal shocks: largely vulnerable, vulnerable and somewhat non-vulnerable. *We have refuted the hypothesis that all FIUs are equally financially independent.*

Table 7.1   FIU figures on budget vulnerability to fiscal shocks, staff composition and separate and independent location

	Budget size in Euros	Own independent budget	Place of the FIU in the organization of the budget-providing institution	Budget vulnerability to fiscal shocks	FIU staff in FTE (in year)	Staff composition in terms of background	FIU premises
AT	975,000*	No	BKA>Economic Crime>Financial Fraud>FIU	Large	13 (2010)	Detectives with financial crime and IT crime training	Within the BKA-Austria
BE	4,257,645	Yes	n/a	Minimal	45 (2012)	Detached prosecutors, police, customs and intelligence liaison officers, financial analysts	Own premises
BG		No	SANS>FIU	Medium	32 (2011)	Law enforcement agents with legal, economic and international relations specialization	Within SANS
CY		No	AGO>FIU	Medium	21 (2011)	Prosecutors, detached custom officers, police officers, financial analysts	Own premises
CZ	1,429,473 (without IT)*	No	MoF> Audit, Finance and Operations Section>FIU	Medium	35 (2011)	Economists, police agents, lawyers	Own premises

Table 7.1 (continued)

	Budget size in Euros	Own independent budget	Place of the FIU in the organization of the budget-providing institution	Budget vulnerability to fiscal shocks	FIU staff in FTE (in year)	Staff composition in terms of background	FIU premises
DK		No	MoJ>State Prosecutor for Serious Economic Crime>FIU	Medium	18 (2011)	Prosecutors, police, tax administration agents	Within the Office of Public Prosecution for Serious Economic Crime
EE		No	PBGB>FIU	Medium	16 (2011)	Police agents (with tax and finance background)	Within the Police and Border Guard Board
FI	1,565,000	Yes	n/a	Minimal	24 (2011)	Police agents (with economic crime experience)	Within the Criminal Intelligence Division of NBI
FR	4,981,688	Yes	n/a	Minimal	73 (2009)	Financial analysts, liaison officers, detached prosecutor	Own premises
DE		No	BKA>Serious Crime>FIU	Medium	17 (2010)	Police officers and other staff of BKA or MoI	Within the National Criminal Police

EL	1,500,000	Yes	n/a	Minimal	29 (2011)	Head prosecutor, officials (Ministry representatives) and detached personnel	Within the AML/CTF SFI Authority
HU	1,000,000*	**	NTCA>Criminal Affairs>FIU	Medium	30 (2010)	Lawyers, economists, customs agents	
IE		No	Garda>National support services>Bureau of fraud investigation>FIU	Large	11 (2011)	Police agents	Within Garda Siochana Fraud Office
IT	207,000 (only expenses)	No[7]	BoI>FIU	Minimal	104 (2011)	Lawyers and economists	Within the Bank of Italy
LV	341,490	Yes	n/a	Minimal	17 (2011)	Police, public prosecutors, finance background	PPO office Latvia (but expected to change)
LT		No	FCIS>Analysis and prevention board> FIU	Medium	10 (2011)	Police officers	Within the FCIS
LU		No		Minimal	14 (2012)	Prosecutors, financial analysts, police liaison officers	Within the Luxembourg Prosecution Office* (2012)

---

7 Despite the FIU's budget being allocated by the Bank of Italy, the vulnerability to fiscal shocks is minimal, as the Bank itself is not considered to be subject to fiscal shocks.

Table 7.1 (continued)

	Budget size in Euros	Own independent budget	Place of the FIU in the organization of the budget-providing institution	Budget vulnerability to fiscal shocks	FIU staff in FTE (in year)	Staff composition in terms of background	FIU premises
MT	330,107	Yes	n/a	Minimal	10 (2011)	Lawyers, financial analysts	Own premises
NL	4,800,000	Yes	n/a	Minimal	56 (2010)	Police liaison, financial analysts	Own premises
PL		No	MoF> Under-secretary of state Inspector General>FIU	Medium	45 (2008)	Lawyers, economists, IT experts	Within the MoF
PT		No	Judicial police> FIU	Medium	30 (2011)	Police officers, tax liaisons	Within the Judicial Police
RO		Yes	n/a	Minimal	96 (2011)	Financial analysts, lawyers, international relations officers	Own premises
SK		No	**	**	30 (2011)	Police officers	Within the Bureau of Combating Organized Crime
SL	691,000	Yes	n/a	Minimal	18 (2010)	Academics – law and economics background	Within the MoF premises

ES	11,000,000	Yes	n/a	Minimal	79 (2011)	Financial and legal experts, detached police agents, tax and customs liaison officers	Own premises
SE	1,400,000*	No	NPB>NBI> Criminal intelligence &Investigations Division>FIU	Large	27 (2009)	Police, financial analysts	Within the National Criminal Police
UK		No	SOCA>Strategy& prevention> Information>FIU	Large	60 (2012)	Police officers, financial analysts	Within the SOCA premises

Note: The following acronyms have been used: SOCA – Serious Organized Crime Agency, NPB – National Police Board, NBI – National Bureau of Investigation, MoF – Ministry of Finance, MoI – Ministry of Interior Affairs, FCIS – Financial Crime Investigation Service, Garda – An Garda Siochana (Irish Police force), NTCA – National Tax and Customs Administration, BoI – Bank of Italy, BKA – Federal Criminal Police, AGO – Attorney General Office, SANS – State Agency for National Security, PBGB – Police and Border Guard Board, AML/CTF SFI Authority – Hellenic Anti-Money Laundering, Counter Terrorist Financing and Source of Funds Investigation Authority; further, '*' marks an approximation of the budget of the FIU and '>' marks the passage to a lower level of hierarchy – such that the institution to the left of the '>' sign is the larger department; '**' marks the fact that we could not collect this information from the national representatives. For more details, see online appendix 7.1 of ECOLEF (2013).

We further examine whether there is any significant relationship between the size of the EU FIU budgets and the wealth of a country or the year it acceded to the EU. We note no statistically significant correlation, and hence *we cannot support the claim that wealthier Member States have allocated higher budgets to their FIUs*. Furthermore, this is consistent with the fact that new Member States do not have lower budgets for FIUs, all else equal.

In terms of the staff numbers for the FIU, we observe large differences across the EU FIUs. The outliers are Italy, with over 100 staff, and Malta and Ireland, who counted less than a dozen employees. The sixth column illustrates the diversity of staff employed by the FIUs with respect to their occupational background. The last column of Table 7.1 introduces a brief description of the FIU premises – and refers mainly to whether the FIU is physically located within the 'parent institution' or whether it has its own geographically separate premises.

We observe that administrative-type FIUs on average have higher staff levels. This leads us to wonder whether administrative FIUs are more bureaucratic on average. A closer look at Table 7.1 however points to another potential explanation. Some FIUs have their own separate premises. In general, these are administrative FIUs, as was also pointed out in the IMF (2004) classification. Table 7.1 shows that administrative-type FIUs (with the exception of Bulgaria, Italy and Poland) have their own separate premises, whereas law enforcement-type FIUs, on average, do not – since they are located within their parent institution. Judicial and hybrid FIUs are somewhat mixed. Table 7.1 shows that the average staff numbers of an FIU with its own (separate) premises is close to 52 employees. Similarly, FIUs that do not have their own separate premises have on average 27 employees. This significant drop suggests that premises matter and that separate premises are on average associated with more staff. The organizational literature argues that firms choose to locate close to each other in order to benefit from other firms' spillovers.[8] This supports our findings, since an FIU that is located close to another department could make use of shared facilities and staff and this would lower its costs. Finally, since most administrative FIUs have their own premises and all the law enforcement FIUs are located within the budget-providing institution, the finding that *administrative FIUs have more staff is most likely to be due to whether the FIU has separate or shared premises*.

Further, we observe that FIUs have more staff in less wealthy Member States. This confirms the economic literature.[9] The latter suggests that

---

[8]   Ellison and Glaeser (1999).
[9]   Sinn (2003).

when capital is scarce, it becomes expensive relative to other factors of production, such as labour. Capital will therefore be replaced with labour in the production of goods and services. Similarly, least wealthy Member States are the least capital-intensive states, and therefore labour intensity is higher because it also replaces missing capital. Comparing across Member States, it is therefore not surprising that FIUs have more staff in less wealthy Member States, if we acknowledge different levels of capital intensity across the EU.

Further, we observe that most FIUs employ a wide array of staff – academics, lawyers, economists, financial analysts, police officers, prosecutors, international relations officers, customs and tax officers and more. Starting with the IMF (2004) classification, we could expect that, since most FIUs in the EU consider themselves administrative, most FIUs employ financial staff only.[10] Table 7.1 disproves this hypothesis. We actually observe that most FIUs have staff of a mixed background. We argue that administrative FIUs have addressed the need to have access to law enforcement data and to be better informed about the subsequent steps in the investigation. They have done so by means of employing detached officers, liaison officers and by appointing former law enforcement agents to head the FIUs. Law enforcement and judicial FIUs seem also to have seen the need to address AML/CTF investigations from several points of view – thereby making more use of financial analysts and liaison officers in combination with the police and prosecution agents that they already employ.

We also looked at whether the type of staff employed by an FIU has an impact on the behaviour of the obliged entities. We observe *a positive and significant relationship between the number of reports sent to an FIU and whether the latter mostly employs staff with a financial background.* This finding seems to support[11] the hypothesis that obliged entities may report differently to FIUs that mostly employ financial staff than to FIUs that mostly employ law enforcement staff. Finally, there also exists a positive significant relationship between the number of reports and the type of FIU. The latter points to the fact that, *all else equal, hybrid FIUs have received more reports from the obliged entities than other types of FIUs.*[12]

---

[10]   We know that this does not take into account the number of FIU staff with the same educational background.

[11]   We did not find a negative significant correlation between the number of reports sent to an FIU and whether the latter mostly employed law enforcement staff.

[12]   This result should be treated with caution as it says nothing about the quality of the reports forwarded by the reporting entities.

7.4   FIU FUNCTIONS: CORE AND ADDITIONAL TASKS AND RESPONSIBILITIES

Article 21 of the Third EU Directive offers the following definition of an FIU: '[The] FIU [. . .] shall be responsible for receiving (and to the extent permitted, requesting), analyzing and disseminating to the competent authorities, disclosures of information which concern potential money laundering, potential terrorist financing or are required by national legislation or regulation. It shall be provided with adequate resources in order to fulfill its tasks.' All EU Member States have transposed this definition into their national legislation. However, a different interpretation of the definition and of the role attributed to the FIU can be seen in each Member State.

Further, Article 35 requires that feedback is given to reporting entities for two purposes: to allow them 'access to up-to-date information on the practices of money launderers [. . .] and on indications leading to the recognition of suspicious activities', and to reflect on the effectiveness of their reports and on their further follow-up. In all Member States, providing feedback to the reporting entities is an additional duty of the FIU.

Table 7.2 reveals for each country which additional duties the FIUs have, compared with the general definition of the Third EU Directive. For exposition purposes we have left out several singular additional tasks that some FIUs have. We nevertheless take stock of these rare additional duties (i.e. environmental crime, as in Sweden; giving recommendations on property seizure, as with Poland and Latvia, etc.) in our analysis. The description of the additional tasks in Table 7.2 is very brief and does not account for national variations. For example, two FIUs that perform supervision of the obliged entities may in effect be performing these tasks differently and to a different extent.

Despite recognizing that not all tasks are similar, we looked into which EU FIUs have more additional tasks than others. Table 7.2 shows that the average EU FIU is given 4.33 additional tasks, and some of the most common additional tasks are drafting AML/CTF legislation, issuing guidelines for the reporting entities on how to report, supervising the reporting entities (either with respect to the AML/CTF obligations or more extensively) and proposing sanctions when noticing irregularities during the supervision controls. Besides this, a handful of FIUs are in charge of coordinating national cooperation in AML matters and some also perform the role of an asset recovery office. Furthermore, almost half of the FIUs use their position as an informational node to research aggregate data that could possibly be related to money laundering and terrorist financing and to assess the AML/CTF threat of the Member State.

Table 7.2 Additional tasks of the FIU

Additional duty	AT	BE	BG	CY	CZ	DK	EE	FI	FR	DE	EL	HU	IE	IT	LV	LT	LU	MT	NL	PL	PT	RO	SK	SL	ES	SE	UK
Supervise REs			X	X	X		X					X		X		X	X	X		X		X	X	X	X		
Propose sanctions			X	X	X		X					X		X		X	X	X		X		X	X	X			
Train supervisors	I	I	I												X				X	I		X					
Supervise the application of the International Sanctions Act				X			X				I	X		X					X		X						
Conduct pre-trial investigations	X			X			X	I	I							X	X						X				

111

Table 7.2 (continued)

Additional duty	AT	BE	BG	CY	CZ	DK	EE	FI	FR	DE	EL	HU	IE	IT	LV	LT	LU	MT	NL	PL	PT	RO	SK	SL	ES	SE	UK
Prosecute ML/TF				X		X											X										
Issue guidelines for REs	X		X	X	I						X	I		X				X	I			X	X	X	I		
Train LEAs	I				X	X			X										X	I		X	X	I			
Draft AML/CTF legislation	X		I	X					I					X	X	X	X	X	X		X	X	I	X	X		
Research ML/TF aggregate data	X		I								X	I		X					I			X			X		
ARO	X				I							I									I	X				X	X

Coordinate national cooperation	X	I	X																			X						X
Conduct ML/TF threat analysis	X	I												X														X
Total (including rare additional duties)	5	4	8	8	5	3	4	1	1	3	4	4	0	4	7	3	4	3	4	4	7	2	8	8	5	4	3	3

Note: "X" designates an additional task being legally imposed on the FIU, "I" marks the indirect imposition of an additional task onto the FIU. Indirect tasks are not legally assigned to the FIU but informally belong to their portfolio. For a more detailed description of the additional tasks that national FIU have, see annex 8.2.

Training sessions organized by the FIU for the reporting institutions as well as for the law enforcement and prosecution authorities reaffirm the FIU's position as a key player in the AML/CTF fight. The broad consensus on giving this additional task to the FIU would also point to a concentration of expertise within this institution as well as to the pivotal role the FIU has, whereby its connection to and communication with all other institutions involved in the AML/CTF fight is vital.

When assessing the extent to which an FIU is burdened by these additional tasks, one has to concede that counting tasks is not the most efficient measurement. National representatives agree that some additional tasks are more resource intensive than others, which is why we expect there not to be a linear relationship between the number of additional tasks and the size of the budget. We therefore content ourselves with looking at the correlation between the number of additional tasks and the size of the FIU budget and the size of the FIU staff. *We find no significant pairwise correlation between the number of additional tasks and the resources – both staff and budgetary – that an FIU disposes of.* This finding seems to support the claim that more additional tasks are not matched with additional resources. This is also confirmed by the numerous complaints about the limited nature of resources, which were presented to us especially by representatives of those FIUs most charged with additional tasks.[13]

In the past decade, eight FIUs (Bulgaria, Greece, Hungary, Italy, Lithuania, the Netherlands, Slovakia and Spain) have undergone major organizational changes.[14] These FIUs have on average 5.4 additional tasks and this is significantly higher than the EU FIU average (of 4.3 additional tasks). This observation seems to confirm the hypothesis brought forward by the institutional literature, namely that *FIUs bring with them some additional tasks from their former organizational structure (since they have the knowledge) and that they are given some extra tasks in the new organizational structure.* Further, there seems to be no connection between the type of FIU and the number of additional tasks. *New EU Member States do not have significantly more or fewer additional tasks than older Member States.* It therefore seems that organizational changes and the national context are the only two indicators that can explain why some FIUs have more additional duties than others.

---

[13] Noting how different tasks can be, we did not explore this hypothesis further, and we advise the reader to keep this limitation in mind when interpreting the results.

[14] For a more detailed overview of the organizational changes that FIUs have gone through, please see table 8.5 of the ECOLEF (2013) report.

Table 7.3   FIU feedback to the reporting entities

	Standard reporting form	Confirmation of receipt	No. of training sessions and workshops	Case-by-case feedback
AT	Yes	yes	49 (in 2011)	
BE	Yes	yes	mostly outsourced	yes
BG	Yes	yes	16 (in 2011)	yes
CY	No	yes	44 (2008, 2009)	yes
CZ	Yes			yes
DK	Yes			yes
EE	Yes	yes	17 (2011)	yes
FI	Yes	yes		yes
FR	Yes	yes		yes
DE	Yes	yes	35 (in 2010)	yes
EL	Yes	yes		no
HU	Yes	yes		no
IE	Yes	no	20	yes
IT	Yes	yes	Numerous	no
LV	No		Many	yes
LT	Yes		12 (2011)	
LU	Yes	yes	20 (2011)	yes
MT	Yes	yes	23 (2011)	yes
NL	Yes	yes	Extensive	no
PL	Yes	yes	30 (in 2011)	yes
PT	Yes	yes	Many	yes
RO	Yes	yes	Many	no
SK	No	yes		yes
SL	Yes		30 (in 2010)	no
ES	Yes	no	many	no
SE	Yes	yes	many	
UK	Yes	yes	many	yes*

Notes: Own, based on information collected in the ECOLEF (2013) project. For a more detailed description of how the national FIUs offer feedback to the obliged entities, see online appendix 7.5 of ECOLEF (2013). UK FIU only provides case-by-case feedback to the top 10 most actively reporting entities.

Table 7.3 depicts the interaction between the FIU and the reporting entities across a few parameters. First of all, in order to ensure that the reporting entities can report effectively, a standard reporting form should be provided to them. We note that such a form is present in almost all EU Member States (except for Cyprus, Latvia and Slovakia). Further, we looked at whether, after reporting, the FIUs provide a confirmation of receipt to the reporting entity. This confirmation should acknowledge the receipt in good order of the report, and should also set out the parameters for future correspondence between the reporting entity and the FIU. For every report sent, the reporting entity gets at least an identification number to use for future reference and the name of the contact person for the specific case. It seems that most EU FIUs provide reporting entities with acknowledgements of receipt upon opening the disclosure of information. Sometimes this is done automatically by the IT system.

Moreover, the third column of Table 7.3 depicts the amount of training and seminars organized by the FIU or where they participated in order to increase awareness among reporting entities or to train them on typologies, risks and ways to report effectively. Finally, we asked Member State representatives to classify the type of feedback they give to the reporting entities – general feedback (by means of annual reports, training and guidelines provided on the FIU website), or individual case-by-case feedback (by means of feedback on and discussion of specific cases, the outcome of their investigations, the contribution of the reporting entity).

Table 7.3 shows that formal contacts between the FIU and the reporting entities are in place in all countries. *All FIUs meet with the reporting entities at least once a year, usually at training sessions.* Moreover, all FIUs publish annual reports, giving general feedback to the reporting entities. Some annual reports are more limited in terms of information – i.e. Ireland and Bulgaria – as they are part of the larger annual reports of the parent institution, and some are very comprehensive. *The largest differences lie in the extent of training given by the FIUs and in the nature of feedback given to the reporting entities.* Some countries are inclined to offer individual feedback, whereas others prefer general feedback.[15]

Furthermore, we observe *no relationship between the size of the Member State and the type of feedback reporting entities receive. We also see no significant pairwise correlation between the type of FIU and the type of feedback the FIUs give to the reporting entities.* Given the large prevalence of case-by-case feedback in Table 7.3, we assume that there is a general trend to increase individual feedback, and that country differences in matters of feedback will therefore diminish.

---

[15]   Individual feedback refers to (in-depth) follow-up of a suspicion report by the FIU. The reporting entity is informed of the outcome of the investigation and on the judicial follow-up as well as on the imposition of punitive measures on the client of the reporting entity – conviction, confiscation etc. Generic feedback refers to a more aggregate feedback on received suspicion reports.

7.5   FIU FACILITIES: ABILITY TO ACCESS RELEVANT DATA AND TO PROCESS LARGE VOLUMES OF INFORMATION

Specialists agree that for a substantial and conclusive analysis of reports, information is key. There are also more types of data which are relevant. Moreover, the speed with which this information is acquired and analysed seems also to be of relevance in the overall investigation process.

Table 7.4 shows the type of access that the EU FIUs have to a basic pool of databases.[16] Access to a database can be direct or indirect. Indirect access (marked as 'request' in Table 7.4) implies intermediated access to a database, in contrast with direct access which can be seen as non-intermediated. Direct access is preferred since it allows the FIU to be flexible in using the information present in the database. Otherwise, intermediated access implies that the FIU asks a question of a third party, not knowing what to expect in terms of an answer. Information loss therefore increases twofold: the FIU must ask the right question to get the right answer and the FIU does not know what the best answer to its question might have been.

As regards the access an FIU has to a database, this may be online or not. The latter merely reflects the speed with which the FIU can collect the information. Direct access, like indirect access, may be online or not. On the issue of the direct or indirect nature of access to a database, liaison officers and detached officers are assumed to ensure direct access for the FIU to these databases. The reason for this is that liaison officers can be assumed to be part of the FIU team and therefore would be able to reduce information loss by allowing the FIU to know what the databases contain and what the best answers to the FIU analysts' questions are.

From Table 7.4 we can conclude that *access to databases is very different across EU FIUs*. Some have a strong preference for online access, whereas others continue to access most databases manually. Some have direct access to most databases – i.e. France, Greece and Latvia – and others have restricted access or even no access to some databases – i.e. Italy. We also observe that *administrative FIUs have managed to overcome their lack of access to police data by using liaison officers*. This gives them access to more than criminal records and therefore considerably increases the

---

[16]   For the purpose of comparison, we chose a set of databases to which we consider access to be of relevance. Databases differ per country and FIUs certainly will have access to broader pools of databases. Nevertheless, pooling these different national databases into seven categories allows for a cross-country comparison.

Table 7.4 EU FIU access to police, real estate, bank, social security, customs, tax and commercial databases

	Police data	Real estate	Bank data	Social security	Customs	Tax	Commercial register
AT	Online direct*	Online direct	Request	Online direct	Request	Request	Online direct
BE	Online direct (*liaison)	Direct	Request	Direct	Online direct (liaison)	Request	Direct
BG	Request	Online direct	Request	Online direct	Direct	Online direct	Online direct
CY	Online direct*	Online request	Request	Direct (liaison)	Online direct (liaison)	Direct (liaison)	Online direct
CZ	Request (online)	Request (online)	Request	Online direct	Direct (liaison)	Request	Online direct
DK	Direct*	Direct	Request	Direct	Request	Direct	Direct
EE	Online direct*	Online direct	Request	Online direct	Request	Online direct	Online direct
FI	Direct*	Direct	Request	Direct	Direct	Direct (liaison)	Direct
FR	Online direct (*liaison)	Direct	Request	Direct	Direct	Direct	Direct
DE	Direct*		Request	Direct			Online direct
EL	Direct * (restricted)	Request	Request	Request	Direct (liaison)	Direct (liaison)	Direct
HU	Direct	Direct	Request	Direct	Direct	Direct	Direct
IE	Online direct*	Direct	Request	Request	No	No	Direct
IT	No	No	Direct	No	Request	Request	Direct

118

LV	Online direct*	Online direct	Request	Online direct	Online direct	Online direct	Online direct	Online direct
LT	Direct*	Direct	Request	Direct	Direct	Direct	Direct	Request
LU	Online direct (*liaison)	Direct	Request	Online direct	Online direct	Online direct	Request	Direct
MT	Direct* (liaison)	Request	Request	Request	Direct	Direct	Request	Direct
NL	Online direct (*liaison)	Direct	Request	Direct	Request	Request	Request	Direct
PL	Online direct		Request	Direct	Request	Online direct	Online direct	Online direct
PT	Online direct (*DCIAP)	Request	Request	Request	Online direct (liaison)	Online direct (liaison)	Online direct (liaison)	Online direct
RO	Direct	Direct	Request	Direct	Direct	Request	Direct	Direct
SK	Direct*	Direct	Request	Direct	Direct	Direct	Direct	Direct
SL	Direct	Direct	Direct	Direct	Request	Request	Direct	Direct
ES	Request*	Direct	Request	Request	Request	Request	Online direct	Online direct
SE	Direct*	Direct	Request	Direct	Direct	Request	Direct	Direct
UK	Direct*	Direct	Request	Request	Request	Request	Request	Request

Notes: In this table '*' under the 'Police data' column marks access by the FIU to a wider pool of police data than criminal records (i.e. criminal intelligence, list of arrested persons, ongoing undercover investigations, ongoing pre-trial investigation) that the FIU can have access to. Social security database includes, among other things, population register and registered state paid benefits. Customs database refers to customs intelligence (i.e. list of people crossing borders and criminal incident database). Tax database refers to recorded tax disclosures – payments and privileges for registered property. Commercial register refers to the companies register, where legal persons disclose their area of activity, financial statements etc. For a more detailed description of the available databases as well as the way national FIUs can access them, see online appendix 7.3 of the ECOLEF (2013).

effectiveness of the FIUs. Moreover, liaison officers have also been used by law enforcement FIUs to improve their access – in particular to tax and customs databases. We note as well that liaison officers are employed by many of the EU FIUs and that, where they do so, these FIUs have, on average, the greatest access to databases.

The Egmont Group has already emphasized, in its 2010 online newsletter, the importance of IT solutions for increasing the effectiveness of the FIUs. Acknowledging this, the Egmont Group has even put in place a system of self-evaluation (FIU IT System Maturity Model) to help FIUs evaluate their standpoint in terms of IT performance and their trajectory should they wish to improve their IT systems. The key domains identified in the FISMM include the collection of reports, processing of reports for analysis, information management and exchange of information. Data-mining systems are put in place to best ensure that unstructured data can be processed fast, with little error and with optimal results. According to the Egmont working group, these systems are diverse across the EU FIUs and for good reason – they need to adapt to national culture, language and the type of information that is available in each Member State.[17]

Table 7.5 shows the different ways in which FIUs receive reports from the obliged entities. To the extent possible, the national representatives have approximated in the first column the percentage of incoming requests that are received electronically. Where such estimation was not possible, we simply depicted the ways in which the FIU receives reports. Furthermore, the second column points to the presence of a data-mining system. To the extent possible we have tried to nominate the system. Where this was not possible, we denoted the presence of a data-mining system by 'own system'. The last column introduces a measure of national internet availability. It measures the number of internet users per 1,000 inhabitants in a country.[18]

We do not delve further into the properties of different data-mining systems, nor do we attempt to classify them according to their information-processing power, user friendliness etc. We assume that readers are aware of the more common data-mining systems – i.e. GoAML, I2, MoneyWeb and iBase – and therefore do not provide an overview of the latter. For the national data-mining systems, such an overview was in any case not available.

---

[17]   Egmont (December 2010) Newsletter, available from: http://www.egmont group.org/library/newsletters.
[18]   Average constructed on the basis of the 2008–11 data provided by the World Bank and downloadable from http://data.worldbank.org/indicator/IT.NET. USER.P2.

Table 7.5   FIU receipt of reports and first analysis

Country	Ways to receive reports	First analysis tool	General internet availability
AT	Electronically and in hard copy	No data-mining system	72.87
BE	70% electronically, 30% in hard copy	No data-mining system in place	66
BG	80% manually, 20% electronically	Own system	39.67
CY	Mostly manually (soon also electronically)	I2	42.31
CZ	90% electronically, 10% in hard copy	I2, Moneyweb, ELO	62.97
DK	Mostly in hard copy	GoAML	85.02
EE	Electronically	RABIS	70.58
FI	Electronically	GoAML	83.67
FR	Electronically and in hard copy	STARTRAC	70.68
DE	Most electronically, a few in hard copy	Own (BKA) system	78
EL	Electronically and hard copy	Own system	38.2
HU	Electronically	HUFO	56
IE	70% electronically, 30% in hard copy	Own system	65.34
IT	Electronically and mail	RADAR	44.53
LV	Electronically and hard copy	?	63.41
LT	Electronically and hard copy	?	55.22
LU	Electronically, fax, mail, delivery in person	Considering installing one	82.23
MT	Manually (delivery in person)	I2	50.08
NL	100% electronically	GoAML	87.42
PL	99% electronically	Own system	53.13
PT	Electronically only	Own system	41.9
RO	Mostly electronically, a few in hard copy	Own system	32.42
SK	Manually or electronically	I2	66.05
SL	Manually	No data-mining system	58
ES	Most electronically, a few in hard copy	Own system	59.6

Table 7.5   (continued)

Country	Ways to receive reports	First analysis tool	General internet availability
SE	Mostly electronically, a few in hard copy	iBase, Analyst Notebook	90
UK	98% electronically and 2% in hard copy	ARENA	78.39

Source: Own made on the basis of ECOLEF collected information. For a more detailed overview of the data-mining systems and on the national FIUs' capacity to filter fast, see online appendix 7.4 of ECOLEF (2013).

Using econometric analysis, we tried to see whether there was a significant relationship between *the size of a country or the general internet availability in a country and the FIU IT intensity, and we observe that there is no significant correlation.* We cannot therefore say that small countries – for instance, Luxembourg – generally receive reports manually. Contrary to what we had expected, we see *no correlation between the employment of data-mining software and the number of reports received by the FIUs.* Furthermore, whether or not FIUs use data-mining systems does not depend on the type of FIU.

Finally, when looking at Table 7.4 we see that the EU FIUs have also recognized the benefits of receiving these reports online, and we can see that most of them receive the vast majority of the reports in electronic format. There also seems to be a general recognition of the need to support the work of the FIU with adequate data-mining software and most FIUs have put in place a data-mining system. Given the diversity of these systems in terms of the analytical possibilities they offer to the financial analysts of the FIU as well as the general trend towards higher reliance on IT filtering systems, we argue that an in-depth comparison at the EU level would be beneficial.

7.6   CONCLUSION

Most Member States agree with the typology originally assigned to their FIUs by the IMF (2004) report. Only a handful of FIUs have changed typology. The majority of EU FIUs are either administrative or of law enforcement type and only four consider themselves to be of the judicial or hybrid types.

The size of the FIU budget does not seem to be correlated with GDP or with the accession year to the EU. Instead the size of the FIU budget and the size of the FIU staff are significantly higher when the FIU has its own separate premises. Since administrative FIUs have, in general, separate premises these are also found to have on average higher budgets and more staff. Further, we find that FIUs with a larger staff are located in less wealthy Member States. This finding is in line with the argument that, when capital is scarce, it becomes relatively expensive and is replaced with labour.

Most FIUs have staff with a mixed background and we find that staff composition is not related to the type of FIU. We argue that this is because a more heterogeneous staff is better able to access and analyse more databases in a shorter time span. We observe that FIU access to databases is very different across the EU. Administrative FIUs have therefore addressed the need to have access to law enforcement data by means of employing inter alia former law enforcement agents whether as liaison officers or in a leading position in the FIU. Consequently, the law enforcement and judicial FIUs seem to have also seen a need to address ML investigations from a financial point of view – thereby making more use of financial analysts, tax and customs liaison officers. Liaison officers are employed by many of the EU FIUs, and these FIUs have, on average, greater access to databases.

Most FIUs have additional tasks and the number of additional duties increases once an FIU undergoes significant organizational changes. We find no evidence that some types of FIUs are more burdened with additional tasks than others. Further, we find no evidence that the number of additional tasks is matched with additional resources. However, since additional tasks are not equally resource intensive, we cannot support the claim that FIUs with more additional tasks are more burdened than the rest, either.

EU FIUs have also recognized the benefits of receiving reports online, and there seems to be a trend towards receiving these reports in electronic format. There also seems to be a general recognition of the need to support the work of the FIU with adequate data-mining software. Supporting the latter claim, most FIUs have put in place a data-mining system.

Formal contacts between the FIU and the reporting entities are in place in all countries. All FIUs meet with the reporting entities at least once a year and publish annual reports to give the reporting entities general feedback. The largest differences however lie in the extent of in-house training given by the FIUs and in the nature of feedback given to the reporting entities. Some FIUs are inclined to offer individual feedback, whereas others prefer general feedback. This does not seem to be related neither to the type of FIU nor to the size of the country.

Finally, it seems that obliged entities may report more to FIUs employing mostly financial staff than to FIUs employing mostly law enforcement staff. It seems that, all else equal, hybrid FIUs have received more reports from the obliged entities than other types of FIUs.

8. Information flows and repressive enforcement

Ioana Deleanu

8.1 INTRODUCTION

Knowing which factors influence the effectiveness of criminal law enforcement allows the effectiveness of the criminal law enforcement system to be enhanced. We take the view that an effective criminal enforcement system is one that effectively enforces criminal penalties such that criminal behavior is deterred. We therefore look at the way various European criminal enforcement systems work and at the roles of the different institutions composing these systems.

In the previous chapter we discussed the role of the FIU – in its core functions as well as those assigned in addition in each Member State. In this chapter, we first explore the forms and functions of the prosecution services and how these impact the effective repression of money laundering. We then use information flow theory to construct a measure of effective communication between the law enforcement agencies involved in the repression of money laundering and show that countries with a higher information flow score have more prosecutions and convictions for money laundering. Finally, we use this information flow index to construct a measure of criminal repression across the EU and discuss several ways to improve country information flow indices in the hope of reducing criminal incentives to commit money laundering.

In the present chapter we test several hypotheses, originating either from the institutional literature or from anecdotal evidence we have gathered while interviewing national representatives of the law enforcement agencies involved in the AML fight. To start with, if countries have in place systems of information flows which facilitate information dispersion and the reduction of information asymmetry between money launderers and the law enforcement authorities, then, all else equal, these countries will have been best able to prosecute and convict on these charges. *Therefore, our hypothesis is that countries with more effective information flow systems have more money laundering prosecutions and convictions.*

From an organizational point of view, there are economies of scale to be gained from clustering prosecutors specializing in money laundering. However, specialized prosecutors who are not geographically clustered are said to be better able to connect with local realities and benefit from the experience of handling other types of criminal offences. The latter argument holds especially when considering that money laundering is often prosecuted in relation to a predicate crime. We therefore test whether *countries where money laundering cases are, in general, handled by a cluster of specialized prosecutors register more money laundering prosecutions and convictions.*

We expect that countries that have adopted a broader definition of money laundering have more prosecutions and convictions, the more effective their national institutions are at cooperating with each other and at passing on money laundering-relevant information. Conversely, ineffective networks underperform most when there is much information to process. For example, in information flows systems that have a bottleneck, problems occur only when the volumes of information are too high for the bottleneck to cope. We therefore expect that *countries that have a broader money laundering definition are better able to discourage criminal behaviour, when the information system they have in place is effective; otherwise the reverse holds.*

We see some best practices that are meant to improve national cooperation and information transmission among the national law enforcement agencies. In some cases, cooperation is facilitated by the institutional setting (i.e. double reporting by the obliged entities and multi-agency dispersal of the FIU analysis) and, in others, cooperation is induced and improved by means of systematic feedback and by employing liaison officers from other key players in the AML repressive system. We therefore *review some of these best practices and discuss the extent to which they are used to improve the effectiveness of national cooperation and information transmission.*

8.2 PUBLIC PROSECUTION: ROLES, ORGANIZATION AND EFFICIENCY IN AML MATTERS[1]

The role of Public Prosecutors

The main task of any public prosecutor is the enforcement of the law, including AML law. The public prosecutor does so by prosecuting cases where the money laundering offence has taken place.[2]

Information is the key to a successful prosecution in any money laundering case. In general, information on suspicious transactions (as well as other information relevant to money laundering cases) can be used in several instances. It can be used to detect money laundering, to investigate a money laundering case, to build a case file against a suspect, and finally it can be used to deliver evidence and proof to the courts. On the basis of the information it collects, the FIU can look for patterns of unusual transactions and therefore detect money laundering. Further, information on suspicious transactions provided by the FIU must be cross-checked against other information (i.e. tax records, police data, real estate records etc.) to confirm the suspicion of money laundering. All this information will thereafter be compiled into a case file against the suspect.[3] At this stage the public prosecutor comes in and decides whether or not to prosecute on the basis of the dossier. Then the case file is placed before the court and, if the court takes the case, the trial procedures may commence.

The prosecutor is thus dependent on information effectively reaching them. This information can pass through many entities before reaching the public prosecutor. At a national level, the prosecutor usually depends on information filtered by the FIU and on information gathered by the investigative authorities. The tax authorities, the financial supervisory authorities and the secret services are also important sources of information for the public prosecutor.

We further see that across Europe there are large differences across the prosecution services with respect to what should be prosecuted and when. We thus examine two principles of mandatory prosecution: the principle of

---

[1] We owe this exposition to Professor François Kristen. The exposition is based on a talk Professor Kristen gave at the ECOLEF Final Conference, December 2012, Amsterdam.

[2] For a broader overview of the tasks and powers of the prosecution services in Europe, see http://www.euro-justice.com/member_states/.

[3] Stessens (2000).

legality and the expediency principle.[4] According to the legality principle, each case which comes to the knowledge of the public prosecutor should be prosecuted. This implies no discretion over the prosecutorial decision. In practice, there are exemptions that make this principle economically feasible (Austria, Czech Republic). By contrast, according to the expediency principle, the public prosecutor has a discretional power to prosecute. In practice, the expediency principle permits the creation of a prosecution policy whereby the public prosecutor has guidelines in order to prioritize prosecution in cases that are in the public interest (Denmark, the Netherlands).

Depending on the principles governing each Member State, the newly criminalized money laundering offence or predicate crime will at some point be carried forward for prosecution.[5] Under the legality principle, the offence will be prosecuted immediately and, under the expediency principle, effective prosecution will depend on the guidelines of the prosecutor's office that prioritize prosecution with respect to the money laundering offence. This is particularly interesting when considering the relationship between the national administration and the prosecution services in each country.

The Organization of the Public Prosecutor's Office

There are several models to be found in Europe.[6] Some countries are governed by the ex officio principle whereby the public prosecutor (PPO) possesses a monopoly on the prosecution decision. In others (i.e. Belgium and France) the public prosecutor prosecutes, but victims of the crime can initiate or even start a prosecution as well. Finally, the public prosecutor can also share the responsibility of prosecution with another authority, such as the police or another specialized law enforcement authority (LEA) (the tax office, the customs authority etc.). On the issue of the enhancement of the effectiveness of the criminal law enforcement system, knowing who can prosecute in each Member State is crucial. If the prosecutor possesses a monopoly, then the focus should be on the public prosecutor and on increasing their capacity. If the prosecution shares this responsibility with another authority, then the focus should be on increasing the effectiveness of the prosecution and of the other specialized law enforcement bodies that can take prosecution decisions.

---

[4] Mansfield and Peay (1987).

[5] This is particularly relevant for the introduction of a new predicate crime – i.e. tax offences.

[6] Tak (2005).

In general, public prosecutors have to be able to prosecute any offence. However, different crimes impose different degrees of specialization and some cases of money laundering might require special training and expertise. In some countries (i.e. the Netherlands, France), public prosecutors must prosecute any money laundering case coming their way. Expertise is thus spread across prosecutors. In others, there exist specialized prosecutorial units that handle the more complicated, the more resource-intensive or the more sensitive cases of money laundering. Expertise is therefore concentrated (i.e. Greece, Malta, Czech Republic).

The relationship between the public prosecutor and the (other) investigation services is different across the EU Member States. In some countries the public prosecutor also investigates and so can investigate money laundering cases. Furthermore, in some jurisdictions, the prosecution can also settle money laundering cases outside court (i.e. the Netherlands). This is one way to lower the workload of the courts and to allow a more effective allocation of court resources. When the prosecution cannot investigate or has limited powers to investigate, the public prosecutor is dependent on law enforcement authorities with investigative powers to collect the needed information in a complete form that could be of use to the public prosecutor. Improving the effectiveness of the criminal enforcement system therefore requires good cooperation between the prosecution and the investigative authorities as well as an efficient system of delegating responsibility.[7]

Increasing the Efficiency of the Criminal Repressive System

Having reviewed *the main* differences in the organization of the public prosecution and prosecutorial procedures, we argue that there are a few things that can help improve the effectiveness of the criminal law enforcement system. A necessary condition is that prosecuting money laundering cases has priority. Then, sufficient resources should be allocated to the entities that are primarily charged with the enforcement of the criminal system with respect to money laundering.

Furthermore, in most cases the public prosecutor plays a central role in the criminal law system, but depends on other authorities in the enforcement of money laundering offences, namely the police and other specialized law enforcement authorities. If the latter have other priorities or do not have sufficient resources, then the public prosecutor lacks information, and is unable to perform its work effectively.[8] On the practical

---

[7] Jehle et al. (2008).
[8] Jehle and Wade (2006).

level it is therefore crucial to improve cooperation between the public prosecutor and other criminal law enforcement authorities and to improve the selection and analysis of information and its distribution among law enforcement entities and the public prosecutor. These aspects are further elaborated in Section 8.3, with a particular focus on information sharing between the prosecution, the law enforcement authorities and the FIU in each Member State.[9]

8.3   INFORMATION FLOWS – A MEASURE OF EFFECTIVE INFORMATION TRANSMISSION FROM REPORTING ENTITIES TO THE NATIONAL COURTS

Information theory studies the decision-making process that underlies transactions where one party has more or better information than the other.[10] The current global AML system is characterized by asymmetric information. In this setting, the national state agencies have imperfect information on the issue of the nature of the financial transactions they oversee nationally and internationally. Money launderers are aware of the illegality of their actions and have an incentive to hide this information from the national law enforcement units.

In a successful informational framework, therefore, government institutions could precisely identify money laundering and could sanction it accordingly. By contrast, an AML system is ineffective when the law enforcement agencies cannot trace the money laundering financial transactions that take place in the national financial system. If the latter is the case, money laundering transactions yield higher benefits than legal financial transactions, and if we assume rational profit-maximizing financial persons, illegal transactions would multiply and eventually legal transfers would no longer exist.[11]

Intelligence gathering is therefore the key to reducing this informational asymmetry. Furthermore, since information has ultimately to reach the entity with the capacity (i.e. resources, expertise etc.) and authority to punish accordingly, intelligence communication is a necessary condition for

---

[9]   In the following analysis we focus almost exclusively on cooperation between the various institutions that are able to effectively contribute to the repression of money laundering.

[10]   Akerlof (1970).

[11]   This is a crude simplification as it would be utopic to imagine a world with only money laundering-related transactions.

this information asymmetry to be effectively reduced, thereby increasing the probability of punishment. In other words, whether or not prosecutors are successful in fighting money laundering also depends on the information they are presented with by the other agencies. Information flow diagrams are used to reflect the communication taking place between different entities within a system.[12] They allow for the identification of the institutions that build repression, and of the way they connect with each other. They also allow us to see how big the informational distance between the money launderer and the repressor is, and what chance the repressor has of punishing/apprehending the criminal. In the EU, there are several types of information flow chains: the cluster police type, the cluster judicial type, the star type and the linear type (see Figure 8.1).

The main differences among the rows of Figure 8.1 are determined by the way the FIU shares information and by the position it has among the law enforcement entities. These differences give rise to different vulnerabilities and inefficiencies for each information flow.

In general, the AML literature recognizes that the reporting entities hold precious, first-hand information about their customers and are therefore best able to distinguish the unusual transactions that their clients might perform.[13] In Figure 8.1, in the left-hand side diagrams we depict, for simplicity purposes, three main sources of information for the FIU: the bullets 'Foreign FIU', 'REs' and 'Other'.[14] Each of these bullets stands respectively for the foreign FIUs as the source of transnational information, the national obliged entities as the source of suspicion reports and the state institutions and other non-obliged entities who uncover money laundering-relevant clues. The bullet 'Other' appears twice in the left-hand side diagrams, as the police has its own sources of information. Information about money laundering offences therefore enters the AML diagrams via different points of access. Differentiating further between the informal sources of the police and of the FIU is not necessary for this analysis.[15]

---

[12] Bruza and Van der Weide (1993).

[13] Schott (2003); Gilmore (1999).

[14] For the analysis we are going to perform, the numbers of bullets informing the FIU are not relevant as long as one type of information chain does not have more informants than the others.

[15] The purpose of the Third EU AML/CTF Directive was to support the development and expansion of the financial gates, as can be seen from the articles justifying the Directive: 'In addition to the criminal law approach, a preventive effort via the financial system can produce results'.

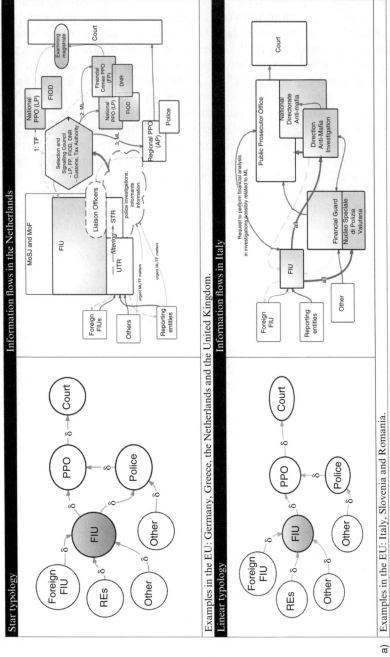

Star typology

Information flows in the Netherlands

Examples in the EU: Germany, Greece, the Netherlands and the United Kingdom.

Linear typology

Information flows in Italy

a) Examples in the EU: Italy, Slovenia and Romania.

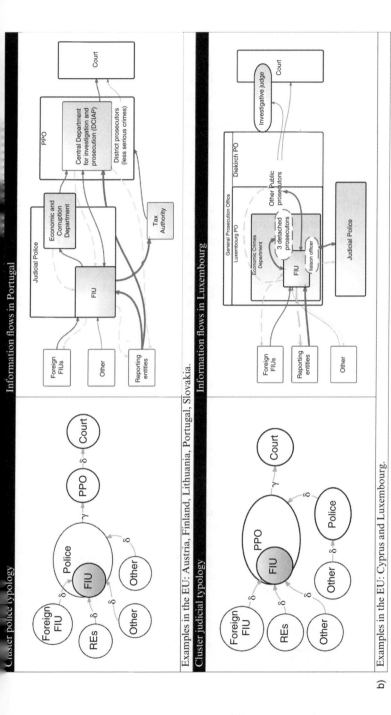

Notes: Own graphs, based on the analysis of the information flows patterns occurring in the EU. All four types of information flows are plotted on the left-handside underneath each other. Next to each type we have plotted the flows of a representative Member State to illustrate the magnitude of the information flow. For a thorough explanation of all 27 EU information flows, see online appendix 8.1 at: http://goo.gl/VZgJb3.

Figure 8.1 Information flow types – generic models and country examples

Once the intelligence reaches the FIU and/or another law enforcement agency, the information asymmetry between the criminals and the repressive system is reduced and follow-up measures to investigate and/or correct behavior can be applied. The information asymmetry thereafter needs to be further reduced such that the prosecutors and courts can effectively apply the punishment (see the arrows in Figure 8.1).

For reasons of simplicity, we have depicted the police and prosecution as two separate bullets without including the many organizational and institutional differences that can occur in the organization of the two institutions (i.e. specialized investigative units handling ML, and other prosecutorial bodies that deal with ML in connection with a specific criminal offence).[16] The same differences (courts of different instances, criminal and administrative courts etc.) are not depicted in the court system – and for that matter the court system is depicted with one single bullet to which ultimately information is transmitted for the purpose of a final decision.

On the issue of information loss/decay, we assume two types. For every flow of information in Figure 8.1, the type is denoted on top of the arrow as δ or γ. When the organization A (i.e. the FIU) transmits information to organization B (i.e. the police), the knowledge pool of B may increase. This increase can be quantified and depends on whether B already had the information and is able to understand and/or use the information. Being able to understand the information sent by A depends on how similar A and B's perceptions are, whereas being able to use the information sent by A depends on whether A sends relevant information or not.

'Limited interaction and a unilateral exchange of ideas' is an information decay factor depicted in Figure 8.1 by δ. If one knows what their interaction partners (i.e. other persons, organizations etc.) think or what their values and value systems are, one can anticipate their future reaction. Knowing what to expect of others increases trust and willingness to cooperate.[17] Correctly anticipating how others will behave depends on how much information one has about them. The underlying assumption here is that the amount of information one holds on others is directly influenced by how connected one is with them.[18] Depending on the institutional setting governing the relations between two organizations (i.e. organization A and organization B), the size of the coefficient can change accordingly. Information transmitted by organization A to organization B has a low

---

[16]   In reality national information flows are much more intricate, as shown on the right-hand side of Figure 8.1.

[17]   Nooteboom (2002).

[18]   Goyal (2007).

informative power when A has no knowledge of B's interests, field of work etc. and does not interact with B. Similarly the informative power increases once A receives periodic feedback from B on the use of this information by B at a later stage. Finally, there is no information loss (δ) when organizations A and B are one, or when members of organization A work within organization B in a liaison/detachment setting.

'Deviant interests' is an *information decay factor depicted in Figure 8.1 with* γ. When entities have deviant interests, information can be lost on purpose. This is because pressure groups – such as lobby groups and other corrupting entities – might be able to impede the transmission of information when this does not serve their interests. When weakness towards such 'corrupt practices' is a persistent factor in the national setting, one may imagine that no institution is safe.[19] The concept of using checks and balances (as originally introduced by Montesquieu) has long been recognized by the UN Office on Drugs and Crime (UNODC) and the World Bank as a fundamental mechanism to improve governance, contain corruption and improve accountability.[20] The underlying idea is that corrupt practices take place more easily within 'closed doors' than otherwise. This means that concentrating power in the hands of too few allows for more deviant interests to go unnoticed.[21]

In the following, we structure the information flow decay (δ) along two axes: national corruption levels and the presence of corruption and checks and balances. We expect high information decay when corruption and lobby groups are powerful and no checks and balances are put in place. Similarly, we expect low information decay when corruption is low and checks and balances are in place. Finally, we assume that the two information decay factors occur independently of each other and have an additive effect.

As illustrated in Figure 8.1, in the *Linear type* the FIU receives information from the reporting entities and from other FIUs, and transmits it further to the PPO. Similarly, the police are informed from their own sources (informants, ongoing investigations etc.) and forward this information to the prosecution. Without proper feedback, this information flow chain is highly vulnerable to the information loss due to limited interaction and unilateral exchange of ideas. *In the Star type* the FIU pools the data it has filtered in a database and makes it available to more

---

[19] See online appendix 8.2, http://goo.gl/VZgJb3.
[20] Available at: http://go.worldbank.org/2GQCH3X4C0.
[21] For a similar discussion on checks and balances and the credibility of the central bank in financial markets, please see Keefer and Stasavage (2002).

LEAs. The FIU is therefore able to transmit this information directly to all LEAs in a star network distribution system. This information flow is also vulnerable to the limited interaction information decay factor, but less so than in the linear cluster because a star distribution implies inherently higher common knowledge. *In the Cluster judicial type* the FIU is part of the prosecution. Information flows have no limited interaction decay as the FIU knows exactly what the other prosecutors need and what it should receive from them. However, it is a case where deviant interests can affect information flows. The lack of checks and balances makes this deviant interests factor larger in countries where corruption is evident than otherwise. *In the Cluster police type* the FIU is part of the police. Whatever information it receives from the reporting entities it keeps internally and sends to the PPO at a later stage. Once again, information has no limited interaction decay but deviant interests can affect the information flows.

From a theoretical point of view, we argue that when deviant interests are present and expected to be large, the star information transmission model is the most efficient. When they are not present and information decay is high, the cluster police information flow model is the most efficient. The linear information flow model without any feedback is the least efficient. Finally, *all models can work equally efficiently if information decay is reduced – i.e. if knowledge flows bi-directionally among interacting entities and if the right checks and balances are in place.*

Information Flow Efficiency of AML Systems – a Look at Europe

Having constructed information flow diagrams for all the EU Member States,[22] we can calculate a measure of information flow efficiency. We use the government effectiveness indicator[23] to approximate, per Member State, the propensity that information is lost, all else equal, when one government institution shares information with another governmental institution in the absence of deviant interests. Further, we use the control of corruption[24] context indicator to approximate the loss of information,

---

[22]   For a detailed list of EU Member States' information flows, see online appendix 8.1, http://goo.gl/VZgJb3.

[23]   The World Good Governance (WGG) government effectiveness indicator captures the 'perceptions of the quality of public services, the quality of the civil service [. . .], the quality of policy formulation and implementation and the credibility of the government's commitment to such policies'; Kaufmann et al. (2010).

[24]   The World Good Governance (WGG) control of corruption indicator captures the 'perception of the extent to which public power is exercised for private

per Member State, all else equal, when two governmental institutions share information in the presence of deviant interests.[25]

Figure 8.2 shows the information flow scores[26] that came out of our analysis of information flow effectiveness in the AML context.[27] The figure reveals the fact that information flows are higher in Western Europe and comparatively lower in Southern and Eastern Europe. Further, we see that there is a positive pairwise correlation (significant at the 95% confidence level) between the effectiveness of the information flows and the average number of prosecutions and convictions that have been reported in the past five years. Though correlation does not imply causality, all else equal, it is more likely that effective information sharing among AML players leads to more prosecutions and convictions than the other way around. *Countries that have no effective information flows have more money laundering prosecutions and convictions.*

Countries effectively sharing information that have a broad ML definition are expected to have more money laundering prosecutions and convictions. This has to do with the fact that a broader definition of money laundering allows for the analysis of a wider pool of data. As long as the system is effective in processing this information, it is more likely that the results will be more prosecutions and convictions. Similarly, in countries where AML players are less effective at sharing information, the adoption of a broader definition of money laundering is expected to reduce the number of money laundering-related prosecutions and convictions. As argued in Section 8.1, the effects of bottlenecks are most visible when more information needs to be processed and therefore more pressure is exerted on the bottlenecks. Countries that have less effective information flows are

---

gain, including both petty and grand forms of corruption, as well as capture of the state by elites and private interests'; Kaufmann et al. (2010).

[25] To avoid temporal fluctuations we use as a proxy the average value these context indicators have taken over the period 2008–11. The proxies are described at the online appendix 8.2, http://goo.gl/VZgJb3.

[26] For parsimonious reasons, we use a single one-size-fits-all proxy for information flow decay per country. This means that we assume interaction among any two members within a country to be equally prone to information decay. This measure of information flow is part of our preliminary research and should be improved by more in-depth research.

[27] The information flow effectiveness of small countries where information is shared well, but where corruption control indices – which are used as proxies for information decay – are low, could be underestimated. Similarly, the information flow effectiveness of countries that have cumbersome information sharing mechanisms but high corruption control indices could be overestimated.

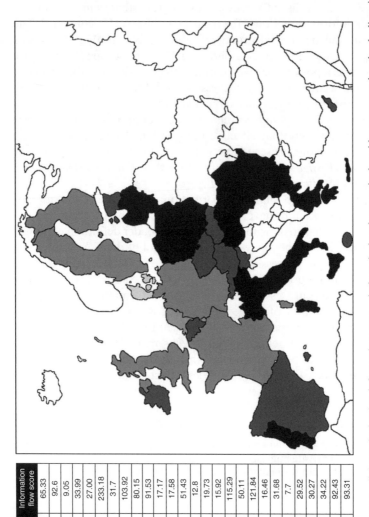

Country	Information flow score
Austria	65.33
Belgium	92.6
Bulgaria	9.05
Cyprus	33.99
Czech Republic	27.00
Denmark	233.18
Estonia	31.7
Finland	103.92
France	80.15
Germany	91.53
Greece	17.17
Hungary	17.58
Ireland	51.43
Italy	12.8
Latvia	19.73
Lithuania	15.92
Luxembourg	115.29
Malta	50.11
Netherlands	121.84
Poland	16.46
Portugal	31.68
Romania	7.7
Slovakia	29.52
Slovenia	30.27
Spain	34.22
Sweden	92.43
UK	93.31

Note: High information score – lightest shades; low information score – darkest shades; the score in the tables correspond to the shadings in the figure.

Figure 8.2 Information flows across the EU

less able to reduce information decay and to avoid bottlenecks. This could not, however, be confirmed econometrically.

8.4 ESTIMATING THE EFFICIENCY OF THE MONEY LAUNDERING REPRESSIVE SYSTEM

Deterrence of criminal behaviour is what criminal systems ultimately aim for. Repressing or deterring money laundering goes one step further than fighting money laundering as it incorporates an element of prevention as well. The effects of expected punishment on criminal behaviour continues to be a growth area in the literature on crime prevention (see Rauhut and Junker (2009), Harbaugh et al. (2011) to name some recent examples). Experiments have shown that punishment alone does not deter crime, and that many other factors play a role. Moreover, deterrence is not straightforward.[28]

As Nobel Prize winner, Gary Becker, described in his seminal work on 'crime and punishment'[29] – a criminal will take into account the size and frequency of punishment before deciding whether to commit the crime. This view is particularly applicable to the cluster of financially profitable crimes that money laundering, to a great extent, is based on and belongs to. Equation 8.1 models the capacity of the AML system to deter money laundering from the perspective of the money launderer. Equation 8.1 expands the equation introduced by Becker (1968), by distinguishing two probabilities: a probability that money laundering is picked up by the reporting entities, by police informants etc. (P_{detect} in Equation 8.1) and the probability (P_{punish} in Equation 8.1) that, once that happens, the prosecution is successful in imposing a punishment (C in Equation 8.1). If the expected punishment is higher than the benefits (B in Equation 8.1) yielded by committing money laundering, then, rational profit-maximizing individuals will commit the crime; otherwise they will refrain from doing so.

$$P_{detect} * P_{punish} * C \sim B \qquad (8.1)$$

Deterrence thus depends on the ability of the AML system to detect and sanction money laundering and should always be discussed from the point

---

[28]   The degree of deterrence does not linearly increase with respect to the punishment and with respect to the probability of being caught and sanctioned.

[29]   Becker (1968).

of view of the money launderers. Effective repression therefore ensures that the punishment is severe enough (C is sufficiently high) and frequent enough (P_{punish} is sufficiently high) to deter criminal behaviour. Effective criminal prevention ensures that the probability of being caught is high enough (P_{detect} is sufficiently high) and that the benefits are low enough to deter criminal behaviour.

Prevention and repression are therefore complementary: prevention can be effective only if repression is also marginally effective, and repression is more effective if prevention is also effective. From this departure point, we look at every national repressive system and describe the way it works.[30] We therefore ask the following questions:

1. What type of punishment can be expected for deviant behaviour in money laundering?
2. What is the probability that punishment will be imposed?

In attempting to answer the first question, we take the legal provisions mentioned in the Criminal Code of each Member State.[31] As the probability that criminal behaviour will be punished in each Member State cannot be found in the statistics we construct a proxy – namely, the value of the information chain that is present in each country. The probability that a criminal will be punished once he commits money laundering is therefore proxied by the probability that financial information from the reporting entities (and others) effectively reaches the organization(s) in charge of imposing the punishment. By 'information effectively reaching the relevant organizations' we assume that this information reaches them in due time, and in such a way that it can be used to secure punishment (as discussed in Section 8.1).

Figure 8.3 offers a measure of 'C', namely the average money laundering punishments across Europe.[32] In constructing the 'average

---

[30] We assume that money laundering prevention is equally efficient across Europe. This means that money laundering yields the same benefits across Europe and that the probability that a money laundering transaction is discovered across the EU is the same. We are aware that this is a simplification.

[31] There are more factors to consider when constructing a measure of sanctions in AML matters: the quality of life in prison, the confiscation of proceeds from crime, the negative impact of a criminal record on future employment possibilities etc. We owe this point to Professor Ernesto Savona, who expressed this view during the ECOLEF Final Conferences, December 2012, in Amsterdam.

[32] In constructing this measure of punishments for money laundering we did not take into account the expected financial loss due to the confiscation of assets involved in committing the crime.

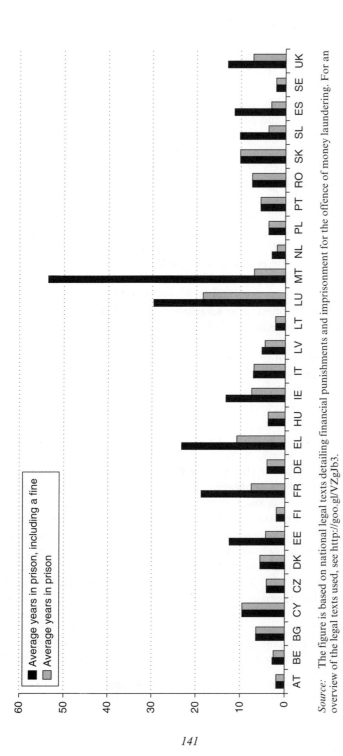

Source: The figure is based on national legal texts detailing financial punishments and imprisonment for the offence of money laundering. For an overview of the legal texts used, see http://goo.gl/VZgJb3.

Figure 8.3   Punishments imposed in each Member State in relationship to money laundering

years of imprisonment' measure we used different national legal texts that criminalize and impose punishments for these two crimes (i.e. the Criminal Code, the Code of Criminal Procedure and the AML/CTF Act). For each Member State we were thus able to calculate[33] an average punishment (prison and fine punishment) for money laundering, taking into account the different degrees of seriousness of the offence, as well as the possible imposition of financial punishments in addition to imprisonment.[34] Alternatively, we could have taken the average of the actual imposed punishments on cases involving money laundering in each EU Member State. This second option was not applied here due to data asymmetry and lack of data.

Figure 8.3 shows that the average imprisonment punishment for money laundering differs significantly among states. If a criminal were therefore to shop for punishments, Austria, Sweden, Finland and the Netherlands would be the most reasonable destinations in which to commit money laundering. Similarly, one would be most reluctant to commit money laundering in Luxembourg, since the average expected punishment is approximately nine times larger than in the first four examples.

Figure 8.4 plots effective money laundering repression across the EU. The effective repression scores are computed for each Member State using the previously referred to information flow score and the money laundering punishment score, according to equation 8.1.

It seems that holding $\frac{B}{P_{detect}}$ constant over the EU Member States, money launderers have less incentive to commit money laundering in the UK, Luxembourg, Denmark or France than in the newer Member States – Romania and Bulgaria, Hungary or Poland. Figure 8.4 reveals a mixed map of Europe, where geographical patterns are no longer so clear. This finding however, rests on a very strong assumption – namely that the probability of being detected when committing money laundering is equal across the EU. One suggestion to overcome this oversimplification is to conduct what is known as 'mystery shopping' – namely to try to pass unobserved using the same technique through the detection mechanisms put in place in all the EU Member States. Seeing how concern is rising over the fact that the present liquidity crisis may drive financial institutions to

---

[33]   For an overview of the punishments that can be imposed in the case of money laundering, when these are simple and/or aggravated offences, see the online appendix 8.3.

[34]   In constructing prison and fine punishment measure, we used the transformation proposed by the Innocence Project (http://www.innocenceproject.org/), namely that one year in prison is worth 50,000 Euros.

Country	Effective repression score
Austria	302.1
Belgium	954.4
Bulgaria	145.0
Cyprus	1739.2
Czech Republic	447.2
Denmark	2448.4
Estonia	584.6
Finland	627.0
France	2665.1
Germany	844.4
Greece	484.8
Hungary	153.9
Ireland	1199.4
Italy	232.3
Latvia	378.7
Lithuania	225.5
Luxembourg	4089.9
Malta	2797.1
Netherlands	1469.8
Poland	176.9
Portugal	541.2
Romania	192.4
Slovakia	639.5
Slovenia	476.1
Spain	648.3
Sweden	312.0
UK	5051.3

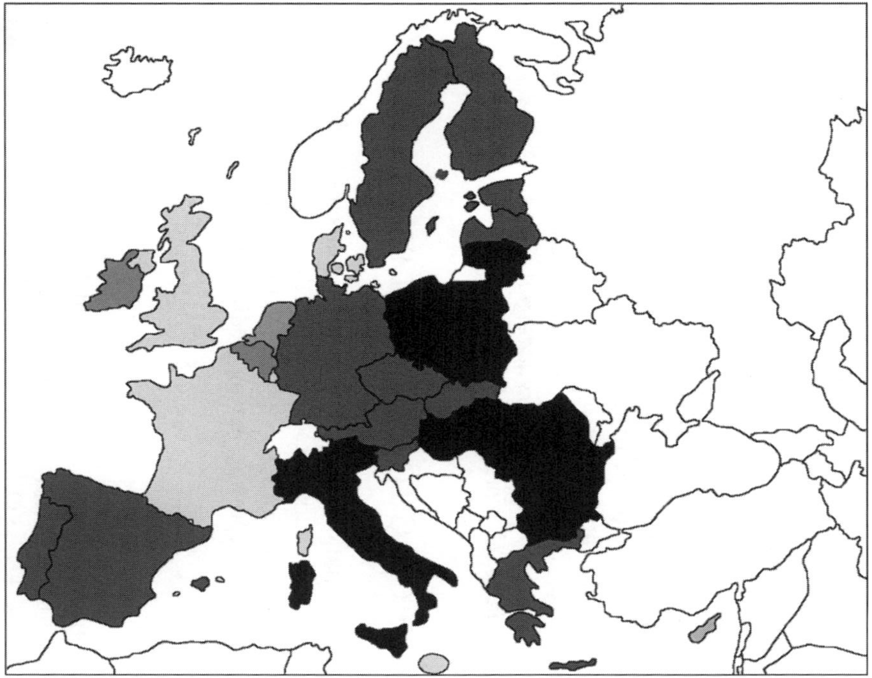

Note: High effective repression score – lighter countries; low effective repression score – darker countries; the values in the table correspond to the shadings in the figure.

Figure 8.4 Effective money laundering repression across the EU

turn a blind eye to illegal money,[35] a 'mystery shopping' assessment might be needed on a more regular basis.

Finally, we also address the hypothesis that Member States that have groups of prosecutors specialized in money laundering also have more prosecutions and convictions for money laundering. Most Member States have specialized prosecutorial bodies that handle the more complex money laundering investigations. These groups of specialized prosecutors are generally located in the largest financial pole of the country and bring together highly experienced prosecutors with financial and organized crime backgrounds. When we correlate the presence of such specialized clusters of prosecutors with the number of prosecutions on money laundering as well as with the number of convictions on money laundering, we do not get any significant results. It seems therefore, that *it may be too early to judge whether these clusters add significant positive value to the overall output of the AML repressive chain.*

8.5   CONVERGING TO SOME BEST PRACTICES

When looking at the national information flows across the EU, we see that all Member States have introduced several methods to increase national cooperation among the key actors in the AML system. This was done either through double reporting, giving feedback and or by introducing checks and balances.

Double Reporting

With the exception of Ireland, Germany and Portugal, all other FIUs are the single national competent authority for receiving disclosures of information (STRs, UTRs or SARs). The Irish FIU shares this duty with a prosecution service, namely the Revenue Commissioners. In Germany, the police (and in two states the prosecution) receive the reports and the FIU receives a copy of the report as well. In Portugal the reporting entities forward their reports to the FIU and to a specialized department within the prosecutor's office.

There are various reasons for this dual reporting. In Portugal this has to do with institutional persistence – the prosecutors had long received disclosures before the establishment of the FIU and would not accept

---

[35]   See statement of the Head of the UNODC, available at: http://www.guard ian.co.uk/global/2009/dec/13/drug-money-banks-saved-un-cfief-claims.

the loss of information that would have been entailed if the FIU had become the sole receiving unit. In Germany the obliged institutions have to double-report due to the different data protection systems that are in place in the federal states. The FIU has access to other databases than the police, and therefore it acts as a distribution centre for information at a federal level. In Ireland the criminal law system has deep common law roots, which means that there are several coexisting prosecuting entities. The Revenue Commissioners use the disclosures of information received from the reporting entities to prosecute in cases where tax evasion has been committed.

It can therefore not be concluded that in all circumstances the decision to impose double reporting was done with an eye to avoiding the concentration of information in the hands of only one institution. This has nevertheless been a secondary effect. When looking at the national estimates for the control of corruption across Member States, double reporting could be argued to have had the largest positive effect in Portugal. The effect should be smaller in Ireland, whose estimated corruption control perception index is very high, and to a lesser extent in Germany where, except for two states, double reporting only disperses information within the same institution: the German police force.

FIUs Need and Want Feedback

During our research we found abundant evidence to support the importance of feedback. First of all, feedback was reported to be crucial in improving the input that the FIU has to offer to the investigative authorities and in helping collect relevant information in due time such that prosecution is successful. Moreover, fine tuning of information received from the FIU is assumed to reduce eventual investigation bottlenecks and possible overloading of other investigative agencies. Finally, feedback is a great tool to ensure that agents that have an intermediate role in producing an outcome share the joy of reaching the outcome – feedback can motivate FIU agents if it makes them feel they have contributed to the successful repression of a 'social bad'.

Another interesting fact we uncovered during this research is that most FIUs are pleased to receive feedback on their analyses. Following the institutional literature, this would indicate that they are ready to take a leading position in the AML fight and to anticipate what is needed from them at a later stage in the investigation. All FIUs that did not have feedback from the PPO wished to receive it. The others were content with the current state of affairs and were looking forward to improving collaboration and to receiving more feedback from the specialized police forces.

Finally, there are three ways to ensure feedback: first, horizontal cooperation – through joint investigation teams or liaison officers, and second, vertical coordination – when feedback is given after an action has been taken by the FIU with a view to potentially similar cases in the future. The first form of feedback is most likely to increase the learning of the FIU, whereas the latter is the least resource intensive on the part of the law enforcement entities (no detached officer needs to be paid for) and is less likely to conflict with national data protection principles. Finally, there is also insider cooperation – when the head of the FIU is appointed from the ranks of the police or of the prosecution to ensure that cooperation increases in the future. Looking at the information flows across the EU, we see *that feedback is given either directly or indirectly to all FIUs.*

Introducing Checks and Balances to Reduce the Concentration of Information within a Single Structure

In some inquisitorial systems, the prosecution makes use of investigative magistrates to avoid being seen as a partial assessor of the situation in which a suspect is involved. Investigative magistrates may have more investigative powers than prosecutors and are there to ensure an impartial judgment. Further, double reporting imposed on the obliged entities can ensure the dissemination of information related to suspicious transactions across institutions. Regardless of the perception of the degree of control of corruption in the country, this can help increase transparency and effectiveness of the information flow system. Finally, when bottlenecks are predicted at the level of an institution, automatic data transfers can be put in place to avoid them. This is detrimental to the filter function of the institution, but can help improve overall information flow effectiveness.

9. International cooperation

Ioana Deleanu and Melissa van den Broek

9.1 INTRODUCTION AND HYPOTHESES

This chapter deals with international cooperation within the AML frame-work.[1] Although the national AML policies of the Member States have so far been the focus of our research, we cannot disregard the fact that international cooperation affects these national policies.

We first look at how international cooperation takes place, within the AML framework. Our first hypothesis is that *cooperation in AML matters takes place only between homologue institutions in the EU*. We then examine international cooperation within the EU and outside the EU. Obviously, there are a lot of international cooperation channels available to European counterparts with the aim of strengthening European cooperation. We therefore hypothesize that, for international FIU cooperation, *cooperation between EU FIUs is easier than cooperation between EU and non-EU FIUs*. The criterion we use to test this hypothesis is the speed of information exchange.

Finally, we hypothesize that *international cooperation takes place mostly among neighbouring countries*. This hypothesis is put forward in the economics literature that makes ample use of gravity models to explain patterns of interaction between countries.[2] Due to data restrictions, this hypothesis will be tested only on the FIUs.

---

[1] This chapter is a modification of ECOLEF (2013), chapter 10.
[2] Gravity models replicate Newton's law of gravity and use it to explain patterns of interaction between agents that depend on their proximity and size. Tinbergen (1962) was the founder of the gravity model of trade, whereby he could predict trade flows between two countries on the basis of their economic mass and the distance between them.

9.2 INTERNATIONAL COOPERATION CHANNELS AND AGREEMENTS

Our research shows that international cooperation takes place, in general, among homologue institutions. Ministries therefore cooperate with other ministries via various EU platforms, FIUs with other FIUs through the use of various mechanisms, and law enforcement authorities with their homologues: the police (law enforcement authorities) with police (law enforcement authorities) and public prosecutor's offices with public prosecutor's offices. There is one exception to this rule: in instances where the FIU belongs to the judicial or law enforcement model, cooperation from the FIU may be sought through judicial and/ or law enforcement cooperation channels. However, it should be noted that these FIUs cannot, strictly in their FIU capacity, formally make use of other channels in international cooperation. Supporting the claim that international cooperation mainly takes place between homologue agencies, the channels designated for communication help maintain information sharing among the same types of authorities, as depicted in Figure 9.1.[3]

EU FIU Platform[4]

The EU Financial Intelligence Units' Platform is an informal group, set up in 2006 by the European Commission, which gathers together representatives of all the FIUs of the EU Member States. The Platform is intended as a forum for discussion on specific aspects related to the application and implementation of the new provisions introduced by the Third Directive, focusing on identifying problems, practical issues and possible solutions.

Recognizing the different types of FIUs and the consequent differences in the legal framework that could disrupt the smooth exchange of information, the Platform is therefore intended to serve as a forum to discuss issues related to differences in the operational structures of FIUs in order to explore the possibilities of a harmonization process, particularly in the field of gathering and interpretation of information for statistical purposes. The European Commission participates in the Platform and provides support.

---

[3] This overview of the channels most used in matters of AML cooperation can also be found in ECOLEF (2013).

[4] Information retrieved from http://ec.europa.eu/internal_market/company/financial-crime/index_en.htm#fiu-platform.

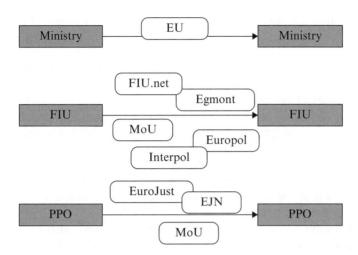

Notes: The figure illustrates a few of the most frequently reported cooperation channels that ministries, FIUs and PPOs use for international cooperation in the AML framework. The list is not exhaustive (e.g. EU FIU and CARIN are not illustrated). MoU stands for memoranda of understanding and EJN stands for the European Judicial Network.

Figure 9.1   International cooperation platforms and agreements

Europol – AWF SUSTRANS and CARIN[5]

Europol is one of the main platforms for sharing information (on AML and other crimes) within Europe. Its mission is 'to support and strengthen action by the Member States' police authorities and other law enforcement services and their mutual cooperation in preventing and combating serious crime affecting two or more Member States, terrorism and forms of crime which affect a common interest covered by a Union policy'.[6] Its tasks are 'the coordination, organisation and implementation of investigative and operational action carried out jointly with the Member States' competent authorities or in the context of joint investigative teams, where appropriate in liaison with Eurojust'.[7]

AWF SUSTRANS (The Analytical Work File for Suspicious Transactions) was formed under Article 10 of the Europol Convention,

---

[5]   Information retrieved from http://www.assetrecovery.org/kc/node/baf520a5-fe6d-11dd-a6ca-f1120cbf9dd3.0.
[6]   Article 88(1) TFEU.
[7]   Article 88(2) TFEU.

which stated that an AWF should be opened for the purpose of analysis, defined as the assembly, processing or utilization of data, with the aim of helping a criminal investigation on the issue of suspicious transactions and money laundering. While primarily designed for the police and law enforcement, law enforcement FIUs can directly benefit from this channel of cooperation. Nevertheless, these intelligence databases are also available to administrative FIUs, where they have liaison officers. For example, the French FIU (TRACFIN) has access to the Europol information exchange system (analysis and data on suspicious transactions) through its police liaison officer. Therefore, liaison officers seconded by the Gendarmerie and police are the inter-agency contacts within the competent judicial departments and responsible for subsequent coordination.

In addition to the SUSTRANS database, Europol also hosts at its headquarters the permanent secretariat of CARIN (Camden Asset Recovery Inter-agency Network). This informal network of contacts was set up in 2004 by Austria, Belgium, Germany, Ireland, the Netherlands and the UK. It is a global network of practitioners and experts intended to enhance mutual knowledge on methods and techniques in the area of cross-border identification, freezing, seizure and confiscation of the proceeds and other property related to crime. Its aim is to improve cooperation among asset recovery offices (AROs) in order to successfully deprive criminals of illicit profits. This is a network which reunites representatives of judicial and law enforcement authorities from the Member States, and is open to FIUs that belong to the judicial or the law enforcement system. Law enforcement FIUs can thus have access to this database as well.

Eurojust

Eurojust includes national representatives from all 27 EU Member States' public prosecutor's offices and national magistrates – and sometimes from law enforcement authorities. Eurojust's mission is to 'support and strengthen coordination and cooperation between national investigating and prosecuting authorities in relation to serious crime affecting two or more Member States or requiring a prosecution on common bases (. . .)'.[8] Article 85 of the Treaty on the Functioning of the European Union (TFEU) describes the tasks of Eurojust that may include:

---

[8]   Article 85(1) TFEU.

- the initiation of criminal investigations, as well as proposing the initiation of prosecutions, conducted by competent national authorities, particularly those relating to offences against the financial interests of the Union;
- the coordination of investigations and prosecutions;
- the strengthening of judicial cooperation, including by resolution of conflicts of jurisdiction and by close cooperation with the European Judicial Network.

Eurojust is the most commonly used cooperation platform for the prosecution and courts within the European Union. Representatives of the national prosecution services across the EU agree that Eurojust is also a good cooperation tool for judicial cooperation in money laundering matters. They report making use of Eurojust in cross-border money laundering cases, as this helps strengthen the criminal investigation and prosecution.

Interpol

Interpol is the world's largest international police organization and this channel too facilitates cross-border police cooperation, supporting the fight against international crime. This channel is reported to be used by the police and by the law enforcement FIUs, in particular when dealing with countries outside the European Union. The Interpol database provides access to classified intelligence on ongoing investigations, known criminals, DNA profiles, etc. Once again, the Interpol channel has been reported to be used actively by various law enforcement FIUs, such as the Austrian, German, Luxembourg, Irish and UK FIUs.

FIU.NET and Egmont Secure Web

There are two channels for the exchange of information between FIUs. These are FIU.NET and Egmont Secure Web (ESW). Irrespective of their types, European FIUs can communicate using FIU.NET. It is a secure and decentralized computer network for the exchange of subject data. FIU.NET is reported to encourage cooperation and enables FIUs to exchange intelligence quickly, securely and effectively.[9] FIU.NET was established in 2000 by France, Italy, Luxembourg, the Netherlands and the United Kingdom and became fully operational in 2002. In 2004 DG MARKT of the European Commission financed the development and expansion of FIU.NET with the aim of intensifying, deepening and

---

[9] FIU.NET, available at: http://www.fiu.net/.

professionalizing FIU cooperation within the European Union. Currently the Final FIU.NET Project 2011–2013 is running. This project is financed by DG Home Affairs of the European Commission.[10] FIU.NET is currently being embedded in Europol. It is scheduled to be completed before January 2014.

An important principle respected by FIU.NET is that the information stays decentralized.[11] This way, FIUs that transmit the information via FIU.NET remain the owners of their information. FIU.NET employs the match system, a well-developed technology that – according to FIU. NET Bureau – allows connected FIUs to match their data with other FIUs in an anonymous way. According to the FIU.NET website, 'FIUs can detect subjects of their interest in other countries even though they were not aware that the subject was trying to hide his proceeds in other countries'.[12] FIUs may decide not to share information with all FIUs, but can each time select those FIUs that they find most suitable. The total number of exchanged requests via FIU.NET was 6,369 in the year 2011. This is double the number in 2007, where the total number of requests was 3,133.[13] EU FIUs thus use FIU.NET more and more. This highlights the true potential that the match system has, and the fact that this potential is increasingly being recognized by EU FIUs.

EU FIUs can also make use of the Egmont Secure Web (ESW). This channel is mostly used for the exchange of information with third-country FIUs. ESW is a secure internet system by which the members of the Egmont Group can 'communicate with one another via secure e-mail, requesting and sharing case information as well as posting and assessing information on typologies, analytical tools and technological developments'.[14]

ESW is a channel open to all EU FIUs. FIU.NET is currently operational in 25 Member States. It is not used by the Czech and Swedish FIUs. While the Czech Republic is not connected to FIU.NET, the Swedish FIU cannot operationalize FIU.NET due to internal regulations of the Swedish National Police Board – to which the FIU belongs. Under the Swedish Police Data Act 1998:662, the FIU is only allowed to store files when cases are still open.[15] In terms of usage, representatives of various FIUs describe the ESW as an email inbox, while FIU.NET has an intranet

---

[10]   FIU.NET, available at: http://www.fiu.net/.
[11]   European Commission (2010b).
[12]   FIU.NET, available at: http://www.fiu.net/.
[13]   ECOLEF (2013).
[14]   Egmont, available at: http://www.fincen.gov/international/egmont/.
[15]   ECOLEF (2013).

and is built in a more sophisticated manner. Ome problem reported with respect to FIU.NET is the fact that some Member States have been temporarily disconnected.

Member States' representatives argue that integrating the two platforms would be highly beneficial. While Egmont only mentions that '(. . .) meetings will take place between the administrators of the Egmont Secured Web (ESW) and the FIU Bureau to create a work plan on how to improve communications between the Egmont Group and FIU.NET',[16] FIU.NET Bureau reported that there already exists a connection between ESW and FIU.NET. FIU.NET cases can already be exported in Egmont files so that the users can exchange FIU.NET cases with FIUs that are not connected to FIU.NET. Furthermore, at the present time the Egmont IT Working Group is doing a feasibility study with the aim of identifying ways that ESW and FIU.NET can further strengthen each other. In this respect, FIU.NET Bureau has reported that they are considering the possibility of integrating ESW mail into FIU.NET, so that FIU.NET users can directly exchange cases with non-FIU.NET FIUs, without having to export them to the ESW format.

Although both channels are actively used by EU FIUs, a large number of FIUs have indicated that they generally prefer to use FIU.NET for exchanging information with EU FIUs. This channel is considered faster and more user-friendly. There are some exceptions. For example, representatives of the Greek FIU have stated they prefer to work with Egmont because that channel has more users. At the Latvian FIU, it is left to the discretion of the employees to use Egmont or FIU.NET. However, the Latvian FIU is of the opinion that Egmont is more advanced than FIU.NET and easier to use.

Informal Contacts vs. Bilateral Cooperation Projects

Informal contacts that run via liaison officers or contacts made during international meetings are reported to be very important as well. Both FIU representatives and public prosecutor's offices representatives value these personal contacts very much, especially as they help speed up the process of collecting information. For FIUs, informal contacts and bilateral projects can also help ensure that more feedback is received on outstanding requests.

---

[16] Egmont, 'Annual Report 2010–2011', available at: http://www.egmont group.org/library/annual-reports.

Various FIU representatives also emphasize the importance of Memoranda of Understanding (MoU) and twinning projects. Formally, most FIUs do not need MoUs for cooperation, since FIU.NET or EGMONT membership will suffice. MoUs, however, are reported to have an important political and diplomatic function and to provide more security about the confidentiality of the data.[17] They are also considered to be signs of permanent and secure cooperation. The Polish FIU has indicated that within the European Union they do not need to sign MoUs with counterparts because Council Decision no. 200/642/JHA, concerning arrangements for cooperation between financial intelligence units of the Member States in respect of exchanging information, functions as the basis for cooperation. For cooperation with third-country FIUs, however, a Memorandum of Understanding is required. The Polish FIU has signed a total of 63 MoUs.[18]

Besides these forms of international cooperation, other reported forms of international cooperation are pilot projects and twinning projects. Under such projects, FIUs visit other FIUs and see how the other FIUs are functioning in order to improve their own performance ('learning curve'). Furthermore, these projects are intended to ease the exchange of larger pieces of information and to cross-check databases containing sensitive information in a secure way. An example is provided by the Dutch FIU, which has set up pilot projects of cooperation with the Swedish FIU and, since 2010, with the Serbian FIU.[19] The Polish FIU reported in its Annual Report 2011 on the twinning project in place with the Romanian FIU.[20] The Spanish FIU has in place a twinning project with the Albanian FIU.

9.3 INTERNATIONAL COOPERATION EASE – WITHIN AND OUTSIDE THE EUROPEAN UNION

We would like to test whether cooperation through FIU.NET is faster than through ESW. For this we could compare the average time responses for requests from EU FIUs and requests from non-EU FIUs.[21] The ECOLEF (2013) report gives information on the self-estimated time-to-

---

[17] CTIF-CFI (2010), p.105.
[18] Polish FIU (2011), 'Annual Report', p. 43.
[19] Dutch FIU (2010), 'Annual Report', p. 40.
[20] Polish FIU (2011), 'Annual Report', p. 43.
[21] Although, of course, we are aware of the fact that EU FIUs cooperation

respond per EU-FIU for requests coming from other EU FIUs and from non-EU FIUs. This data is available for 18 EU FIUs.

Only three FIUs (Cyprus, Germany and Luxembourg) indicated a time difference between responding to EU FIUs requests and third-country FIU requests. The Cypriot FIU indicated that priority is given to EU FIUs requests over other non-EU FIU requests. The German FIU indicated an average response time of a maximum of one week for requests from EU FIUs, but indicated that no time frame could be provided for answering requests coming from non-EU FIUs. The Luxembourg FIU indicated a response time of 24 hours for EU FIUs and a response time of 24 hours to one week for non-EU FIU requests. The Luxembourg representatives further indicated that the Luxembourg FIU responds to an FIU request through FIU.NET, on average, in 1–2 days and to a request made through ESW within 2–4 days.

The other 15[22] FIUs responded that there was no difference in response times. Also the answers on average response time varied a lot. Two FIUs answered between 24 hours and 30 days, and seven Member States indicated 'within 30 days'. Some Member States were able to provide an average. The Czech FIU indicated that it replies within one week to international FIU requests. The Danish FIU indicated an average response time of 3 working days. The Irish FIU replies within 3–5 working days. The Dutch FIU's average response time is 5 working days, that of Estonia 14 working days, and the Maltese FIU on average replies within 6 working days. On average, the Swedish FIU responds to international exchange requests within 3 working days. Finally, the UK FIU is reported to respond within an average of 22 working days.

The Maltese and Swedish FIUs were also able to indicate the average time response from other FIUs to their own requests. For the Maltese FIU this was 37 working days; while the Swedish FIU has to wait 14.3 working days on average to receive a reply to its requests. Both numbers are considerably higher than the average response times indicated by the FIUs. On the basis of the set of data obtained, we cannot confirm that international FIU cooperation between EU FIUs is faster than with non-EU FIUs.

---

may also take place through Egmont and that not all EU-FIUs have been linked to FIU.NET.

[22] Belgium, Bulgaria, the Czech Republic, Denmark, Estonia, Ireland, Lithuania, Malta, the Netherlands, Portugal, Romania, Sweden, Spain and the United Kingdom.

9.4   HINDRANCES TO INTERNATIONAL COOPERATION

There are six hindrances to international cooperation, both for international FIU and international judicial cooperation. The hindrances to international cooperation expressed by national representatives are language barriers, time delays, generic information, differences in data protection standards, non-efficient *national* cooperation and the lack of a legal basis in all EU Member States' legislation that allows FIUs to block or freeze suspicious transactions on their own motion for a certain period of time.

The extent of hindrances to international cooperation differs: while Western European Member States indicate that they do not encounter any serious hindrances in international cooperation, most Central and Eastern European Member States indicate that they face a number of difficulties in international cooperation. However, since most country representatives here were asked to give an opinion on the extent to which they encounter difficulties in international cooperation – without having to attribute the source of the problem to their side or to the side of their collaborators – one cannot say that cooperation with Central and Eastern European Member States is more difficult than with Western European Member States.

Eastern European Member States were the only ones to report language barriers as a serious hindrance in international cooperation. In general, however, English is commonly employed as the language of international cooperation. Sometimes, however, there is evidence that Member States cooperate with each other by using their own languages. For instance, the Portuguese and Spanish FIUs explain that in practice they send each other requests for information exchange and responses to requests in their own languages to each other. They report that this does not lead to any difficulties in cooperation between the two FIUs.

Time delays seem to be most commonly felt as the main hindrance to international cooperation. It seems that this problem is more prevalent in international judicial cooperation than in international FIU cooperation. The translation of judicial documents, letters rogatory, and documentation that may serve as evidence takes considerable time. This also explains why mutual legal assistance (MLA) takes a lot longer than FIU international cooperation. Whereas above we could see that FIU international cooperation is usually a matter of days, it seems that MLA cooperation takes months – if not years. In any case, both FIU and PPO representatives indicated that the processing time always depends on the complexity of the cases and on the amounts of information that are requested to be gathered.

Generic information sometimes plays a role in international cooperation, although various representatives have stated that this holds especially for cooperation with non-EU countries. Generic information refers to information that is quantitative but not qualitatively significant for the requesting party. Formally, an authority may have replied to a request, while – for whatever reason – it did not really give an answer to the request itself. This problem is seen as the main hindrance to international cooperation by Western European Member States. Our assumption is that the problem of receiving general information is averted and/or avoided by the use of informal contacts.

Non-efficient national cooperation is also mentioned by various Member States' representatives as hampering international cooperation. This statement usually concerns the non-efficient national cooperation of other Member States, whereas own national cooperation structures are at the same time often praised.

Data protection is a matter that receives attention from the cooperation channels outlined above. We received anecdotal evidence in the field of FIU international cooperation on differences with respect to data retention. For example, where record-keeping periods differ between Member States, this may result in a situation where no information can be provided in response to a request. For international FIU cooperation, various representatives explained that this is why information is only exchanged with FIU.NET or Egmont partners, or with FIUs with which Memoranda of Understandings have been signed.

The issue of the inability of some EU FIUs to block or freeze suspicious transactions without the prior approval of a judiciary authority has been researched by CARIN since 2010. Members of the network have observed that if all FIUs had the power to block or freeze suspicious transactions on their own motion for a minimum (standard) period of time, then national coordination and international cooperation would significantly improve. The issue is particularly relevant for money flows that only briefly transit a Member State and that are otherwise difficult to seize and confiscate. Based on the data collected by CARIN in 2010, only 14 of the 27 EU FIUs had the power to freeze or block suspicious transaction on their own motion. Moreover, the freezing and blocking periods varied from a couple of days to several months.[23]

---

[23] The EU FIUs that could block and freeze suspicious transactions on their own motion in 2010 were: Belgium, Cyprus, the Czech Republic, Denmark, Estonia, Finland, Hungary, Ireland, Latvia, Lithuania, Luxembourg, Poland, the Slovak Republic and Slovenia.

9.5   INTERNATIONAL FIU COOPERATION IN PERSPECTIVE

One of the hypotheses we wanted to test in this chapter is whether international cooperation between FIUs takes place mostly between neighbouring countries. Table 9.1 provides a systematic grouping of the top cooperation partners that the FIUs have. The table is based on information gathered from FIU annual reports, MONEYVAL, FATF evaluations and ECOLEF (2013). Unfortunately a great deal of data is missing, which makes our results sensitive at this point.

In Table 9.1 when requests are incoming from or outgoing to a neighbouring FIU, the name of the respective FIU is in bold type. For some countries, in particular Cyprus, Malta and the UK, due to their insular geography, this is not done. The table nevertheless shows visually that neighbours play a very important role in FIU cooperation. Moreover, based on information readily available in this table, we were able to graph the interaction patterns in this network.

Figure 9.2 graphs the interaction patterns between the EU FIUs and their most prominent foreign cooperation partners. The figure is based on the data presented in Table 9.1. Some countries have not reported their most important cooperation partners, so Figure 9.2 cannot offer a robust picture of international cooperation among the EU FIUs. In Figure 9.2, the UK is by far the country with the highest connectivity – and this means that most other FIUs send requests for cooperation to the UK. Similarly, Luxembourg, Belgium, Italy and Spain are popular cooperation partners for other EU FIUs. Finally, once again, we see that geographical proximity and cultural and historical ties matter – as Member States cooperate very closely with their former colonies and with their direct neighbours.

9.6   CONCLUDING REMARKS

There are a variety of judicial and FIU international cooperation channels in the field of fighting money laundering. International cooperation takes place between homologues. The only exception is where judicial or law enforcement FIUs seek cooperation with the police (law enforcement authorities) and judicial authorities through Europol, Interpol or Eurojust.

In matters of international cooperation on money laundering cases, there are six most recognized hindrances, encountered by both FIUs and judicial authorities. These hindrances are the language barrier, time delays in gathering and providing a reply to a request, generic information that

Table 9.1 Countries to which EU FIUs send most requests and from which they receive most requests

	Top 5 incoming requests	Top 5 outgoing requests	Average response time by FIU
AT		1. **DE** 2. **Switzerland** 3. **IT** 4. UK 5.Russia	
BE	1. **LU** 2. **FR** 3. **NL** 4. Jersey 5. UK	1. **NL** 2. **FR** 3. **DE** 4. **LU** 5. ES	
BG			
CY	1. **UK** 2. **ES** 3. **EL** 4. Russia 5. Ukraine	1. **UK** 2. Russia 3. United States of America, 4. **DE**	
CZ			5 days
DK			3 days
EE	1. **LV** 2. FI 3. **Russia**	1. **LV** 2. **Russia**	14 days
FI			
FR			
DE	1. **LU** 2. **BE** 3. SK 4. **Switzerland** 5. FI		
EL			
HU			
IE			3 to 5 days
IT	1. **LU** 2. **FR** 3. SK 4. **BE** 5. **SL**	1. **LU** 2. **San Marino** 3. ES 4. CY 5. **Switzerland**	
LV	1. Ukraine 2. Moldova 3. **Russia** 4. **LT** 5. **EE**	1. **EE** 2. PL 3. **LT** 4/5. **Belarus/Russia**	
LT			
LU	1. **BE** 2. **FR** 3. **DE** 4. ES 5. FI	1. **UK** 2. **DE** 3. **FR** 4. IT 5. ES	
MT	1. **LU** 2. UK 3. BE 4. LT 5. Montenegro	1. **UK** 2. DE 3. AY 4. IT 5. PL	6 days
NL	1. **BE** 2. FI 3. LU 4. FR 5. ES	1. **BE** 2. **DE** 3. LU 4. ES 5. FR	5 days
PL	1. LU 2. BE 3. UK 4. **SK**	1. UK 2. CY 3. LV 4. **DE** 5. **CZ**	
PT	1. LU 2. BE 3. UK 4. Jersey 5.**ES**	1. **ES** 2. Brazil 3. FR 4. UK 5. IT /Switzerland	
RO		1. IT 2. CY 3. United States of America 4. British Virgin Islands 5.UK	
SK	1. **CZ**2. **HU** 3. **PL** 4. **Ukraine** 5. EE / Montenegro	1. DE 2. **HU** 3. RO 4. UK 5. **CZ**	

Table 9.1   (continued)

	Top 5 incoming requests	Top 5 outgoing requests	Average response time by FIU
SL	1. **Croatia** 2. **IT** 3. Serbia 4. UK 5. Russia	1. **Croatia** 2. **IT** 3. Serbia 4. UK 5. Russia	
ES	1. UK 2. BE 3. FR 4. **PT** 5. LU	1. UK 2. IT 3. **FR** 4. United States of America 5. NL	
SE	1. NL 2. **DK** 3. DE 4. EE 5. UK		3 days
UK	1. LU 2. Jersey 3. Guernsey 4. Isle of Man 5. BE	1. ES 2. NL 3. FR 4. United States of America 5. Gibraltar	22 days

Notes: For illustration purposes we make use of ISO codes only for EU Member States. Countries that receive or transmit information to another country with which they share an inland border are depicted in bold.

is sometimes given to a specific request, differences in data protection standards among cooperating jurisdictions, non-efficient national cooperation and the lack of a legal basis in all EU Member States' legislation that allows FIUs to block or freeze suspicious transactions on their own motion for a certain period of time.

The hypothesis that international FIU cooperation between EU Member States is easier than with third countries could not be confirmed by the data concerning average response times by FIUs. This is because the data was insufficiently specified and not varied enough. Finally, we hypothesize that international cooperation takes place mostly with neighbours. Due to data asymmetry it is hard to prove the validity of this statement. Therefore, at this point, we can only argue that neighbours play a significant role in FIU cooperation.

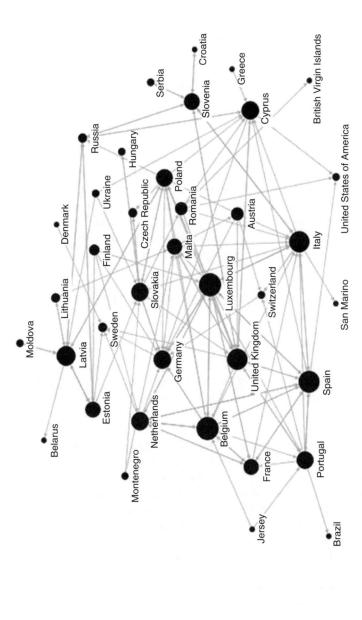

Notes: The arrows mark the direction of the FIU requests. The size and shade of the nodes are directly proportional to how connected the dots are: small dark nodes seldom transmit or receive information, whereas large light nodes receive or transmit most information.

Figure 9.2   Patterns of international cooperation involving EU FIUs

10. Collection of statistics

Joras Ferwerda

10.1 INTRODUCTION

We classify the statistics on AML policy into two types. First, we identify what we call output statistics, which are the result of the AML policy. The main output statistics that we discuss are reports sent to the FIU, the number of prosecutions and the number of convictions for money laundering. In addition to these output statistics we identify input statistics, which are the resources spent on AML policy, such as the budget of the FIU and other relevant institutions. After discussing both types of statistics we will conduct a statistical analysis to classify the Member States.

10.2 OUTPUT STATISTICS: REPORTS SENT TO THE FIU

The most widely available statistic on anti-money laundering policy seems to be the number of reports sent to the FIU. The EUROSTAT report on money laundering in Europe[1] is basically the only report with a reasonable amount of cross-country statistical information on anti-money laundering policy indicators. This EUROSTAT report identifies the number of reports sent to the FIU as its first key indicator. However, at the moment it is still very hard to use this statistic as an actual indicator for anti-money laundering policy. An increase in the number of suspicious transaction reports (STRs) can be the result of greater anti-money laundering efforts, a different counting rule, or an increase in the amount of money laundering. Moreover, an increase in the number of reports does not lead per se to better money laundering prevention or more convictions for money laundering, because it can also mean that the FIU is overloaded with patchy useless information, leading to an actual decrease in effectiveness.[2] The EUROSTAT report also mentions that

---

[1] EUROSTAT (2010).
[2] Takáts (2007).

the figures reported vary greatly, even allowing for the different sizes of the respective financial markets, with extremely high figures reported by some countries (NL, LV and UK). This is because concepts and counting rules are not uniform across the EU. FIUs tend to process transactions received in STRs as cases. Relevant cases are sent to the Law Enforcement Authorities. Some FIUs record all related STRs as one case, while others only count the first case-opening STR. For some Member States (CY, FI, UK) the concept is interpreted as a Suspicious Activity Report (SAR), which may include activities, not related to any particular monetary transaction, but to e.g. the opening of a bank account, restructuring a company, providing insurance products etc. One Member State (NL) records Unusual Transaction Reports (UTR) which, if found to be suspicious, may be sent to the law enforcement authorities.

Although SARs are only used explicitly in some EU Member States, it is also possible to report activities like opening a bank account in many other Member States (e.g. Malta, Italy and Portugal).

Section 3.2.2 shows that the reports used by various European countries in the prevention of money laundering are of a very distinct nature in six different respects:

(1) the type of report (some reports refer only to cash transactions, while others refer to all transactions; some reports refer only to transactions, while others refer to any activity);
(2) subjective grounds of suspicion (the level of necessary knowledge when defining a transaction as suspicious);
(3) objective grounds of suspicion (the reporting threshold of the amount of money involved in a transaction, for which a report must be filed);
(4) the definition of a transaction (specifying which activities constitute transactions);
(5) the inclusion of attempt (including an attempt at a transaction even when stopped) and
(6) the data collection methodology (making a report for each transaction or bundling the transactions of one money laundering operation together).

This would support the conclusion that at the moment different countries' statistics on the number of reports disclosed to FIUs cannot actually be compared with each other and cannot be used as an indicator for money laundering or anti-money laundering policy.

Although the FATF seems to be aware of the problems with this statistic, we see that they still use this statistic to compare countries with each other and use it as an indicator for the effectiveness of their anti-money laundering policy (see the examples below).

Example 1: STRs in Denmark and Hungary

In the Third Mutual Evaluation Round on the Kingdom of Denmark, the FATF compared the Danish level of STR reporting on the basis of statistics with a great number of other European and non-European countries. The FATF mentioned the fact that a comparison based on absolute numbers alone would not provide a good comparative basis, but still undertook this comparison.[3] The FATF concluded that the number of reports was significantly lower in Denmark than in the countries being compared. Although the statistics were not a conclusive factor, the FATF noted the low level of STR reporting as a shortcoming of Recommendation 13 that consequently lowered the compliance rate.

Denmark was for instance compared with Hungary. While the number of reports in 2004 for Hungary was 14,120, the number of Danish reports was 413. Although this divergence is indeed considerable and cannot be fully explained, it is not so surprising when the definition of STRs in the two countries is considered. While in Denmark the level of knowledge required for reporting was based on a suspicion of money laundering in connection with a criminal offence punishable by imprisonment of one year or more,[4] the applicable AML/CTF Act at that time in Hungary referred to 'any data, facts or circumstances indicating money laundering', thus setting a lower threshold of suspicion than in Denmark.[5]

This may have been one of the reasons that explain the different reporting numbers and shows that the absolute number of reports only cannot be compared.

Example 2: German STRs and UK SARs

In the German FATF evaluation of 2010, the FATF expressed its concerns about the effectiveness of the German reporting system.[6] It compared the absolute number of reports with those in France, Italy, the United Kingdom and Canada. These countries were chosen because they are

---

[3]   In fact, it then continued to compare the number of STRs by commercial banks, arguing that those institutions would be defined similarly across countries and would have more experience of AML/CTF reporting. See FATF (2006a), pp. 116–17.

[4]   FATF (2006a), p. 116.

[5]   See MONEYVAL (2005), p. 42. The definition in the current AML/CTF Act has remained unchanged in this respect.

[6]   FATF (2010e), p. 170.

'FATF member countries with a substantial financial sector'.[7] However, the table in the report showed that the number of reports in the United Kingdom diverged considerably from the number of reports in Germany (in 2008, 210,524 reports in the UK against 7,312 reports in Germany).[8]

This difference can be explained by various factors, as indicated in Table 3.1. For example, one sees that the level of knowledge required for disclosing a report to the competent authorities is actually somewhat higher in Germany. Moreover, in the United Kingdom activity has to be reported, while the reporting obligation in Germany is confined to transactions.

Moreover, though this is not clear from the table, an interesting difference from the reporting obligation in Germany is that in the United Kingdom the basis for reporting lies in several provisions of the Proceeds of Crime Act (POCA), and hence in criminal law. Of the four applicable provisions (Sections 327–30 POCA), the first three relate to all people and not only to the institutions subject to the Money Laundering Regulations 2007. Therefore, the scope of application is considerably wider in the UK than in Germany, where only institutions subject to the AML/CTF Act have to send a (copy of the) report to the FIU.

Here, too, it can be concluded that due to the various differences in the reporting systems in Germany and the United Kingdom, the absolute number of reports cannot be compared with each other. The FATF indeed gave consideration to the fact that variation in reporting levels is due to differences in the regime design and methods used to count STRs, but the number of German reports was so low that assessors found it difficult to conclude that the German system was adequate.[9]

Example 3: UTRs

In the Netherlands the type of report used is called an unusual transaction report (UTR). Only after analysis by the FIU may these reports be declared suspicious. The unusual character of a transaction generally has a lower threshold of knowledge or suspicion of money laundering than applies to the STRs used in other European countries (see Table 3.1). Moreover, while STRs in most countries are merely based on subjective suspicion, Dutch UTRs may also be disclosed in case of objective thresholds. To make it even more interesting, the objective thresholds differ

[7] Ibid.
[8] Ibid.
[9] Ibid., p. 171.

per category of institutions. For example, money transfers offices must disclose a UTR to the FIU in case of cash transactions of 2,000 Euros or more, while sellers of high-value goods have to report to the FIU in cases of transactions where vehicles, vessels, art objects, precious metals, gems and jewellery are paid in total or partially by means of cash, where the amount to be paid is 25,000 Euros or more.[10]

Another country that uses UTRs is Latvia. Both UTRs and STRs have to be reported to the FIU. However, the meaning of UTRs in Latvia is entirely different from the meaning of UTRs in the Netherlands. In Latvia, UTRs are only disclosed in case of objective indicators (thresholds).[11] And, as in the Netherlands, the thresholds vary according to the category of institutions.[12] For example, the (cash) threshold for the sale or purchase of precious metals, precious stones and articles is 10,000 LATs (approximately 12,000 Euros). Money transfer offices must disclose a UTR to the FIU in case of cash transactions of 25,000 LATs or more (approximately 30,000 Euros).[13] When comparing the thresholds with the thresholds set by the Dutch legislator for similar categories of entities, one will notice that they diverge considerably.

All in all, merely comparing UTRs with STRs in absolute numbers is thus impossible. In the first place because the level of knowledge is considerably lower in the case of UTRs and in the second place because UTRs are not limited to subjective suspicion only, but may relate to threshold reporting as well. Likewise, a comparison of the number of UTRs in the Netherlands with the number of UTRs in Latvia would also not reflect the real situation, because the thresholds set differ considerably and in the Netherlands UTRs are also based on a subjective suspicion.

Example 4: Polish STRs and SARs, UK SARs

Poland has a rather unique AML/CTF reporting system as regards the type of reports used. Besides STRs, SARs (suspicious activity reports) also

---

[10] Annex to Implementing Decree of the Dutch AML/CTF Act (Uitvoeringsbesluit Wet ter voorkoming van witwassen en financieren van terrorisme, Stb. 2008, 305).
[11] In that respect, for comparative purposes it would have been more convenient to call them cash transactions reports.
[12] Cabinet of Ministers Regulation No. 1071 On the List of Indicators of Unusual Transactions and the Procedure according to which Reports on Unusual and Suspicious Transactions shall be made, approved by the Cabinet of Ministers on 22 December 2008.
[13] Financial and Capital Market Commission (2010), p. 15.

form part of the system. Seemingly, the only difference between the two types of reports is the number of transactions involved in the report. If a report concerns a suspicion of money laundering in the case of a specific transaction, the STR format is used. When a suspicion of money laundering arises only after a series of transactions, the SAR format is used.

While STRs relate to just one suspicious transaction, a comparison of Polish STRs with STRs in other countries would not provide the full picture, because in other countries an STR may contain several individual transactions.

With respect to the SARs, Table 3.1 indicates that there are no similarities whatsoever with the SAR as used in the United Kingdom. As explained above, the SAR reporting system in the United Kingdom is entirely based on criminal law. Therefore, it is not only the persons that are subject to the Money Laundering Regulations that have an obligation to report, but all people should report if they wish to have a defence against any of the principal money laundering offences stipulated in Sections 327–29 POCA.

Hence, a direct comparison based on absolute numbers of SARs between these countries would not be possible.

Example 5: Polish and Slovenian Threshold Reports

Poland also has a reporting threshold in place. All transactions above the equivalent of 15,000 Euros and 1,000 Euros in the case of some categories of institutions must be reported to the FIU. This low threshold, combined with the fact that it is not restricted to cash transactions, means that the Polish FIU received information on about 31 million transactions contained in no fewer than 82,000 threshold reports in 2009.[14] This is considerably different from the threshold reporting system in Slovenia. In this country, cash transactions exceeding 30,000 Euros have to be disclosed to the Slovenian FIU. Up until 2008 the threshold was equivalent to 21,000 Euros, but the Slovenian legislator raised the threshold after consultation with the obliged institutions to lower their burden.[15] In 2009, 16,846 cash transactions were reported to the FIU.[16] Once again the incomparability

---

[14]   General Inspector of Financial Information on implementation of the Act of 16 November 2000 on counteracting money laundering and terrorism financing in 2009 (FIU (2009), Annual Report, at § 1.2).
[15]   Indicated by several stakeholders during interviews held in the course of the ECOLEF project.
[16]   Office for Money Laundering Prevention, Data from the report on activities of the Office for Money Laundering Prevention of the Republic of Slovenia for the year 2009, at § 2.1.

of absolute numbers becomes clear: the 16,846 cash transactions reported in Slovenia are in no way proportionate to the 31 million transactions reported in Poland.

Last Remark on the Number of Reports

As a last remark on this statistic, we have to report that during our research we discovered that the EUROSTAT report[17] had the number of STRs in Hungary wrong. In table 15, EUROSTAT reports that the amount of STRs in 2007 is 13 and in 2008 it is 62. This is, according to the Hungarian representatives, probably the number of cases forwarded by the FIU to the LEAs. The actual number of STRs received by the Hungarian FIU was 9,480 in 2007, 9,940 in 2008 and 5,440 in 2009.

10.3   THE WAY FORWARD: HOW TO MAKE THESE STATISTICS CROSS-COUNTRY COMPARABLE?

The most intuitive solution is to push for uniform legislation such that the notion of a report is a uniform concept in all the countries in the world. This of course needs to be done by means of legislative changes, which takes time and effort, and political negotiations are involved. Changing the classification schemes of administration might involve other policy fields as well and might be very difficult. Therefore, this policy option might be a long-term solution or even a utopian ambition.

Alternatively, we propose a restructuring of the current units of measurement such that they are better comparable across countries; more specifically: to measure and compare the amount of money and the number of natural persons involved in the suspicion reports, instead of the number of reports. Clearly there will still be some degrees of freedom on how to interpret money laundering tasks and time devoted to it, but at least it would take away the differences in the data collection method, which is the least transparent characteristic of the current reports sent to the FIU.

We made a start by taking stock of which countries already have statistics on the numbers of people and the amount of money involved in the number of reports. Table 10.1 shows these statistics next to the average number of reports that are sent to the FIU each year.

---

[17]   EUROSTAT (2010).

Table 10.1   Average number of reports per year sent to the FIU

	STR	SAR	UTR	CTR	No. of people in reports	Money in reports (€m.)
Austria	1,055					
Belgium	14,052	773				
Bulgaria	737			248,636		311
Cyprus		262				
Czech Republic	2,184					
Denmark	1,440					
Estonia	4,452			9,124	18,500	3,191
Finland		13,356				
France						
Germany	8,753				16,480	
Greece	1,655					
Hungary	9,243					
Ireland	12,500					
Italy	17,485					
Latvia	22,031			14,962		
Lithuania	198					
Luxembourg		1,402			2,898	1,229
Malta	69				101	
Netherlands			224,615			
Poland	46,992	1,836		25,746,538		
Portugal	989			13,944	2,853	
Romania	2,217					
Slovakia			2,017			5,790
Slovenia	182			31,643	206	118
Spain	2,906					
Sweden	9,408					
United Kingdom		224,799				

Source: Own database, which is a collection of data collected by online surveys, interviews and desk research on mutual evaluation reports, annual reports of relevant institutions and EUROSTAT (2010). For visibility reasons the numbers reported are averages over the statistics available for the period 2005–10.[18] STR = suspicious transaction report, SAR = suspicious activity report, UTR = unusual transaction report and CTR = currency transaction report. For some countries (BE, CZ, DK, IE, NL, RO, SL, ES and SE), this statistic could include (a small number of) reports on the suspicion of terrorist financing. No. of People in reports means the average total amount of persons mentioned in the reports per year. Money in reports is the average summation of all the value of the transactions reported to the FIU per year. The money in reports in Bulgaria represents the amounts as per newly initiated cases by the FIU for each year on the basis of the reports. These amounts only roughly coincide with the actual amount per STR.

[18]   This is a rather crude calculation method to increase data availability. To give some additional insight into our calculation method, let us use two examples.

Output statistics: Cash Declarations at the Border

Apart from these reports sent to the FIU by reporting entities, we also have, in the Cash Control Report,[19] statistics on the number of cash declarations at the border. Moreover we have statistics on the number of false cash declarations, i.e. where (more) cash is detected, which might be an even better indication of money laundering. The advantage is that the thresholds and definitions of these reports are uniform across Europe, which means that the drawbacks of the reports sent to the FIU by reporting entities are not present for these reports. This makes the statistics on cash declaration reports much more comparable across countries, but we should remember that these statistics do not represent any money laundering activities per se and are therefore mere indications.

Output Statistics: Number of Prosecutions and Convictions

Another statistic that seems to be a logical choice when looking for an indicator for the effectiveness of the fight against money laundering is the number of persons prosecuted/convicted for money laundering. One of the main problems with this statistic is that, when criminals are convicted of money laundering, they are often also convicted of the predicate crime in the same court case. The question then arises whether the convicted criminal will be registered as being convicted for only the predicate crime or also for money laundering. The same holds for the number of prosecutions. Another issue with this statistic is that courts in different EU Member States interpret the term money laundering differently, as has already been pointed out in Chapter 6. The major difference in this respect is of course the criminalization of self-laundering, which could be corrected for, since most Member States that have this statistic can differentiate as to whether the conviction is for self-laundering or third-party laundering

---

If we have statistics for a certain country available only for the year 2008 (like Greece), then we present that number in the table. If a country has statistics for the years 2007, 2008 and 2009, then we take the average over those three years and present that average in the table. A potential drawback of this calculation method is that some statistics might be somewhat biased for comparability purposes, because the statistics represent different years. If, for instance, the numbers are rising over time throughout Europe, then the countries with data available only in later years are biased upwards, while countries with data available only in the early years are biased downwards. Due to data unavailability it is hard to identify whether such a trend is present.

[19]   European Commission (2010a).

(13 of the 17 countries were able to differentiate[20]). Moreover, an increase in the number of prosecutions and convictions for money laundering does not have to be the result of more effective anti-money laundering policies, since the increase could also be caused simply by an increase in money laundering. Nevertheless, one could still compare this statistic with the number of STRs to measure the effectiveness of the investigation and prosecution stages in the fight against money laundering. This was also the general idea of EUROSTAT when they started to collect these statistics.

Representatives of the Member States have indicated to us that we should be extremely cautious about comparing the number of reports with the number of convictions or prosecutions for several reasons. First of all, many reports sent to the FIU could eventually result in only one conviction, while the opposite is also possible: one report could lead to many convictions. Statistics on how many reports led to how many convictions are rare among the EU Member States. Second, the investigation and prosecution process of a money laundering case could be extremely time-consuming, especially when international cooperation is required. This means that one can still not conclude how many reports that were sent to the FIU in, for instance, 2007 were used to convict money launderers, since some reports might still be under investigation or the case might still be pending in court. Third, a report in a certain country might not lead to a conviction in the same country. It could be that a certain country received a report and did excellent (resource-consuming) investigation work which eventually resulted in the money launderer being convicted in another country. Fourth, convictions can also be the result of regular police work and therefore do not originate from the reporting system.

With all these remarks at the back of our minds, we show in Table 10.2 how many prosecutions and convictions for money laundering and terrorist financing occurred in the EU. Additionally, we report the percentages of numbers of prosecutions compared to the number of reports sent to the FIU, and how the number of convictions relates to the number of prosecutions.

We can conclude from Table 10.2 that the number of prosecutions in Germany is extremely high. A German representative explained to us that this has to do with the fact that prosecutors have an obligation to prosecute any suspicion in cases brought to their attention (principle of compulsory prosecution). This is also clear from a comparison of the number of reports with the number of prosecutions. According to this statistic, there are more prosecutions in Germany than there are reports on

---

[20]   See EUROSTAT (2010), table 9.

Table 10.2 *Average number of prosecutions and convictions for money laundering*

	Prosecutions	Convictions	Prosecutions / reports*100%	Convictions / prosecutions * 100%	Convictions per FIU employee	Convictions per million inhabitants	Interpretation of ML definition
Austria	17	10	1.57	60.24	0.77	1.22	Normal
Belgium	1.37		9.60				Normal
Bulgaria	129	12	17.45	9.49	0.38	1.71	Broad
Cyprus	43	24	16.44	56.74	1.16	22.13	Very broad
Czech Rep.	8	27	0.35	348.39	0.77	2.65	Normal
Denmark	532	503	36.95	94.49	27.93	91.14	Very tight
Estonia	17	6	0.01	1200.00	0.38	4.64	Tight
Finland	54	14	0.40	25.00	0.56	2.57	Very tight
France	186	186	0.80	99.73	2.54	2.87	Very tight
Germany	10.1	381	116.22	3.75	22.41	4.67	Very tight
Greece	42	34	2.54	80.95	1.17	3.16	Normal
Hungary	5	4	0.05	91.07	0.14	0.43	Normal
Ireland	9	5	0.04	55.55	0.45	1.12	Very tight
Italy							Very tight
Latvia	15	25	0.07	171.19	1.49	11.38	Normal
Lithuania	2	1	0.89	71.43	0.13	0.35	Tight
Luxembourg	48	2	3.42	4.58	0.16	4.42	Very broad
Malta	5	2	6.92	31.25	0.15	3.69	Normal
Netherlands	592	486	0.26	82.20	8.69	28.98	Very Broad

Poland	87	35	0.34	39.85	0.77	0.90	Normal
Portugal	107	7	10.79	6.33	0.23	0.63	Normal
Romania	27	7	1.22	24.07	0.07	0.30	Normal
Slovakia	60	10	2.96	17.28	0.34	1.89	Normal
Slovenia	13	1	6.89	4.00	0.03	0.25	Normal
Spain	104		3.56				Normal
Sweden	94	36	1.00	38.03	1.32	3.94	Very tight
UK	2.16	1.003	0.96	46.24	13.72	16.09	Broad

Source: Own database, which is a collection of data collected by online surveys, interviews and desk research on mutual evaluation reports, annual reports of relevant institutions and EUROSTAT (2010). For visibility reasons the numbers reported are the averages of the statistics available in the period 2005–10.[21] The reports statistic that is used is the aggregate of the number of STRs, SARs and UTRs. CTRs are not included because of their (even more) distinct nature. The broadness of the money laundering definition comes from our own research described in Chapter 6 (France is not classified).[22]

[21] This is a rather crude calculation method to increase data availability. To give some additional insight into our calculation method, let us use two examples. If we have statistics for a certain country available only for the year 2008 (like Greece), then we present that number in the table. If a country has statistics for the years 2007, 2008 and 2009, then we take the average over those three years and present that average in the table. A potential drawback of this calculation method is that some statistics might be somewhat biased for comparability purposes, because the statistics represent different years. If, for instance, the numbers are rising over time throughout Europe, then the countries with data available only in later years are biased upwards, while countries with data available only in the early years are biased downwards. Due to data unavailability it is hard to identify whether such a trend is present.

[22] The population statistics used are from Heston et al. (2011).

suspicions of money laundering. This probably has to do with the fact, mentioned above, that prosecutions and convictions can be the result of regular police work and therefore do not necessarily originate from a report sent to the FIU. We also see such extreme statistics (more than 100%) for certain countries when comparing the number of prosecutions with the number of convictions. This could be due to the above-mentioned observation that convictions might happen in a different year from a prosecution.[23]

As an aside, we have to report that during our research we found that the EUROSTAT (2010) had the number of convictions for the Czech Republic wrong. In its table 9, EUROSTAT reports that the number of convictions in the Czech Republic is more than 600 each year, while table 10 mentions that the total number of sentences is between 21 and 31. The Czech representatives indicated that more than 600 convictions a year is definitely not correct, and that the total number of sentences seems to be the correct statistic. This would mean that the number of convictions in the Czech Republic are 21 in 2003, 26 in 2004, 31 in 2005, 29 in 2006 and 21 in 2007.

Now that we have the statistics on the number of convictions, the question arises as to whether we are able to explain the differences between Member States. Why are there so many convictions in the UK, Denmark and the Netherlands and why is the number of convictions in Lithuania and Slovenia so low? The first idea that comes to mind is of course that bigger countries have more crime in absolute terms and that they therefore have more convictions in absolute terms. Something else that comes to mind is that the money laundering definition is interpreted differently in different Member States (see Chapter 6) and that countries with a broader definition probably have, all else equal, on average more ML convictions. To verify these hypotheses, we show in Table 10.2 the number of convictions related to the size of the country and the size of the FIU and classified by the broadness of the money laundering interpretation.

We can see from Table 10.2 that the big difference in the number of money laundering convictions indeed diminishes when we take into account the size of the country (measured in FIU staff or the number of inhabitants). While the difference between the lowest and the highest absolute number of money laundering convictions is of a factor of around 2,000, for relative conviction statistics this difference is of a factor of

---

[23]   Note that we use averages to calculate these statistics, so the years from which we use data might differ not only from country to country but also between certain statistics within a country.

around 1,000 and 400, respectively, in relation to the number of FIU staff and the number of inhabitants. This hypothesis is also supported by a statistical analysis with pairwise correlations that show very significant positive relations between the absolute number of money laundering convictions and GDP and population statistics.[24]

The idea that the differences in convictions for money laundering are related to the broadness of the money laundering definition is not confirmed. Although the numbers 2 (NL), 3 (CY) and 4 (UK) in terms of relative number of convictions have a broad or very broad money laundering definition, the contrary is true for the number 1 (DK). Actually, Table 10.2 shows that the countries with a tight money laundering definition have, in both absolute and relative terms, quite a high number of money laundering convictions. Also a statistical analysis with pairwise correlations shows that the broadness of the money laundering definition does not explain the differences in conviction statistics significantly.[25]

This leaves us with the question of what else can explain why the number of money laundering convictions is high in certain countries and low in others. We therefore conduct a statistical analysis with pairwise correlations between the number of convictions for money laundering and all the other statistics that we gathered in this project (over 200 variables). We report the most interesting results here. The absolute number of convictions for money laundering is positively significantly related to the amount of threat, the corruption index of the World Bank, the number of suspicion reports sent to the FIU[26] and the number of prosecutions for money laundering.[27]

The fact that the number of convictions is related to the amount of

---

[24] The correlation between the number of convictions and GDP is 0.6066 with a P-value of 0.0008. The correlation between the number of convictions and population is 0.5238 with a P-value of 0.0050.

[25] The absolute number of convictions is significantly related only to the dummy variable for a broad money laundering definition (coefficient of 0.4914 with a P-value of 0.0092) and not with the other four dummies for categories of the broadness of the money laundering definition.

[26] The reports statistic that is used is the aggregate of the number of STRs, SARs and UTRs. CTRs are not included because of their (even more) distinct nature.

[27] The correlation with threat is 0.5051 with a P-value of 0.0072, with corruption 0.4246 with a P-value of 0.0273 (note that a higher score for corruption means better governance performance against corruption), with the average number of reports (STR+SAR+UTR) for the years available is 0.7955 with a P-value of 0.0000 and with the number of prosecutions is 0.4211 with a P-value of 0.0287. When we correct the number of convictions for money laundering for the size of the country by dividing the number by population, the correlation with threat

threat confirms the consideration above that this statistic might not per se say something about the effectiveness of the AML system, but it could also be related to the underlying unknown amount of money laundering in the country.

The relation between money laundering and corruption has been debated in the literature. Walker (1995 and 1999) assumes that criminals do not like (excessively) corrupt countries, because corruption increases the costs of laundering due to necessary side payments and bribes. On the other hand, a very low corruption level might make it difficult to find facilitators for laundering, increasing the transaction costs of laundering. The corruption–laundering literature is ambiguous about the relation. Chaikin and Sharman (2009) give an overview of the various theoretical links between corruption and money laundering. Dreher and Schneider (2010) find this ambiguity empirically for the shadow economy: corruption reduces the shadow economy in high-income countries, but increases it in low-income countries.[28] Our empirical results in this project suggest that there is a positive relation between convictions for money laundering and governance performance against corruption. Hence, in countries where corruption is under better control, the number of convictions is higher. We could come up with different reasons why this would be the case. Probably the most intuitive reason is that when the government has better control over corruption, it probably also has better control over money laundering. Alternatively, one could argue that, in countries with more corruption, money launderers might be able to bribe the police officer who is about to catch them.

The initial idea of EUROSTAT when drafting their report[29] was to show statistically the chain of how reports lead to prosecutions and how many of these prosecutions lead to conviction. This approach has been opposed very often by representatives of the countries we visited (see also the introduction to this section on the number of prosecutions and convictions for money laundering). Our statistical analysis suggests that these statistics are related when we do not correct for the size of the country. When we do correct for the size of the country – by dividing all three statistics by population – the number of reports is no longer significantly related to the number of convictions, which seems to support the view of many representatives that one cannot simply compare the number of reports

---

becomes 0.1281 with a P-value of 0.5242 (hence insignificant), and with corruption becomes 0.4574 with a P-value of 0.0165.

[28]   Ferwerda et al. (2013).
[29]   EUROSTAT (2010).

with the number of convictions. The number of prosecutions and the number of convictions for money laundering continues to be significantly related when corrected for size.[30]

EUROSTAT (2010) also collected statistics on the number of prosecutions and convictions for money laundering. We were able to improve these statistics in two ways. First, we have more recent statistics. Second, we also have the number of prosecutions for Austria, Denmark, France, Greece, Hungary, Ireland and United Kingdom and the number of convictions for Denmark, Greece, the Netherlands and Slovakia, data that was missing in the statistics of EUROSTAT.

10.4 INPUT STATISTICS: STAFF AND BUDGET OF THE FIU

Since output statistics for anti-money laundering policy (like the number of reports sent to the FIU or the number of prosecutions and convictions for money laundering) always have the problem that an increase in the statistic can come from an increase in the amount of money laundering or from an improved policy response,[31] it is perhaps better to use input statistics (like resources spent fighting money laundering) as an indicator for the amount of effort made by Member States to fight money laundering. We have tried to gather the following input statistics:

● AML budget of the responsible ministry/ministries;
● FIU budget;
● FIU personnel;
● law enforcement agencies' (LEAs) budget for fighting ML;
● LEAs' personnel for fighting ML;
● budget for judiciary to be spent on AML;
● judiciary personnel for AML;
● reporting costs for obliged entities;
● training and compliance costs for obliged entities;
● budget supervisory institutions for AML;
● personnel for AML in supervisory institutions.[32]

---

[30] The correlation between prosecutions/population and convictions/population is 0.4368 with a P-value of 0.0227.
[31] This is a common problem with crime statistics in general.
[32] Note that these statistics are also gathered for the cost-benefit analysis in Chapter 12.

We conclude that the best available input statistic is the amount of personnel in the FIU. All countries are able to provide such a statistic. As can be seen in Table 10.3, some countries were also able to provide us with the budget of the FIU.

Although not all countries were able to provide us with statistics regarding the budget of the FIUs, we can make an estimate based on the number of employees. During our first Regional Workshop we agreed with the country representatives that most of the budget is spent on personnel costs, as in other intelligence-based institutions such as universities. Let us assume that 80% of the budget of each FIU is spent on personnel costs. Furthermore, let us use EUROSTAT statistics on the average gross monthly earnings of legislators in every EU Member State[33] to correct for differences in salaries in the different Member States. Then we can calculate that, for the 11 countries for which we have budget statistics, on average the annual budget per employee is about 15 times the gross monthly earnings of a legislator. If we assume that this average relation applies also to the countries for which we do not have budget statistics, we can calculate an estimated budget for these countries. The statistics gathered and the results of our estimations are shown in the online Table 10.1 (see http://goo.gl/VZgJb3).

Our estimates suggest that the cost of having an FIU is probably the highest in Italy with its high number of employees and its relatively high wage level. Unfortunately we do not have statistics on the number of prosecutions and convictions in Italy to see whether this leads to economies of scale or is due to the inefficiency of the FIU.

To make the statistics better comparable across countries of very different size, we also show the amount of FIU personnel per million inhabitants and how much the FIU costs on average for each inhabitant per year. These statistics seem to indicate that FIUs have so-called economies of scale, which means that the more inhabitants a country has, the lower the costs per inhabitant are. In this sense, having an FIU is relatively costly for the smaller countries. The five EU Member States with the least inhabitants (Cyprus, Estonia, Luxembourg, Malta and Slovenia) have the highest number of FIU staff per million inhabitants.

Since price levels differ among EU Member States, it would be unfair to look only at absolute FIU budgets. It is more expensive in Sweden to fight money laundering simply because everything is more expensive than,

---

[33]   See Eurostat Pocketbooks (2009), table 7.1, for gross monthly earnings by occupation in Euros in 2006.

Table 10.3   Number of staff and budget of the FIU

Country	Staff (in FTE)	Budget (in Euros)	Total budget estimate	Staff (per m.)	Price for FIU (per person per year)	Corrected price for FIU (per person per year)
Austria	13		1,375,238	1.6		
Belgium	45	4,257,645	4,843,125	4.1	€0.39	€0.44
Bulgaria	32		275,400	4.4		
Cyprus	21		1,703,756	19.4		
Czech Rep.	35	1,429,473	983,719	3.4		
Denmark	18	No budget	2,000,700	3.3		
Estonia	16		362,700	12.3		
Finland	24	1,565,000	2,196,450	4.6	€0.30	€0.37
France	73	4,981,688	6,524,831	1.1	€0.08	€0.09
Germany	17		1,872,975	0.2		
Greece	29	1,500,000	1,812,863	2.7	€0.14	€0.14
Hungary	30	1,000,000***	711,563	3.0	€0.10	€0.07
Ireland	11		990,825	2.6		
Italy	104	207,000	10,992,150	1.7		
Latvia	17	341,490	265,200	7.6	€0.15	€0.11
Lithuania	10		157,875	2.8		
Luxembourg	14		1,947,488	28.5		
Malta	10	330,107	402,375	24.7	€0.82	€0.67
Netherlands	56	4,800,000	4,226,250	3.4	€0.29	€0.32
Poland	45		1,288,406	1.2		
Portugal	30		1,814,063	2.8		
Romania	96		1,643,400	4.4		
Slovakia	30		694,688	5.6		
Slovenia	18	691,000	999,338	9.0	€0.34	€0.28
Spain	79	11,000,000	5,941,294	1.7	€0.24	€0.24
Sweden	27*	1,400,000**	2,393,550	3.0	€0.15	€0.19
UK	60		6,044,625	1.0		

Source: Statistics collected by the ECOLEF project, via interviews, online questionnaires and regional workshops, except: * = FIU Sweden (2009), p. 22 and ** = FATF (2006d). *** = this figure is estimated using the overall budget of the Customs Criminal Investigations Bureau (CCIB); representatives of the Hungarian Ministry of Finance and the Hungarian FIU have said that it seems to be a reasonable estimation. Note that the staff statistics come from different years. Most are from 2011, exceptions being AT 2010, BE 2012, FR 2009, DE 2010, HU 2010, LU 2012, NL 2010, PL 2008, SL 2010, SE 2009, UK 2012. The number of staff for Ireland does not contain the 7 police officers that work alongside the FIU in what is called the Money Laundering Investigation Unit (MLUI). The budget for the Czech Republic omits IT costs and the budget for Italy includes only expenses. FTE = full-time equivalent, per m. = per million inhabitants. The corrected price for FIU is calculated with price level statistics in 2010 (the US price level is the benchmark with 100).[34]

[34]   The population statistics used are from Heston et al. (2011). We use the

for example, in Poland. We therefore correct for these differences in price levels by using the price level statistics of the World Penn Table.[35]

We have found it hard to collect the other input statistics mentioned above. Most institutions (ministries, LEAs, judiciary and supervisors) have many more tasks and do not have a separate budget for AML and are unable to make any reasonable estimation for it. For obliged entities these statistics might even be kept secret, because it could be sensitive information for competitors.

EUROSTAT (2010) also collected statistics on the number of staff in the FIU. We were able to improve these statistics in two ways. First, we have more recent statistics. Second, we also have data for the number of staff for Austria, Belgium, Hungary, Ireland, Italy and Poland that was missing in the statistics of EUROSTAT.

10.5   CLUSTER ANALYSIS

In this section we want to find out whether we can cluster countries based on the statistics we have gathered. The statistical method that we have chosen for this clustering is hierarchical agglomerative cluster analysis with Ward's algorithm. Hierarchical agglomerative cluster analysis is the dominant method in clustering and results are usually stable according to Leschke (2005).[36] In comparison with other algorithms, Ward's has proved to generate very good results in most cases.[37] The Ward's method is designed to optimize the minimum variance within clusters by making use of the error sum of squares or within group sum of squares.[38] Those cases that result in the minimum increase in the error sum of squares are joined in a cluster. This method leads to relatively homogeneous clusters.[39] The 29 variables listed with their characteristics in Table 10.4 are the basis for the cluster analysis.[40]

---

most recent population statistics that were available from this source, which are from 2009. Also their most recent price level statistics are used, which are from 2010.

[35]   Heston et al. (2011).
[36]   Leschke (2005).
[37]   Aldenderfer and Blashfield (1984), pp. 60–61 and Backhaus et al. (2000), p. 366.
[38]   Aldenderfer and Blashfield (1984), pp. 42–3.
[39]   Leschke (2005).
[40]   We selected primarily ratios and classifications to prevent big countries having high values for all variables and therefore automatically being grouped together.

Table 10.4 The selected variables for cluster analysis

Variable	Obs	Mean	Std. Dev.	Min	Max
GDP (in million US$)	27	609,175.7	911,378.9	7,955	3,353,000
Threat estimation Walker	27	65.88889	41.0884	15	156
WB index Government Effectiveness	27	1.159767	0.617317	−0.2190219	2.246964
WB index Corruption	27	1.026053	0.8175407	−0.2003449	2.421083
FATF compliance score	27	57.71581	4.86711	45.58465	72.68007
Number of suspicion reports/GDP	27	0.070859	0.1665722	0.0019848	0.8392635
Cash declarations (in €)/GDP	27	6,735.738	15,729.29	2.988389	61,512.86
Detected cash declarations (in €)/GDP	27	38.92524	65.66886	0	297.3413
Prosecutions/suspicion reports	27	0.0901902	0.2287483	0.0001376	1.162177
Convictions/prosecutions	27	0.127371	0.2605056	0.0374521	1.272727
EU founder	27	0.2222222	0.4236593	0	1
EU member in 1990	27	0.4444444	0.5063697	0	1
EU member in 1995	27	0.5555556	0.5063697	0	1
EU member in 2004	27	0.9259259	0.2668803	0	1
Supervision model FIU	27	0.2962963	0.4653216	0	1
Supervision model Internal	27	0.1851852	0.3958474	0	1
Supervision model External	27	0.0740741	0.2668803	0	1
Supervision model Hybrid I	27	0.1851852	0.3958474	0	1
Supervision model Hybrid II	27	0.2592593	0.4465761	0	1
FIU staff	27	35.55556	26.28151	10	104
Administrative FIU	27	0.5185185	0.5091751	0	1
Law enforcement FIU	27	0.3333333	0.4803845	0	1

Table 10.4 (continued)

Variable	Obs	Mean	Std. Dev.	Min	Max
Judicial FIU	27	0.0740741	0.2668803	0	1
Hybrid FIU	27	0.0740741	0.2668803	0	1
ML definition very narrowly interpreted	27	0.2222222	0.4236593	0	1
ML definition narrowly interpreted	27	0.0740741	0.2668803	0	1
Normal ML definition	27	0.5185185	0.5091751	0	1
ML definition broadly interpreted	27	0.0740741	0.2668803	0	1
ML definition very broadly interpreted	27	0.1111111	0.3202563	0	1

Source: Own database, which is a collection of data collected by online surveys, interviews and desk research on mutual evaluation reports, annual reports of relevant institutions and EUROSTAT (2010) or otherwise the source listed here.[41,42] GDP statistic comes from the World Penn Table.[43] WB stands for World Bank. Government Effectiveness and Corruption are the Worldwide Governance Indicators from the World Bank.[44] The reports statistic that is used is the aggregate of the number of STRs, SARs and UTRs. CTRs are not included because of their (even more) distinct nature. Obs stands for the number of observations (in this case countries), Std. Dev. stands for standard deviation, Min stands for the minimum value and Max stands for the maximum value.

41 UNODC (2011).
42 Cluster analysis needs a full data set. We therefore had to interpolate some missing values. The following interpolation has been done: France gets a normal ML definition (not broad, not tight); France gets 23,420 reports (STR+UTR+SAR), the average of the other 26 countries; Italy gets 229 prosecutions, the average of the other countries (Germany is left out of this average calculation, because it is such an outlier for this statistic); Italy, Spain and Belgium get 112 convictions, the average of the other 24 countries.
43 Heston et al. (2011).
44 Available at: http://info.worldbank.org/governance/wgi/index.asp.

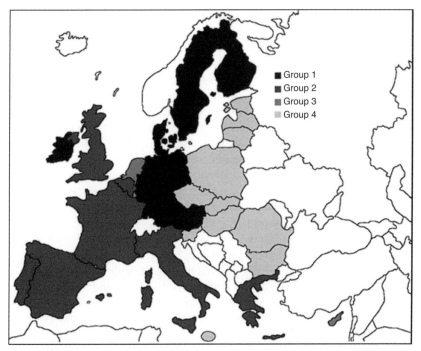

*note, colors used do not refer to a scaling value.

Group 1:	AT, DE, DK, FI, IE, SE
Group 2:	BE, EL, ES, FR, IT, PT, UK
Group 3:	CY, LU, NL
Group 4:	BG, CZ, EE, HU, LT, LV, MT, PL, RO, SK, SL

Figure 10.1   Identified groups by the statistical cluster analysis

All variables are standardized to z-scores with mean zero and standard deviation one, such that all variables have equal importance in the cluster analysis. The resulting four groups[45] are shown in Figure 10.1.

The clear homogeneity that we can see in group 1 is that almost all of the countries have a law enforcement type FIU, a very tight money laundering definition and the hybrid II supervision model. The countries in group 2 were all members of the EU when the Maastricht Treaty was signed in 1992 and almost all have a normal money laundering definition

---

[45]   Note that this is a purely statistical classification based on the 29 variables that are used. It is up to the researcher to decide what the appropriate number of groups is. We chose to select four groups, in line with the number of supervision models and FIU types.

and an administrative type of FIU. The countries in group 3 all have a very broad money laundering definition. The countries in group 4 are all so-called new members of the EU and most have a normal money laundering definition. We use correlations to find out whether the countries within each group are homogeneous on the other aspects. The countries in group 1 have on average a significantly higher government effectiveness index, a significantly higher corruption control index and significantly more prosecutions/GDP.[46] The countries in group 2 have on average significantly higher GDP and significantly more FIU staff.[47] The countries in group 3 have no significant correlation with any of the variables, probably due to the limited number of countries. The countries in group 4 have on average significantly lower GDP, a significantly lower government effectiveness index, a significantly lower corruption control index and significantly less money laundering threat.[48]

Apart from these characteristics we identify more similarities within certain groups. The countries in group 1 all experience or experienced pressure from the FATF for not having self-laundering criminalized. Apparently, the international standards for money laundering policy do not fit well within their legal system. In some countries in group 2 domestic cooperation might be harder due to the size of the country (such as Spain, France and Italy) and/or distinct regions within the country (such as Belgium, Spain, Italy and the UK). Group 3 consists of relatively small countries with a throughput of large financial flows. Group 4 are mostly Eastern European countries that are relatively recent members of the EU and might therefore face pressure on their institutions to implement and deal with a lot of new international laws and regulations on all kinds of topics (food, health, environment, child labour, etc.). Apparently, these diverse contexts, where countries deal with their own challenges, show up in different statistics to such an extent that a purely statistical analysis groups countries accordingly.

---

[46] The correlation of group 1 with the government effectiveness index is 0.5934 with P-value 0.0011, with the corruption control index it is 0.5874 with P-value 0.0013 and with Prosecutions/GDP 0.4051 with P-value 0.0361.

[47] The correlation of group 2 with GDP is 0.4920 with P-value 0.0091 and with FIU staff it is 0.5607 with P-value 0.0023.

[48] The correlation of group 4 with GDP is -0.4644 with P-value 0.0147, with government effectiveness index it is -0.6211 with P-value 0.0005, with corruption control index it is -0.6530 with P-value 0.0002 and with threat it is -0.6530 with P-value 0.0002.

10.6   CONCLUSION

Although there are quite a lot of statistics available on AML policy, their cross-country comparability is questionable. The number of reports sent to the FIU is one of the best available indicators, but there are many factors that have to be taken into account when trying to compare these statistics across countries. We identified differences on six aspects, namely the type of report (STRs, UTRs, etc.), the subjective grounds of suspicion (level of knowledge), the objective grounds of suspicion (threshold), the definition of a transaction (narrow or broad), the inclusion of attempt and the data collection methodology of these reports.

Another important indicator is the number of prosecutions and convictions for money laundering. Because these numbers differ greatly between countries, we tried to find out what can explain these differences. As expected, larger countries have more prosecutions and convictions, but to our surprise how broadly the money laundering definition is interpreted is not related to the number of prosecutions and convictions. Moreover, our statistical analysis shows that countries more threatened by money laundering have more convictions for money laundering, which could indicate an appropriate response to this threat. Our statistical analysis also shows that less corrupt countries have more money laundering convictions, which indicates that countries better able to fight corruption are also better able to fight money laundering.

A better indicator for AML policy effort in countries might be how much money is spent on AML policy. The main indicators in this category (mainly because of their availability) seem to be the budget and personnel of the FIU. We were able to gather statistics on the number of personnel working at the FIU for all 27 EU Member States. We were able to collect budget statistics for the FIU in 11 countries and used this information to make an estimation of the FIU budget in all 27 EU Member States. According to our estimations, Italy should have the highest budget due to their high number of employees with a relatively high wage. We showed that there are certain economies of scale associated with having an FIU, and that therefore an FIU is relatively costly for smaller countries, like Cyprus, Estonia, Luxembourg, Malta and Slovenia.

In this chapter we tried to improve on the EUROSTAT (2010) statistics. We were successful in three ways. First, we were able to collect more recent statistics. Second, we also have the figures for number of prosecutions in Austria, Denmark, France, Greece, Hungary, Ireland and United Kingdom and the number of convictions in Denmark, Greece, the Netherlands and Slovakia that were missing in the EUROSTAT statistics. We also have data for the number of staff in Austria, Belgium, Hungary,

Ireland, Italy and Poland that was missing in the EUROSTAT statistics. Third, we corrected the figures for the number of STRs in Hungary and the number of convictions for money laundering in the Czech Republic which were incorrect in the EUROSTAT report.

We have used the statistics we collected during the project to conduct a cluster analysis. Our cluster analysis shows that in terms of AML policy the 27 EU Member States consist of four groups which have their own distinct characteristics. We identify a group of countries (AT, DE, DK, FI, IE, SE) that experience or experienced international pressure due to the fact that they were unable to transpose international standards adequately into their legal system, a group of countries (BE, EL, ES, FR, IT, PT, UK) in which domestic cooperation might be harder, a group of relatively small countries with large financial flows going through (CY, LU, NL) and a big group of mostly Eastern European countries that are relatively recent members of the EU. Apparently, these diverse contexts in which countries deal with their own challenges show up in different statistics to such an extent that a purely statistical analysis groups countries accordingly.

11. Effectiveness: threat and corresponding policy response
Ioana Deleanu and Joras Ferwerda

11.1 INTRODUCTION

Chapters 3 to 10 have described the different aspects of AML/CTF policy in detail. These chapters show that AML/CTF policy has quite a lot of different and important elements that, together, represent the total policy response. In this chapter we try to bring all this information together in order to explore to what extent the policy response towards money laundering is effective in relation to the money laundering threat the country is facing, which was calculated in Chapter 2.[1]

11.2 METHODOLOGICAL APPROACH

Since AML policy has such multiple and varied dimensions, which cannot be encompassed in a single measurement of policy response without great loss of accuracy, we select the most suitable indicators for a good policy response. We therefore plot these indicators, one by one, next to the ML threat to explore how these two variables are related. The suitable indicators analysed in this chapter represent AML policy and have a logical hierarchy and are furthermore selected based on data availability and cross-country comparability. It is conceptually hard to compare an indicator for AML policy with threat estimation because the units of measurement are by definition completely different. The visual exploratory approach we use in this chapter can indicate whether the policy

---

[1]   Note that our analysis focuses here on money laundering only. There is insufficient data on terrorist financing to perform a similar analysis for terrorist financing at this point. However, the same methodology could be applied in the future when more data on terrorist financing policy is available and when we have more insight into what determines the threat of terrorist financing in the different EU Member States.

response is proportional, but cannot be seen as an exact measurement.[2] The exploratory analysis is based on a figure which has along the horizontal axis a policy response indicator (in which a higher score is a better policy response), with threat (either in millions of Euros or as a percentage of GDP) on the vertical axis. We consider the diagonal area in this figure an appropriate policy response in the sense that a country in this area has a policy response that is more or less proportional to the threat it is facing. Member States that are plotted in the bottom-right-hand corner are playing safe, since their policy response is more than proportional to the threat they are facing. We consider countries plotted in the top-left-hand corner to be at risk of having a less than proportional policy response.

11.3   THE SELECTED INDICATORS FOR POLICY RESPONSE

We selected the following variables to represent the policy response: FATF compliance score, legal effectiveness score, timeliness of implementation, FIU response score, international cooperation score, information flow score and the number of convictions for money laundering. We give a small overview of these indicators, which elements of AML policy they cover, how they are measured and what their downsides and merits are.

FATF Compliance Score

Our first indicator for policy response is an FATF compliance score, because these recommendations were actually the starting point for our research. The FATF/MONEYVAL evaluate all countries on the extent to which they are compliant with each of the 40 FATF recommendations. In constructing the FATF compliance measure we simply added up the scores for each recommendation (by giving 3 points when a country is fully compliant, 2 when it is largely compliant, 1 when partially compliant and 0 when non-compliant), based on the latest Mutual Evaluation Report for each country. The advantage of using FATF compliancy scores is that they are available for all Member States and that all Member States are scored on the same basis. The downside of this measure is that national

---

[2]   The results of our analysis are for instance sensitive to the scaling of the axes and are primarily a relative score. We therefore made all indicators for AML policy response take only positive values, with the characteristic that more is always better, and have (0,0) at the origin (bottom-left-hand corner) of the graphs.

scores come from different time periods (some are almost ten years old), are being awarded by different teams, offer mainly a measure of 'law in the books compliance' and not of 'law in action compliance', are not completely cross-country comparable,[3] and assume that every recommendation is of equal importance in terms of having an effective AML policy – which is obviously not the case. The FATF does not take into account to what extent a country is threatened by money laundering.

If a country were to be fully compliant with all 40 recommendations of the FATF, it would receive a FATF compliance score of 120 (40 times 3). The 27 EU Member States receive scores of between 42 (for Luxembourg) and 95 (for Hungary). When assessed for threat (see Figure 11.1), none of the EU Member States is in the black zone (at risk). Only Luxembourg, due to its bad compliance score, is in the grey zone, no matter whether threat is measured as a percentage of GDP or in millions of Euros. Latvia and Estonia face a relatively high level of threat (if calculated as a percentage of GDP), but are nonetheless in the grey zone due to their relatively good compliance score. The same holds for UK when threat is measured in millions of Euros.

Legal Effectiveness in Preventive AML Policy

Our next indicator is a measure of the legal effectiveness of the substantive norms in preventive AML policy. This indicator is based on the analysis in Chapter 3 of this book. In Chapter 3 we identified, besides the general factors that negatively influence the legal effectiveness of Member States' AML/CTF policies, a number of potential legal hindrances to preventive AML policy for each Member State. We constructed an index of legal hindrances for every country using the following weights: 1 for technical hindrances, 3 for fundamental hindrances and 2 for other hindrances. We were then able to create a scale of legal hindrances across the European Union using this indicator. The scale was proven not to be overly sensitive to the chosen weights. As a last step, we took the inverse of this legal hindrance measure to obtain the legal effectiveness measure presented in Figure 11.2 and in online appendix 11.2 at http://goo.gl/VZgJb3.

The advantage of using such a measure is that it is easily constructed once one has identified the legal hindrances present in the preventive

---

[3] A member of a FATF evaluation team has indicated that the situation of the country (like the state of its economy) is considered when giving the compliance score. This would mean that a poor country could get a rating of largely compliant for a certain recommendation, while a richer country with the exact same policy might get a rating of only partly compliant.

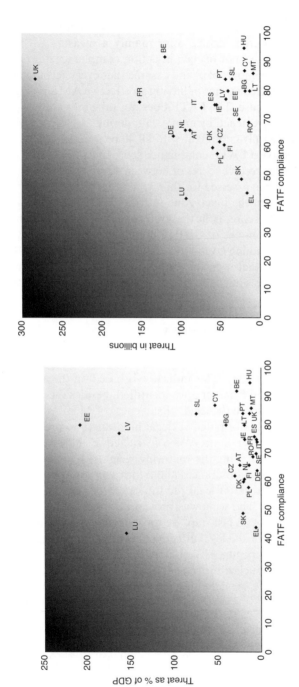

Source: Created by the authors, based on the following data: for threat estimations, see Chapter 2; the FATF compliance score is a simple addition of the compliancy scores given by the FATF for the different recommendations. To make this addition possible we transformed the scores into numbers. Fully compliant = 3, largely compliant = 2, partially compliant = 1, non-compliant = 0 and not applicable = 3 (because N/A is usually given where the recommendation is not necessary; for example, in countries where trusts are not permitted, there is no need to comply with recommendation 34; legal arrangements are beneficial to owners, so it is as good as fully compliant). Online appendix 11.2 lists the exact scores for all Member States (see http://goo.gl/VZgJb3).

Figure 11.1 Visual representation of threat vs. FATF compliance score

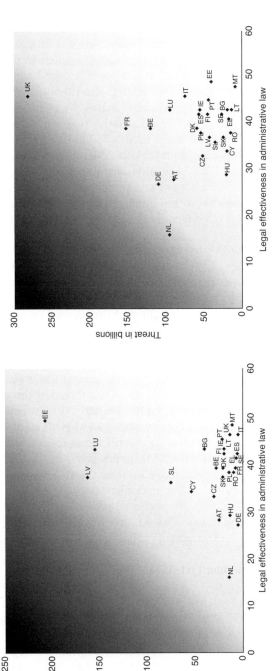

Source: Created by the authors, based on the following data: for threat estimations see Chapter 2; the legal effectiveness score is based on the findings of Chapter 4. For each country, the legal hindrances were identified and classified into: technical, fundamental and other. After performing a robustness analysis it became clear that a robust ranking of Member States according to their hindrances can be obtained by assigning the following weights to each hindrance: 1 for technical hindrances, 3 for fundamental hindrances, 2 for other hindrances that are not fundamental or technical in nature. The inverse of this measure of legal hindrances is presented in the graphs above as legal effectiveness to make sure that we apply a consistent methodology, with a policy response indicator for which more is better on the x-axis. Online appendix 11.2 lists the exact scores for all Member States (see http://goo.gl/VZgJb3).

Figure 11.2   Visual representation of threat vs. legal effectiveness

AML policy of the Member States. The disadvantages are that it is a crude exercise in translating qualitative into quantitative information, the weights attached to each of the hindrances are open to discussion and also that the categorization of hindrances has a direct effect on the index as well as an indirect effect on the country rankings. Furthermore, there is a lot of data asymmetry between the Member States. First, for some Member States there is a lot more information publicly available than for other Member States. Second, for some Member States the information available was far more outdated than for other Member States. For example, some FATF or MONEYVAL evaluations date from 2006. In the case of Member States for which more and more recent information is available, we also know more about hindrances. This generally means they end up with a lower legal effectiveness score. We acknowledge this methodological issue.

The Member State identified as having the least legal hindrances was Estonia, which obtained a score of 49 out of a maximum of 50. Having had a very recent FATF evaluation, the Netherlands was the Member State where we were able to identify most legal hindrances. The Netherlands received a score of 20. We took into account that there could be many more hindrances that were overlooked which is why the Netherlands is not considered to be a country with a nil legal effectiveness policy indicator (see Figure 11.2). When compared with our measures of threat, we see that, despite having a potentially excellent preventive legal framework, Estonia's policy response is only proportionate to the threat of money laundering when seen as a percentage of GDP. Similarly, Luxembourg and Latvia seem to have a proportional policy response, whereas all other Member States have taken more than proportional measures to ensure the legal effectiveness of their preventive AML policy given the threat of money laundering they face as a percentage of their GDP. Figure 11.2 also shows that Member States with a strong legalistic background have a proportional and somewhat less than proportional policy response when looking at threat in billions of Euros. This has to do with the fact that these countries are also the most threatened economies.

Third EU Directive Implementation Timeliness

Our next indicator is to what extent the Third EU Directive was implemented on time. Chapter 4 discusses implementation delays in detail; here we use this information as an indicator for AML policy response.

The advantage of this indicator is that it is easily obtainable, easy to calculate and available for all 27 EU Member States. The disadvantage is that implementation delays do not necessarily represent any resistance or inefficiency on the part of a certain country, but could have quite basic and pragmatic causes, such as delays caused by a change in parliament.

Figure 11.3 shows that France is most at risk (in the black zone) for this indicator, mostly due to the fact that it has the highest implementation delay in the EU: 991 days. The small Member States with a relatively high amount of threat (when measured as a percentage of GDP: Estonia, Latvia and Luxembourg) were relatively fast with the implementation, which is a proportional policy response in our Figure 11.3. Next to France, Belgium is the only country that also has a less than proportional policy response, mainly due to a relative high implementation delay of more than two years.

AML FIU Policy Response

In constructing the AML policy response indicator for the FIU we made use of a factor analysis using several indicators described in Chapter 7 of this book: the FIU budget securitization score, the FIU data access score, the FIU feedback score and the suspicion reports receiving and processing score.

The FIU budget securitization measure depends on the FIU's financial independence and is also affected by the type of organization the FIU is accountable to. We operationalize the FIU's budgetary independence by giving 4 points to FIUs who have a completely separate budget which they can administer themselves, 3 points to FIUs that receive their budgets from another organization but are within the first decision tier in the organogram, 2 points to FIUs that receive their budgets from another organization but are within the second decision tier in the organogram and finally, 1 point to FIUs that receive their budgets from another organization and are within the last decision tiers in the organogram. We operationalize the measure of FIU accountability by giving 2 points if the institution to which the FIU is accountable is the national parliament or a ministry and if the organization in charge of appointing the head of the FIU is either the government, the parliament or a ministry, and 1 point if the institution to which the FIU is accountable to is the police or the prosecution office, and when members of these institutions also appoint the head of the FIU.

The data access score is constructed on the basis of the type of access that FIUs have to several databases: direct or on request, online or not (see Table 7.4). Based on the importance that FIU representatives in general gave to direct information access versus online access, we gave 10 points for online direct access – thus recognizing that this is the best form of access, 9 points for direct but not online access – since this form

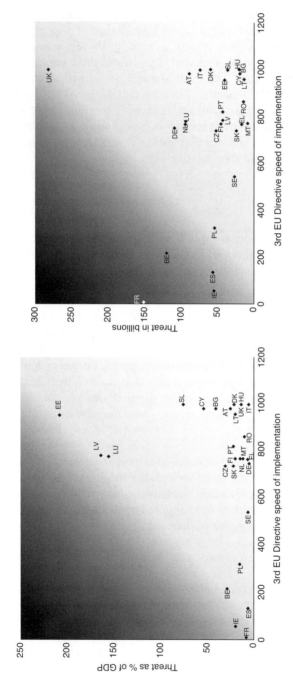

Source: Created by the authors based on the following data: for threat estimations see Chapter 2; the speed of implementation is calculated by subtracting the implementation delays shown in Figure 5.1 of this report from 1000. The subtraction ensures the x-axis represents a policy response indicator for which more is better; the subtraction from 1000 has the effect of making all scores positive (the maximum delay in the EU is 991 days for France) and therefore we can have (0,0) at the origin (bottom-left-hand corner). Online appendix 11.2 lists the exact scores for all Member States (see http://goo.gl/VZgJb3).

Figure 11.3   Visual representation of threat vs. implementation timeliness

of access is only lacking speed, 5 points for indirect access – as more information and time can be lost with this lack of transparency, and no points when the FIU has no formal or informal access to a database.

The suspicion reports receiving and processing score is based on the way reports are received and analysed by the FIUs – by mostly electronic means or mostly manually, and with or without the help of data-mining systems (see Table 7.5). We aggregated this data into three categories for suspicion reporting – high speed (when the Member State representatives suggested that the FIU receives only electronic reports or mostly electronic reports), medium speed (when the Member State representatives suggested that the FIU receives electronic, paper and fax reports) and low speed (when the Member State representatives suggested that the FIU mostly receives STRs as paper copies or by fax). Similarly, for data mining there are two groups: FIUs that have a data-mining/analysis system and FIUs that do not, at the time we conducted this research.

The FIU feedback score is based on whether FIUs provide standard reporting forms to the reporting entities, have helpful websites with readily accessible annual reports where reporting entities can report online, give regular training sessions and workshops and confirm the receipt of a suspicion report (see Table 7.3).

These indices are the results of crude exercises of translating qualitative information into quantitative data and are also subject to data asymmetry between the Member States. In order to reduce these disadvantages, we used a factor analysis method to construct a general measure of FIU AML response. A description of the factor analysis can be found in online appendix 11.1. The advantages of this method are that it takes away some of the variation in these indices which could be due to either index construction or data availability, and that it allows for cross-country comparability across all of the FIUs of the European Union.

According to this factor analysis, the Italian FIU has the lowest policy response which means that it has a proportional policy response if threat is measured as a percentage of GDP and a less than proportional policy response when threat is measured in billions of Euros. Similarly, the UK FIU has an under-proportional FIU response, although this is mostly due to the high threat its economy faces.

International Cooperation Score

Money laundering is for the most part an international crime, which makes international cooperation in the fight against money laundering an important element. Chapter 9 of this book analyses the international cooperation of the 27 EU Member States in the form of the signature,

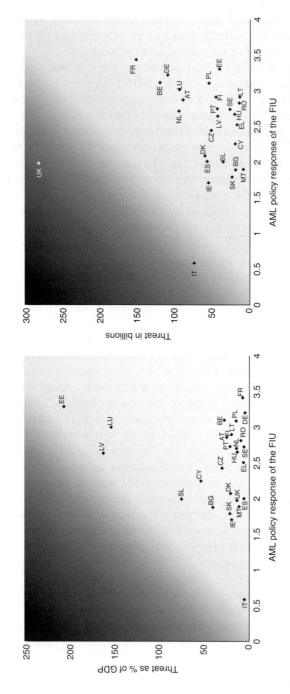

Source: Created by the authors, based on the following data: for the threat estimations see Chapter 2; the AML policy response of the FIU is based on a factor analysis on four ECOLEF constructed indices that were introduced in Chapter 7. Online appendix 11.1 describes the factor analysis (see http://goo.gl/VZgJb3). The AML policy response of the FIU measure ranges from −2 to +2, but is transposed to vary from 0 to 4, so that we have, consistent with the other graphs, (0,0) at the origin (bottom left-hand corner). Online appendix 11.2 lists the exact scores for all Member States (see http://goo.gl/VZgJb3).

Figure 11.4   Visual representation of threat vs. FIU score

ratification and implementation of the principal international conventions in the AML/CTF field. This overview is the basis for the construction of the policy indicator for international cooperation that we analyse here. Signature of a convention is awarded 3 points, ratification 2 points and full implementation 1 point. The total maximum score is 33 points, based on 6 points for the Vienna Convention, UN Terrorist Financing Convention and Palermo Convention and 5 points for CoE 1990, the Merida Convention and CoE 2005 (NB: full implementation is only analysed for the Vienna, the Terrorist Financing and Palermo Conventions).

This indicator is available for all Member States and is straightforward to calculate, but the disadvantage of this indicator is that it only shows 'compliance in the books', which might be quite different from actual performance in international cooperation.

Due to the relatively high scores for international cooperation by the EU Member States, most countries are in the white zone and, hence, on the right-hand side. Only Estonia, Luxembourg and the UK are in the grey zone due to their relatively high levels of threat (either measured as a percentage of GDP or in billions of Euros).

AML Information Flow Scores

In constructing the information flow score, we could not rely too much on statistics, since there are virtually no such statistics available across the EU. This measure was constructed on the basis of the four types of information transmission chains that were identified in each country in Chapter 8, correcting for additional information transmission mechanisms (such as double reporting and liaison officers). We further used government effectiveness and corruption perception indicators available for all the EU Member States as proxies for the two types of identified information loss described in the value of the network calculations – limited interaction and deviant interests, respectively.

The advantages of this policy response indicator are the cross-country comparability and the identification of best practices in information transmission within a country. The disadvantages are that there is a great deal of data asymmetry across the Member States, that the proxies used for information decay may not reflect the different information decay that may occur when investigative agents cooperate and that these models are overly simplified and do not take into account other types of barriers to criminal apprehension (such as resources, priorities of the law enforcement entities).

The maximum information flow score occurs in a star information flow chain with the best corruption perception and government effectiveness

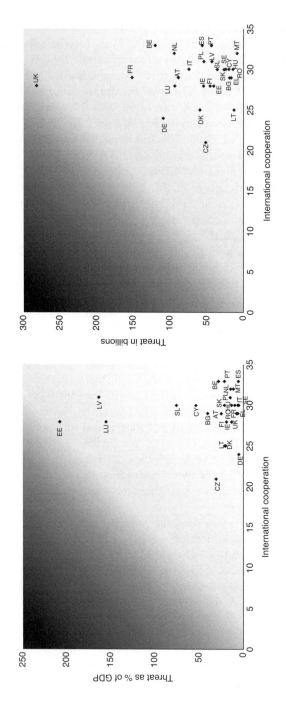

Source: Created by the authors, based on the following data: for the threat estimations see Chapter 2; for the international cooperation score see Chapter 9. See online appendix 11.2 lists the exact scores for all Member States (see http://goo.gl/VZgJb3).

Figure 11.5 Visual representation of threat vs. international cooperation

scores and in our sample they vary between 233 (Denmark) and 7.7 (Romania). Despite the large differences in the information flow scores, most countries have proportional policy responses considering the money laundering threat levels they are exposed to (see Figure 11.6). Exceptions are the small countries with a high exposure to threat as a percentage of GDP – Estonia and Latvia and the large financial centres such as the UK, when threat is expressed in billions of Euros. For Italy, the information flow scores reveal that national cooperation in AML matters may be under proportional to the threat, if this is expressed in billions of Euros.

ML Convictions

One of the goals of anti-money laundering policy is of course to catch money launderers and convict them. We therefore see the number of money laundering convictions as one of the most important indicators measuring the result of anti-money laundering repression policy, even though cross-country comparability is still dubious, as mentioned extensively in Chapter 10.

Denmark has a relatively high number of money laundering convictions per year and relatively low levels of threat (both measured in billions and as a percentage of GDP) and is therefore the only country that is on the safe side (in the white zone) in both graphs. Although the UK has by far the most convictions per year, when compared with the threat it is facing (measured in billions of Euros), this policy response is only proportional.

11.4 RESULTS

When plotting and analysing the results for all Member States of our visual exploratory approach for all our selected indicators for the policy response, we can identify for each country whether their policy response is either over-proportional (white), proportional (grey) or under-proportional (black) for each part of the policy response. These results are shown in Table 11.1.

As can be seen from the table, Denmark is the only Member State that is fully in the white zone – hence, on the safe side – for all the indicators of policy response both in relation to threat measured as a percentage of GDP and measured in millions of Euros. Not only does Denmark have a relatively low amount of threat, it also scores quite well for all the indicators we selected. Remarkably though, Denmark has been criticized by the FATF for not criminalizing self-laundering. Our analysis does not indicate that this severely limits their ability to fight money laundering.

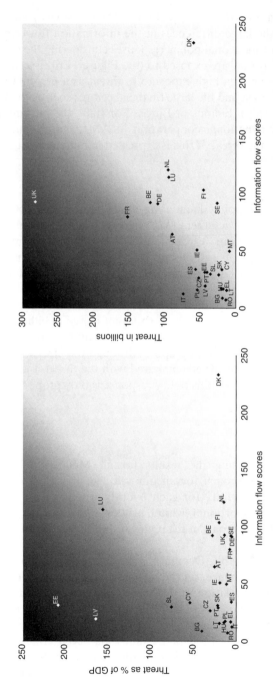

Source: Created by the authors, based on the following data: for the threat estimations see Chapter 2; for the information flow score see Chapter 8. For Estonia, Denmark, Finland, Latvia, Lithuania and Sweden, the analysis of the information flow chains was performed at a much more superficial level than for the other Member States, due to the timing of our research. Furthermore, information flows in the UK will change in the near future. See online appendix 11.2 lists the exact scores for all Member States (see http://goo.gl/VZgJb3).

Figure 11.6   Visual representation of threat vs. information flow score

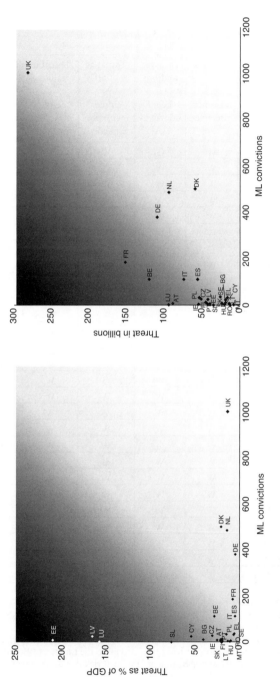

Source: Created by the authors, based on the following data: for the threat estimations see Chapter 2; the data used to calculate the average number of money laundering convictions per year in the period 2005–10 is specified in Chapter 10. See online appendix 11.2 lists the exact scores for all Member States (see http://goo.gl/VZgJb3).

Figure 11.7 Visual representation of threat vs. number of ML convictions

Effectiveness of EU anti-money laundering policy

Table 11.1   Overview of the extent to which the policy response of EU Member States is proportional to the threat

	Threat as % of GDP vs. FATF compliance score	Threat in millions vs. FATF compliance score	Threat as % of GDP vs. Legal effectiveness	Threat in millions vs. Legal effectiveness	Threat as % of GDP vs. Implementation timeliness	Threat in millions vs. Implementation timeliness	Threat as % of GDP vs. FIU response score
AT	W	W	W	G	W	W	W
BE	W	W	W	W	G	B	W
BG	W	W	W	W	W	W	W
CY	W	W	W	W	W	W	W
CZ	W	W	W	W	W	W	W
DK	W	W	W	W	W	W	W
EE	G	W	G	W	G	W	G
FI	W	W	W	W	W	W	W
FR	W	G	W	G	G	B	W
DE	W	G	W	G	W	W	W
EL	W	W	W	W	W	W	W
HU	W	W	W	W	W	W	W
IE	W	W	W	W	G	G	W
IT	W	W	W	W	W	W	G
LV	G	W	G	W	G	W	G
LT	W	W	W	W	W	W	W
LU	G	G	G	W	G	W	G
MT	W	W	W	W	W	W	W
NL	W	W	G	G	W	W	W
PL	W	W	W	W	G	G	W
PT	W	W	W	W	W	W	W
RO	W	W	W	W	W	W	W
SK	W	W	W	W	W	W	W
SL	W	W	W	W	W	W	G
ES	W	W	W	W	G	G	W
SE	W	W	W	W	W	W	W
UK	W	G	W	G	W	G	W

Source: Created by the authors, based on indicators developed in the ECOLEF project. See online appendix 11.2, http://goo.gl/VZgJb3, for a description of how we establish each ranking. W = the white zone, which indicates that a country is on the safe side by having an over-proportional policy response to the threat it is facing, G = the grey zone, which indicates that the policy response is more or less proportional to the threat and B = the black zone, which indicates that the Member State might be at risk due to having an under-proportional policy response to the threat it is facing.

Threat in millions vs. FIU response score	Threat as % of GDP vs. Information flow score	Threat in millions vs. Information flow score	Threat as % of GDP vs. International cooperation score	Threat in millions vs. International cooperation score	Threat as % of GDP vs. Number of convictions	Threat in millions vs. Number of convictions
W	G	G	W	W	G	B
W	G	G	G	W	G	B
W	G	G	W	W	G	G
W	G	G	W	W	B	G
W	G	G	W	W	G	G
W	W	W	W	W	W	W
W	B	G	W	W	B	G
W	G	G	W	W	G	G
W	G	G	W	W	G	B
W	G	G	W	W	G	G
W	G	G	W	W	G	G
W	G	G	W	W	G	G
G	G	G	W	W	G	G
G	G	B	W	W	G	G
W	B	G	W	W	B	G
W	G	G	W	W	G	G
W	G	G	G	W	B	B
W	G	G	W	W	G	G
W	W	G	W	W	W	G
W	G	G	W	W	G	G
W	G	G	W	W	G	G
W	G	G	W	W	G	G
W	G	G	W	W	G	G
W	G	G	W	W	B	G
W	G	G	W	W	G	G
W	G	G	W	W	G	G
B	G	B	W	G	W	G

For the rest of the Member States we see in general quite a mixed picture, with most countries ending up in the grey zone for some indicators, while being on the safe side (in the white zone) for most of the indicators. None of the Member States ended up consistently in the black zone. Actually, the Member States that ended up most in the black zone did so only twice (out of the 14). Estonia ended up least in the white zone, simply because – according to our estimations – the country is so much threatened by money laundering, especially when it is measured as a percentage of their GDP. This is the result of a relatively small country (Estonia) being located next to a very big country with a significant amount of crime and, therefore, criminal proceeds (Russia).

11.5   CONCLUSION

One of the critiques of the FATF mutual evaluations is that they do not take into account to what extent a country is threatened by money laundering. In this chapter we explore to what extent the policy response of the EU Member States relates to the size of the money laundering threat it faces. To do so, we mapped all Member States in a graph with threat and a policy response indicator on the axes. In our analysis, countries with high levels of threat and a relatively weak policy response end up in the black zone, which we typify as being at risk, because the policy response is under-proportional. The countries with low levels of threat and a relatively strong policy response end up in the white zone, which we typify as being on the safe side, because the policy response is over-proportional. When the policy response is more or less proportional to the threat, countries end up in the grey zone. This visual exploratory approach shows that most EU Member States are generally on the safe side (in the white area), with only a few Member States ever ending up in the black zone. Although the EU Member States perform relatively well in our analysis, almost all of them can improve on certain indicators. The positive exception here is Denmark, which has been criticized by the FATF for not criminalizing self-laundering, but which in our analysis has not only relatively low levels of threat, but also relatively good scores for all our policy response indicators.

12. Cost-benefit analysis

Joras Ferwerda

12.1 INTRODUCTION

Although cost-benefit analysis is a standard way of evaluating current and new policies in almost all policy fields, it is extremely rare in the area of anti-money laundering policy.[1] Whitehouse[2] concludes that 'The cost of compliance is increasing rapidly but it would be a brave person who steps up to say that it is too high a price to pay for countering terrorism and serious crime.'

In this research project we tried to gather statistics to do a cost-benefit analysis for the countries in the EU-27 regarding their AML/CTF policy. Unfortunately it turned out to be hard to gather these statistics or to make reasonable estimates for them. For most components we were able to gather statistics for only a few countries and the countries for which we could find statistics differed from component to component. Since this meant that we could not perform a cost-benefit analysis at all, we decided to do a cost-benefit analysis for a hypothetical country which combines the information that we gathered for the 27 EU Member States. To correct the statistics for size and price level, our hypothetical country has a population of 10 million people and a price level of 100. The average population in the EU-27 is around 18.5 million, but since a number of countries have a population of around 10 million (Belgium, Czech Republic, Greece, Hungary and Portugal),[3] we choose this nicely rounded number for our hypothetical country. International price level statistics normally take the level of the US as 100. The simple average in the EU-27 is only about 5% lower. Bulgaria has the lowest price level in the EU with 53, while Denmark has the highest at 146. The price level of Greece is the closest to the price level of our hypothetical country – 98.5.[4] What we will do is

---

[1]   Gill and Taylor (2002), p. 44.
[2]   Whitehouse (2003), p. 144.
[3]   Population statistic from 2010 from Heston et al. (2011). The values are also listed in online appendix 12.1 (see http://goo.gl/VZgJb3).
[4]   Price level statistic (p) from 2010 from Heston et al. (2011). The values are also listed in online appendix 12.1 (see http://goo.gl/VZgJb3).

take all the possible statistics we have for every component of the cost-benefit analysis and correct them to match the size and price level of our hypothetical country. Online appendix 12.1 shows these correction factors for each Member State (see http://goo.gl/VZgJb3). Consequently, we take the average of the statistics available as our best estimate and use the lowest and highest statistics to indicate the bandwidth of the estimations. Although such a procedure does not meet the standards for a cost-benefit analysis,[5] it allows us to illustrate the order of magnitude of the different statistics and makes it easily visible for which components we do not have statistics at all.

Before starting to identify the components and associated data, we should identify what we want to assess exactly. We can calculate how much it has cost to set up an AML/CTF policy and compare that with how much we have benefited from it (let us call this the 'historical approach'), but we can also assess which costs we would save if we were to stop the current AML/CTF policy and what benefits we would lose consequently (let us call this the 'current approach'). Although these two methods both measure the costs and benefits of AML/CTF policy and although they seem to be much the same, there is one important difference: with the 'historical approach' we would include the set-up costs of the policy, while we would not include these costs in the 'current approach'. These set-up costs may be quite substantial, since they include not only the work of the FATF associated with devising an international policy, but also include costs such as setting up an FIU in every country in the world, implementing new laws in the legal system, training personnel in law enforcement agencies as well as reporting institutions and many more efforts. The 'historical approach' would tell us whether starting AML/CTF policy has been a good idea, while the 'current approach' considers whether we should continue the current efforts. Geiger and Wuensch[6] conclude that anti-money laundering regulation is extended rather than being thought over, and ask themselves why a review does not take place. In this light it seems most fruitful to concentrate on the 'current approach' for now, since it is more policy relevant.

Based on a literature review, conducted interviews and discussions during the regional workshops, we identify the following components for the cost-benefit analysis.

---

[5] The results can for instance be biased when certain costs or benefits are not proportional to population (because of fixed costs or economies of scale for example) or when the countries that provided data are not representative of the EU-27.

[6] Geiger and Wuensch (2007), p. 100.

The possible cost components of anti-money laundering policy are:

- ongoing policy making;
- sanction costs (repressive);
- FIU;
- supervision;
- law enforcement and judiciary;
- duties of the private sector;
- reduction in privacy;
- efficiency costs for society and the financial system.

The possible benefit components of anti-money laundering policy are:

- fines (preventive and repressive);
- confiscated proceeds;
- reduction in the amount of money laundering;
- less predicate crimes;
- reduced damage effect on real economy;
- less risk for the financial sector.

Although there is still very little information on the costs and benefits of anti-money laundering policy,[7] let us discuss each component briefly and report what we do know. Note that this cost-benefit analysis is at the country level and not at the level of the particular institutions involved. It is also interesting to look at the costs and benefits of anti-money laundering policy for individual institutions, because this might determine their incentive to cooperate. For such analyses, see the work of Takáts[8] and Harvey.[9]

12.2   THE COSTS OF AML/CTF POLICY

Ongoing Policy Making

Since we are leaving out the set-up costs (see discussion above), we only consider the ongoing policy-making costs. Normally this constitutes only some policy staff at the relevant ministry. Estimations of these costs are

---

[7]   Gill and Taylor (2002), p. 44.
[8]   Takáts (2007).
[9]   Harvey (2004).

often hindered by the fact that the policy staff are not responsible only for anti-money laundering policy, which means it is necessary to estimate the time they spend on anti-money laundering policy.

To find out the level of these costs in the 27 Member States, we asked the relevant ministry or ministries the following questions in an online survey and in a personal interview if the online survey was not answered.

> What is the overall budget for the year 2010 at your Ministry (and other Ministries, if applicable) for AML/CTF policy? (Please provide the overall budget which includes personnel and specify the currency, in case you do not have a statistic, please estimate the amount and indicate this with an asterisk (*) after the number)
> What is the number of staff dedicated full time (or full-time equivalent) on money laundering and terrorist financing matters at your Ministry (and other Ministries, if applicable)?

The responses of the countries are shown in the online appendix 12.2 (see http://goo.gl/VZgJb3).

Our initial idea was to estimate the budget using data on the number of staff for the last couple of countries that were not able to answer this question. For an idea of how this would work, see the estimations for the budget of the FIU explained in Chapter 10. Unfortunately, the data we gathered here falls far short of what would be necessary to make such estimations. We are left with three relevant answers that can be used to estimate the ongoing policy-making costs for our hypothetical country: 75,000 Euros in Estonia, 980,000 in Ireland and 131,194 in Sweden. Hence, when corrected for the price level and size of these countries, our best estimate for the ongoing policy costs of our hypothetical country is 896,754 Euros with a bandwidth of 116,762–1,813,000 Euros.[10]

FIU

Every country in the world has set up an FIU to receive reports on money laundering and terrorist financing suspicions from banks and other reporting institutes. Since the whole FIU is normally focused on AML/CTF, we should count all costs of the FIU and can therefore have a good estimation

---

[10]   Example of how these numbers are calculated: first, the three relevant budgets are multiplied by the overall correction factors mentioned in online appendix 12.1 (see http://goo.gl/VZgJb3). This means we have three estimates of this budget: 760,500; 1,813,000 and 116,762. The average of these three numbers is 896.754, which is our best estimate. The lowest (116,762) and highest (1,813,000) estimates indicate the bandwidth.

of these costs based on the budget of the FIU, which is sometimes even publicly available. As already reported in Chapter 11 and also shown in online appendix 12.3 (see http://goo.gl/VZgJb3), we have data on the budget of the FIU for 11 countries and estimated a budget based on the number of employees for the remaining 16 countries. Since we reduce this data to one best estimate, there is no need to use the estimated budgets.

Hence, after correcting for the size and price level of our hypothetical country, our best estimate of FIU costs for our hypothetical country is 2,892,349 Euros, with a bandwidth of 685,460–9,860,636 Euros.

Supervision

Estimating the supervision costs of AML/CTF policy is rather difficult, because AML/CTF is normally just one of the supervision tasks of each supervisor. Moreover, the supervision of the AML/CTF duties of the private sector is normally fragmented over different supervisory authorities, based on the type of institution under supervision. This would not normally be a problem if we were able to get data for all the supervisory institutions. Unfortunately this is not the case. We asked all supervisors in all 27 EU Member States the following two questions via an online survey and sometimes also in a face-to-face interview.

> What is the annual overall budget at your authority for supervising AML/CTF regulations? (Please provide the overall budget which includes personnel and specify the currency, in case you do not have a statistic, please estimate the amount and indicate this with an asterisk (*) after the number)
> How many persons work in your organization in total in full time equivalence (so two half time employees count as one full time employee)?

The responses of the countries are shown in the online appendix 12.4 (see http://goo.gl/VZgJb3).

Because there is not a single country for which we have data for all supervisors, we have to devise a way to make an estimation for all the supervisors in total. If we had a good way of knowing the size of the different supervisors in each country, then we would be able to estimate the share of a single supervisor for the overall supervision costs. The staff would be a good indicator for this, but this information is also not available for a single country for all supervisors. We therefore assume that all supervisors are of equal size and expect that, because we use an overall average, the extreme values cancel each other out. This would also be indicated by an increased bandwidth. After calculating the supervision costs for nine countries, corrected for the number of supervisors and the price level and population of our hypothetical country, our best estimate for supervision costs is 14,332,941 Euros with a bandwidth of 291,906–112,200,000 Euros.

Law Enforcement and Judiciary

Although the total budget of law enforcement agencies and the judiciary is often public, separating out specific AML costs is hard. Many investigations and court cases have money laundering as just one of the crimes. The question then is, if money laundering were left out of the package of crimes that are investigated/prosecuted, how much money would be saved? Such a question seems to be impossible to answer. In the hope that some countries collect statistics on this, we asked the following questions via an online survey and sometimes in face-to-face interviews:

> What is the overall budget for the year 2010 for law enforcement in general (public prosecutor, police and other investigating authorities) in your country? *(Please provide the overall budget which includes personnel and specify the currency, in case you do not have a statistic, please estimate the amount and indicate this with an asterisk (*) after the number)*
> Which share of the annual overall budget of law enforcement is spent on AML/CTF? *(Please provide us with an estimate of the percentage, and specify for different law enforcement authorities in case you think their share differs)*
> What is the number of staff dedicated full time (or full-time equivalent) to money laundering and terrorist financing in law enforcement agencies?
> What is the overall budget for the year 2010 for the judiciary in general in your country? (Please provide the overall budget which includes personnel and specify the currency, in case you do not have a statistic, please estimate the amount and indicate this with an asterisk (*) after the number. In case you have difficulties to estimate this, keep in mind that the percentage of time the staff spends on AML/CTF might be a good benchmark)
> Which share of the annual overall budget of the judiciary is spent on AML/ CTF? *(Please provide us with an estimate of the percentage. In case you have difficulties to estimate this, keep in mind that the percentage of time the staff spends on AML/CTF might be a good benchmark)*
> What is the number of staff dedicated full time (or full-time equivalent) to money laundering and terrorist financing in the judiciary?

The responses of the countries are shown in the online appendix 12.5 (see http://goo.gl/VZgJb3).

Although we have the overall budget for LEA and the judiciary for some countries, in none of them do we have a statistic on the amount spent on AML/CTF. In Hungary we know how much is spent by the police, which is quite useful, but the amount spent by the public prosecutor's office is missing. We therefore assume that the amount spent on AML/CTF is proportional to the overall spending of the police and the public prosecutor.

In Hungary 7.57 times more is spent by the police than by the PPO. Using this proportion, we would have an estimate for our hypothetical country on the amount spent by LEAs on fighting money laundering of 1,423,565 Euros. If, on the same reasoning, we use the fact that the amount spent by the judiciary is about 28% of the spending by LEAs, our estimate for the amount spent by the judiciary on AML/CTF is 400,245 Euros.

Sanction Costs (Repressive)

AML policy has two types of sanctioning: the preventive and repressive aspects of the policy. The sanctions in the preventive part of the policy are sanctions against banks and other reporting institutions for not perform-ing their AML duties appropriately. Since this is normally done by the supervisors of these reporting institutions, these costs are not considered here to prevent double counting. The sanctions in repressive policy are the sanctions against the money launderers. The main costs here are probably the prison costs of locking up the money launderers, but we can also con-sider the costs of chasing money launderers to pay their fines for example, although we can expect that these costs would be relatively low.

To have at least a basis for estimation, we asked the following questions via an online survey and sometimes in face-to-face interviews:

> What is the average imprisonment duration regarding sanctions for natural persons for the offence of money laundering in practice? *Please estimate if you do not have statistics and indicate this with an asterisk (*) after the number.*
> - Suspended imprisonment
> - Unsuspended imprisonment
>
> What is the average imprisonment duration regarding sanctions for natural persons for the offence of terrorist financing in practice? *Please estimate if you do not have statistics and indicate this with an asterisk (*) after the number.*
> - Suspended imprisonment
> - Unsuspended imprisonment

The responses of the countries are shown in the online appendix 12.6 (see http://goo.gl/VZgJb3).

Of course, only unsuspended imprisonment is relevant for our estima-tion of the prison costs. We can have an estimate of the costs of having a criminal in prison for a day, but the important question here is: would this criminal also be in prison if he or she had not been convicted of money laundering? This question seems to be impossible to answer, because money laundering is often only one of the offences for which the defendant is prosecuted. In Ireland the representatives indicated to us that they nor-mally do not add money laundering to a prosecution which also involves the predicate crime because this complicates the case needlessly. Also in countries where self-laundering is not criminalized we would expect that money laundering prosecutions and convictions do not include the predicate crime. But unfortunately, none of these countries was able to answer our questions on the average duration of imprisonment. We therefore only have the Irish estimate to work with. According to the Irish Prison Service,[11] the average annual cost of incarcerating a person in prison in 2009 was 77,222 Euros and since Irish representatives indicated an average unsuspended imprisonment for money laundering of three years, a money laundering conviction costs on average an estimated 231,666 Euros. The average number of convictions in Ireland is five per year in the period 2005–10. This means that the annual prison costs for Ireland would be estimated at 1,158,330 Euros, which means that, correcting for size and price level, the estimate for our hypothetical country is 2,142,911 Euros.

Duties of the Private Sector

This component comprises all the costs reporting institutions incur in fulfilling the duties as described in the Third EU Money Laundering Directive. These costs seem to receive most attention in the literature. Alexander[12] says about this component that these duties for the private sector comprise 'those tangible operational costs that relate to investments that institutions will make in the form of physical and human capital required to carry out the compliance function. This is a task based on the assumption that laundering activity will be evidenced via some unusual account transaction that the banks will be able to detect through their "inside knowledge" of all financial transactions. It is without a doubt an immense task to pick out the illegal from the multitude of legitimate financial transactions that pass through the system.' Harvey[13] mentions that 'many costs of compliance are not additional but are part of due diligence activity'. A PwC report[14] notes that 'the costs of AML to a firm will vary enormously between different industry sectors'.

We identified and tested three ways of estimating these costs. Our first intuitive approach is in line with how we calculate most of the components for this cost-benefit analysis. We asked a number of reporting institutions in every Member State to answer the following two questions.

---

[11]   Irish Prison Service (2010), p. 4.
[12]   Alexander (2000), pp. 9–27.
[13]   Harvey (2004), p. 341.
[14]   PriceWaterhouseCoopers LLP (2003), 'Anti-Money Laundering Current Customer Review Cost Benefit Analysis', report prepared for the FSA.

How much does it cost, on average, to file one report to the FIU? *(This figure should include all possible costs related to filing a report, like personnel, material etc. Please specify per type of report, the currency and in case you do not have a statistic, please estimate the amount and indicate this with an asterisk (*) after the number)*

How much do you spend annually on total training costs (and compliance systems, if applicable) for AML/CTF policy? *(Please specify the currency and in case you do not have a statistic, please estimate the amount and indicate this with an asterisk (*) after the number)*

The responses of the countries are shown in the online appendix 12.7 (see http://goo.gl/VZgJb3).

There are several reasons why it is hard to use these answers to derive an estimation of these costs. First of all, the response rate is very low, although this could have been expected.[15] Second, countries have a clear incentive to overestimate the amount. Third, it is hard to extrapolate from the costs for one institution to an estimate for the whole sector, and even more complicated to come to an estimate for all reporting entities in a certain country. We therefore explored a second approach in which we use earlier estimates from a cost-benefit analysis in the UK. This cost-benefit analysis was associated with the Money Laundering Regulations 1993 and consisted of only the costs and benefits for the reporting institutions. The results of this cost-benefit analysis are estimates for the total amount of costs for different types of company: a large building society, a large unit trust and PEP plan management company, a large life assurance/pensions company and a medium-sized motor finance house. Unfortunately, these different types of company do not even come close to covering all reporting entities in the UK or any other Member State. Moreover, there is no precise description of the characteristics of these types of companies, which makes it hard to classify companies in a certain country accordingly. We therefore tried to find a reasonable estimate based on a literature review and found a report that estimated the total costs for reporting entities in the Netherlands for their reporting and identification duties at 40.1 million Euros in 2007.[16] Since we lack other opportunities for estimation,

---

[15] To make a similar type of estimate for a cost-benefit analysis as the Annex of the UK's Money Laundering Regulations 1993, HM Treasury sent out 1,000 requests, to which only 60 responded and of which only one respondent attempted to quantify these costs.
[16] Brief van de Algemene Rekenkamer, Bestrijden witwassen en terrorismefinanciering, Tweede Kamer der Staten-Generaal, vergaderjaar 2007–2008, 31 477 no. 1. This letter reports the estimate and cites another source, namely Financiën (2007), Vaststelling van de begrotingsstaten van het Ministerie van Financiën

we correct this estimate for our hypothetical country to come up with an estimate of 22,055,000 Euros for the duties of the private sector.[17]

Reduction in Privacy

The screening of all financial transactions to filter the ones related to money laundering, together with the additional customer due diligence that is required of reporting entities, is, at least in theory, a reduction in privacy, which we could see as a social cost of AML policy. Whether this reduction in privacy is severe and how much it matters is extremely difficult to measure or estimate. Geiger and Wunsch[18] also mention a reduction in privacy as a cost of AML policy.

Efficiency Costs for Society and the Financial System

The AML policy that is executed by banks and other reporting entities focuses on criminals, but harms legitimate users/customers in more or less the same way. Increased customer due diligence, for instance, is needed for all customers. Moreover, the financial transactions of criminals can be delayed for further analysis, but also other people might have their transactions delayed inadvertently. One could argue that the costs of the AML duties of reporting entities are passed on to their customers in higher prices, but we exclude this here because we already mentioned above these costs of AML duties for reporting entities. The efficiency costs for society due to AML policy can be quite substantial, but they will be very hard to measure or estimate. The delay of a financial transaction may have very severe effects (like stopping an important business deal), but may also be completely harmless (as when transferring money from a checking account to a savings account). The same holds for intensified identification duties. It could for instance hamper financial inclusion in Africa – because banking with a mobile phone now first needs identification – while it could

---

(IXB) voor het jaar 2008. Tweede Kamer, vergaderjaar 2007–2008, 31 200 IXB, no. 2. Den Haag: Sdu, in which we were unable to find the cited estimate.

[17]   This estimate is probably an underestimate, since Institut der deutschen Wirtschaft Köln, Consult GmbH (2006), Bürokratiekosten in der Kreditwirtschaft, p. 9 estimates the costs for AML for the financial sector in Germany at 775 million Euros (the estimate for our hypothetical country would be 93 million Euros). Unfortunately, this report focuses on the financial sector only and since there is no estimate for the other reporting institutions in Germany, we could not use this report directly for an estimation of our component 'duties of the private sector'.

[18]   Geiger and Wuensch (2007), p. 98.

also be completely harmless if identification would be needed anyway (for instance when doing a real estate transaction at a notary's). Other scholars also mention these costs, but none has been able to estimate it in any way,[19] except for the study by Transcrime that estimated it for a small part of AML/CTF policy, namely the transparency requirements in the company/corporate field and banking sector.[20]

12.3 THE BENEFITS OF AML/CTF POLICY

Fines (Repressive)

There are two types of fine in AML policy. One of these falls under preventive policy, namely fines for reporting entities that do not comply with their duties, and one falls under the repressive part of the policy, namely fines for money launderers who are caught. According to Harvey,[21] reporting institutions mainly get fined for lack of compliance and not for the presence of money laundering. The fines are benefits in the AML/CTF framework, but they are at the same time costs for the reporting entities. Since we consider both components, they will always cancel each other out, no matter the size. Therefore there is no need to estimate these benefits. Hence, in this section we only consider the fines in the repressive part of the AML/CTF policy; the fines that money launderers have to pay.

On the fines for money launderers, we asked the following questions via an online survey and sometimes in face-to-face interviews.

> What is the average size regarding (criminal) fines for natural persons for the offence of money laundering in practice? Please estimate if you do not have statistics and indicate this with an asterisk (*) after the number.

> Does there exist corporate criminal liability, that is: the criminal sanctioning of legal persons, with regard to the offences of money laundering? If YES: What are the corresponding minimum and/or maximum of criminal fines?

> What is the number of administrative sanctions for money laundering on an annual basis between 2005–2010 (specified per year), and what is the number of natural persons and the value involved? Please estimate if you do not have statistics and indicate this with an asterisk (*) after the number.

The responses of the countries are shown in the online appendix 12.8 (see http://goo.gl/VZgJb3).

---

19   See for example Masciandaro (1998) and Geiger and Wuensch (2007).
20   Transcrime (2007).
21   Harvey (2004).

The online appendix 12.8 (see http://goo.gl/VZgJb3) shows that we do know for many countries how often criminal fines are imposed, but since we do not have any information on the (average) size (amount), we do not have enough information to make an estimate here. For criminal fines for corporate criminal liability and administrative law sanctions, our data availability is the worst; we did not get a single statistic for these. It should be noted that, even if we had more statistics here on the amount of the fines imposed, these numbers would not necessarily benefit our analysis, because we do not know whether these fines are actually paid.

Confiscated Proceeds

Once a money launderer is caught, he faces the risk of having his proceeds confiscated. This is an important measure in the fight against money laundering, and crime in general, because it could take away the incentive of the criminal and at the same time could generate income for the state.

Regarding the confiscation of proceeds, we asked the following questions via an online survey and sometimes in face-to-face interviews.

> What is the average size regarding confiscation of proceeds for natural persons for the offence of money laundering in practice? Please estimate if you do not have statistics and indicate this with an asterisk (*) after the number.[22]

> How many money laundering prosecutions have led to a conviction on an annual basis between 2005–2010 (separated per year), in how many convictions was confiscation of proceeds imposed and what was the total value? Please estimate if you do not have statistics and indicate this with an asterisk (*) after the number

The responses of the countries are shown in the online appendix12.9 (see http://goo.gl/VZgJb3).

It is apparent from the online appendix 12.9 (see http://goo.gl/VZgJb3) that we have three countries for which we have statistics on the amount confiscated for money laundering. These statistics show that the amounts differ greatly from year to year, but since we took an average for the period 2005–10, these extreme values are not shown in the table. The main

---

[22]   Initially the idea was to use this statistic in combination with the number of convictions to get a reasonable estimate for the total amount confiscated per year. It turned out that this question was only answered by the countries that had exact statistics on confiscation, which are publicly available. Since there is no need to make an estimate when exact statistics are available, in the end the answers to this question were not used in our research.

question now is to what extent the proceeds would be confiscated if there were no AML policy. Most of the convictions in these three countries are for self-laundering, which means that these proceeds might also be confiscated based on a conviction for the predicate crime. We therefore adjust the statistics to take this into account by multiplying the statistics by the share of convictions for third-party money laundering.[23] After also correcting for the size and price level of our hypothetical country, our best estimate for the annual amount of confiscated proceeds is 474,294 with a bandwidth of 14,715–1,039,896 Euros.

Reduction in the Amount of Money Laundering and Terrorism

Harvey[24] concludes that 'there is presumed to be an inverse relationship between the degree of regulation and the amount of money laundering taking place. While there is theoretical support for this approach, it has not been empirically tested on a wide scale, nor has account been taken of changes in money laundering behavior resulting from changes in regulatory requirements'. Also Geiger and Wuensch[25] conclude that 'whilst this deterrence mechanism sounds logically reasonable, its effectiveness and efficiency for fighting predicate crime is doubtful'. We are also unable to estimate to what extent this goal of AML policy is reached.

Effects of Money Laundering: Fewer Predicate Crimes, Reduced Damage Effect on Real Economy and Less Risk for the Financial Sector

The literature on money laundering mentions many indirect effects. A comprehensive literature review yields 25 effects that money laundering can have on the real economy and the financial sector, shown in the online appendix 12.10 (see http://goo.gl/VZgJb3). Money laundering can affect the real economy by distorting consumption, savings, investment, inflation, competition, trade and employment. Furthermore, money laundering can affect the financial sector with an increased risk for the solvency,

---

[23] The amount confiscated then becomes for Bulgaria 175,000 in 2006, 207,500 in 2007, 11,400 in 2008, for Cyprus 0 in 2005, 0 in 2006, 0 in 2007, 1.584 in 2008 and for Latvia 58.000 in 2005, 4.419 in 2006, 0 in 2007 and 0 in 2008. Shares of convictions for third-party money laundering are calculated from EUROSTAT (2010). When it was not possible to distinguish the conviction statistics between self-laundering and third-party laundering, we assumed a 50–50 division between self-laundering and third-party laundering.

[24] Harvey (2004), p. 343.

[25] Geiger and Wuensch (2007), p. 92.

liquidity, reputation and integrity of the sector. On the other hand, money laundering could also be good for the economy, for example because it increases the profits for the financial sector and leads to a greater availability of credit. The literature is therefore still uncertain as to whether money laundering would have a net positive or negative effect on the economy in the long run.

Hardly any of the effects listed in the literature have empirical support. Most of them are theorized and, in some cases, seem to have no traceable source at all. Bartlett[26] might be a good example of this, with explanations like 'it is clear from available evidence', without ever mentioning this evidence. Empirical research on the effects of money laundering is mainly hampered by the lack of a reliable estimate of the amount of money laundering in every country in every year.[27] Unger et al.[28] conclude that 'most literature on money laundering effects is pure speculation [. . .] one source refers to the other source, without much of an empirical solid back up'. Geiger and Wuensch[29] conclude, based on research by Baker,[30] Cuellar[31] and Bolle,[32] that the empirical evidence suggests that the relationship between detecting money laundering and an increased chance of detecting the predicate crime is only weak, if verifiable at all. All these effects of money laundering are in need of empirical testing and at this stage it is impossible to make any reasonable estimate for the size of these effects for our hypothetical country.

12.4 CONCLUSION

Table 12.1 summarizes our estimates for annual costs and benefits in our hypothetical country. As can be seen from the table, it is possible to estimate most of the costs, but hardly any of the benefits. This would mean that the cost-benefit dilemma for AML policy is reduced to the question: are we willing to spend almost 44 million Euros, with a reduction in privacy and efficiency costs, for unknown benefits? To answer with the words of

---

26 Bartlett (2002).
27 Levi and Reuter (2006), p. 294.
28 Unger, B., Rawlings, G., Siegel, M., Ferwerda, J., de Kruijf, W., Busuioc, E.M. and Wokke, K. (2006), 'The Amounts and Effects of Money Laundering', Dutch Ministry of Finance report.
29 Geiger and Wunsch (2007), p. 94.
30 Baker (2005).
31 Cuellar (2003).
32 Bolle (2004).

Table 12.1   Estimates of the annual costs and benefits of AML policy (in Euros)

Costs	Best estimate (Bandwidth)	Benefits	Best estimate (Bandwidth)
Ongoing policy making	896,754 (116,762–1,813,000)	Fines	Unknown
FIU	2,892,349 (685,460–9,860,636)	Confiscated proceeds	474,294 (14,715–1,039,896)
Supervision	14,332,941 (291,906–112,200,000)	Reduction in the amount of ML	Unknown
Law enforcement	1,423,565 (single estimate)	Less predicate crimes	Unknown
Judiciary	400,245 (single estimate)	Reduced damage effect on real economy	Unknown
Sanction costs (repressive)	2,142,911 (single estimate)	Less risk for the financial sector	Unknown
Duties of the private sector	22,055,000 (single estimate)		
Reduction in privacy	Moral cost		
Efficiency costs for society and the financial system	Unknown		
Total cost estimate	44,143,765 + 2 unknown	Total benefit estimate	474,294 + 5 unknown

Note: These are estimates for a hypothetical country with 10 million people and a price level equal to the US. The numbers are for illustrative purposes only, since all estimates are very sensitive to many possible biases and estimation procedures.

Whitehouse:[33] 'it would be a brave person who steps up to say that it is too high a price to pay for countering terrorism and serious crime'.

Apart from the actual estimation of costs and benefits, this exercise also shows that the main costs of AML/CTF policy seem to be the duties of the reporting sector and its supervision. In our estimation these two components are responsible for 84% of all the costs that could be estimated. Furthermore, we can conclude that the information available for a cost-benefit analysis is very limited (illustrated by the many components

[33]   Whitehouse (2003), p. 144.

220   *Effectiveness of EU anti-money laundering policy*

that are based on single estimates) and very diverse (illustrated by the wide bandwidths for certain components).

With the correction factors (reported in online appendix 12.1 at http://goo.gl/VZgJb3) that we used to correct the national data to the size and price level of our hypothetical country, we can estimate the costs and benefits for each country in the EU-27 and for the EU as a whole, as shown in Table 12.2. It should be noted that extrapolation of already sensitive estimates increases the sensitivity even more.

Table 12.2   Estimates for the annual costs and benefits of AML policy for each country and the whole EU (in Euros)

Country	Estimated costs of AML/CTF	Estimated benefits of AML/CTF
Austria	39,331,650 + 2 unknown	422,591 + 5 unknown
Belgium	52,109,975 + 2 unknown	559,885 + 5 unknown
Bulgaria	16,697,035 + 2 unknown	179,398 + 5 unknown
Cyprus	4,749,348 + 2 unknown	51,028 + 5 unknown
Czech Republic	34,239,484 + 2 unknown	367,879 + 5 unknown
Denmark	35,545,389 + 2 unknown	381,910 + 5 unknown
Estonia	4,355,149 + 2 unknown	46,793 + 5 unknown
Finland	28,707,338 + 2 unknown	308,440 + 5 unknown
France	320,821,916 + 2 unknown	3,447,008 + 5 unknown
Germany	378,177,540 + 2 unknown	4,063,254 + 5 unknown
Greece	46,737,736 + 2 unknown	502,164 + 5 unknown
Hungary	30,925,483 + 2 unknown	332,273 + 5 unknown
Ireland	23,870,414 + 2 unknown	256,471 + 5 unknown
Italy	286,270,198 + 2 unknown	3,075,774 + 5 unknown
Latvia	7,480,286 + 2 unknown	80,370 + 5 unknown
Lithuania	10,304,206 + 2 unknown	110,712 + 5 unknown
Luxembourg	2,517,861 + 2 unknown	27,053 + 5 unknown
Malta	1,477,812 + 2 unknown	15,878 + 5 unknown
Netherlands	80,858,428 + 2 unknown	868,767 + 5 unknown
Poland	109,126,093 + 2 unknown	1,172,484 + 5 unknown
Portugal	44,676,164 + 2 unknown	480,014 + 5 unknown
Romania	60,662,875 + 2 unknown	651,780 + 5 unknown
Slovakia	18,516,679 + 2 unknown	198,949 + 5 unknown
Slovenia	7,404,790 + 2 unknown	79,559 + 5 unknown
Spain	201,599,523 + 2 unknown	2,166,046 + 5 unknown
Sweden	49,501,570 + 2 unknown	531,860 + 5 unknown
UK	260,394,648 + 2 unknown	2,797,759 + 5 unknown
EU-27	2,157,059,590 + 2 unknown	23,176,102 + 5 unknown

13. Summary and conclusions

Brigitte Unger

Member States differ in the way in which they respond to money laundering threats. Policy responses to laundering activities range from the implementation of the Third Directive and the criminalization of money laundering and terrorist financing to the enforcement of preventive policy, prosecution and, ultimately, the conviction of launderers and terrorists.

The book therefore comprises five steps or building blocks:

- the threat of money laundering;
- the legal implementation of AML policy;
- the execution of AML policy;
- the enforcement of AML both nationally and internationally; and
- an effectiveness evaluation and cost-benefit analysis.

13.1 THE THREAT OF MONEY LAUNDERING

Using a range of different methods, including a gravity model, we find that the threat of money laundering is greatest in the United Kingdom, Luxembourg and other Western European countries, as a result of their relatively sophisticated financial markets, their relatively high GDP per capita levels, their high trade volumes, and cultural links to a wide range of countries which generate proceeds of crime. Hot money will generally flow from Eastern Europe to the west and from the rest of the world to Europe's financial centres, in search of safer havens for investment. The main bulk of money laundering in million Euros was identified in the financial and commercial centres of Europe. This means that these countries have to make more policy effort to combat laundering than Eastern and Southern EU countries (see Chapter 2).

In order to take into account differences in country size, we measured the threat of laundering in two ways. First, we measured it in absolute volume (threat in million Euros). Second, we corrected for the size of the country (threat as a percentage of GDP). The picture changes dramatically, when expressed as a percentage of each country's GDP.

It is especially the smaller EU Member States, surrounded by much larger countries the latter generating large amounts of money potentially available for laundering, that are threatened with being overwhelmed by criminal money (e.g. Estonia and Latvia by Russian money), while the medium-sized and large Member States face the highest volume of laundered money (see Chapter 2).

The difference between big financial centres and cash-intense economies also implies that the strategies on how to combat laundering will have to differ between these two groups. For cash-intense economies the reduction of cash payment possibilities seems the most obvious cure. In this regard Estonia, with its focus on electronic payment and electronic storage of documents ('e-government'), is an example of a country which has managed to reduce cash payments very substantially. The efforts of Belgium, Bulgaria, Greece and Italy, which introduced or sharpened cash bans, have also to be mentioned here.

13.2   LEGAL IMPLEMENTATION OF AML/CTF POLICY

With regard to the legal effectiveness of the AML policy, various aspects are studied in this book, including legal implementation of the substantive norms, implementation of international conventions, and the timeliness of the implementation of the Third EU Directive.

According to our definition, a policy is legally effective when the norms are applied and obeyed. Legal effectiveness is understood narrowly and as a functionality: if a rule is in force (and applied/obeyed), it functions and therefore a norm is effective. More broadly, a policy is legally effective when there are no legal hindrances that make reaching the policy goal more difficult, nor are there other factors with legal consequences that negatively influence the application of the law.

With respect to the substantive norms in the preventive AML policy, this book concludes that these norms are to a large extent harmonized within the European Union. National variations do exist, but in all Member States' AML legislation the basic obligations of customer due diligence, reporting, record-keeping and internal policy are present. The differences in wording between Member States are demonstrated by the implementation aspects of extensions to the scope of obliged institutions, the reporting obligation and the legal-privilege exemption.

The legal effectiveness of the preventive AML policies of the Member States can be negatively impacted by both general and country-specific factors. General factors include diverging norms from the FATF

Recommendations and the Third EU Directive, and the existence of very general definitions, open norms and interpretation difficulties. Examples are found in the varying definitions of ultimate beneficial ownership, politically exposed persons, trust and company service providers, and tipping-off.

Furthermore, virtually all Member States face, to a certain extent, some legal hindrances. These are sometimes specific to a single country and sometimes specific to a group of countries. Some hindrances are of a mere technical nature, while other legal hindrances are of a more fundamental nature. More fundamental legal hindrances concern, for example, gaps in the scope of obliged institutions and broad legal-privilege exemptions. There is also evidence to suggest the existence of practical hindrances, such as a low level of awareness or application of AML obligations by some types of obliged entities and professionals in various Member States (see Chapter 3).

This book assesses some implementation aspects in the light of a proposal for a Fourth EU Directive. The proposal makes changes to a wide range of aspects, including – inter alia – the risk-based approach, the inclusion of tax crimes as a predicate offence to money laundering, the definitions and obligations concerning politically exposed persons and ultimate beneficial ownership, simplified due diligence, record-keeping, internal policies and procedures. It seems that the proposal takes into account extensions to the scope made by Member States, as some have now been incorporated in the proposal. The proposal also removes the diverging standards of the FATF Recommendations and Third EU Directive with respect to the matter of simplified due diligence.

In terms of international cooperation, the fact that Member States have not signed, ratified, or fully implemented the relevant international conventions may be considered a factor that negatively impacts the legal effectiveness of their AML policies. Relevant international conventions are the main international conventions addressing money laundering and terrorist financing, and referred to in the evaluations of the FATF and MONEYVAL. Analysing the status of implementation, ratification and full implementation of these conventions, Belgium, Portugal and Spain are considered the most legally effective. These Member States have signed and ratified all relevant international conventions and there are no deficiencies in their implementation. Least effective are Denmark, Lithuania, Germany and the Czech Republic.

13.2.1. Timeliness of Implementation

The book finds that the Third EU Directive has been implemented and transposed relatively smoothly, and in a timely manner, compared with other EU Directives. The Member States considered the Directive as well prepared and expected. There were some minor problems, such as how to interpret Ultimate Beneficial Ownership, but altogether the Third Directive can be seen as a smoothly implementable (transposable) Directive. However, as FATF standards were in place already and had to be dealt with, Member States faced conflicting standards between the hard law of the EU and the soft law of the FATF. Following the first could still mean painful economic sanctions by the latter.

Time delays in implementation seem mainly to have been due to domestic factors and not to external factors or factors related to the quality of the Directive itself. The number and type of implementation authorities, and methods of implementation applied, have not appeared to be significant in explaining the non-timeliness of some Member States. Key findings were:

- older Member States show statistically significantly more delay than newer Member States;
- Member States with internal supervisory architecture (professional associations) show statistically significantly higher delays (see Chapter 4).

13.3 THE SUPERVISORY ARCHITECTURES

While the substantive norms have to a large extent become harmonized within the European Union, the contrary is observed with respect to the procedural norms. This is however not surprising, since European Union law is implemented, applied and enforced within the framework of the national laws of the Member States, which means that national rules of procedure apply. This has the effect that AML supervisory architectures across the Member States are different. In turn, these differences potentially create difficulties in supervision and enforcement in cross-border situations where businesses and professionals operate in more than one Member State.

This book takes a systematic approach to the different AML supervisory architectures, designing (institutional) models of the supervisory architectures of the Member States. Four models of AML supervisory architectures can be identified: the FIU model, the external model, the internal model and the hybrid model. These different models have different inherent strengths and weaknesses, which are discussed in Chapter 5 of this book. This chapter also categorizes all 27 EU Member States into each of the four models.

13.4 THE DEFINITIONS OF MONEY LAUNDERING IN PRACTICE

Although the FATF 40 Recommendations, the EU Directive, and other international conventions all require various essential elements of money laundering to be criminalized, there remains a considerable divergence in practice between the criminal provisions in the Member States.

One area of considerable divergence is shown in which crimes are predicate crimes for money laundering. Only the proceeds of defined (predicate) crimes which underlie the money laundering definition can be prosecuted for laundering. Seven countries – Malta, Romania, Slovakia, Spain, Belgium, the UK and Ireland – have an all crimes approach. This means that no matter the underlying offence, a person can be prosecuted for money laundering. Bulgaria and Italy also have an all crimes approach, but in Italy this only applies to crimes committed intentionally and therefore crimes by negligence are excluded, while in Bulgaria it applies to all crimes except insider trading. France and the Netherlands have a serious crimes approach, covering all crimes that are punished with a certain severity. Greece and Luxembourg have opted for a combination of a list of predicate offences and a threshold approach.

Numerous significant differences were identified in the definitions of money laundering, which, in practice, could pose problems in international cooperation. One key area of difference is between countries that have, or have not, criminalized 'self-laundering', where disposing of the money is done by the same person who acquired the proceeds by committing a crime. The mere possession of criminal proceeds is not considered money laundering in most Member States, with Luxembourg and the Netherlands (in certain cases) as exceptions. The intention to hide and the knowledge, and/or reasonable grounds (and (gross) negligence), of the fact that the proceeds come from criminal activity in case of third-party money laundering is required in all Member States, but there are large interpretation variations as to what should be considered 'concealment' (hiding the proceeds) (see Chapter 6).

13.5 THE EXECUTION OF AML/CTF POLICY: THE ROLES AND RESOURCES OF FIUs

This study has built upon, and improved, the classification devised by the IMF (2004), whereby FIUs are allocated to a specific type given their location, access to police data and investigative powers – law enforcement, administrative, judicial and hybrid. The majority of EU FIUs are either administrative (BE, BG, CZ, FR, EL, IT, LV, MT, PL, RO, SL, ES) or law enforcement (AT, DK, EE, FI, DE, IE, LT, PT, SK, SE, UK), and only four consider themselves to be of the judicial (CY, LU) or hybrid (HU, NL) types. Most countries, except for the Netherlands, Denmark, Hungary, Latvia and Greece confirmed the classification of FIUs done by the Egmont group.

Staffing and budgets vary considerably from country to country, and show little relationship with GDP, or with the year of accession into the EU. There is also considerable diversity of staff employed by the FIUs with respect to their occupational background. They include among others:

- detectives with financial crime and IT crime training;
- detached prosecutors, police, customs and intelligence liaison officers;
- financial analysts, economists, lawyers and tax administration agents.

We observe that administrative types of FIUs on average have higher staff numbers, which appears related to the fact that they tend to have their own separate premises. The average staff numbers of an FIU with its own (separate) premises is close to 52 employees, while those that do not have their own premises on average have 27 employees. Further, we observe that FIUs have more staff in less wealthy Member States, reflecting higher labour intensity where capital is scarce.

In addition to the basic task of 'receiving (and to the extent permitted, requesting), analyzing and disseminating to the competent authorities, disclosures of information which concern potential money laundering, potential terrorist financing or are required by national legislation or regulation' (Article 21 Third EU Directive), some FIUs are expected to perform some or all of the following tasks:

- supervise (some) reporting entities;
- propose sanctions;
- train supervisors on AML matters;
- supervise the application of the International Sanctions Act;
- conduct pre-trial investigations;
- prosecute money laundering;
- issue guidelines for reporting entities;
- train law enforcement agencies on AML matters;
- draft AML/CTF legislation;
- research ML/TF aggregate data;
- fulfil the role of an asset recovery office;

- coordinate national cooperation on AML matters;
- conduct ML/TF threat analysis;
- start an investigation on their own motion.

FIUs that have undergone a substantial organizational change bring with them additional tasks from their former organization into the new one and tend to have significantly more additional tasks than FIUs which have not been restructured. However, no significant relationship is found between staff numbers or budgets and the numbers of tasks the FIU is required to perform (see Chapter 7).

13.5.1 Access to Information and Feedback

Access to databases is very different across EU FIUs. Some have a strong preference for online access, whereas others are still manually accessing most databases. Some have direct access to most databases – i.e. France, Greece and Latvia – while others have indirect (intermediated) access and even no access to some databases – i.e. Italy. We also observe that most administrative FIUs overcome their lack of direct access to police data by using liaison officers, giving them access to more than criminal records and therefore considerably increasing their effectiveness. Liaison officers have also been used by law enforcement FIUs to improve their access – in particular – to tax and customs databases. Where liaison officers are employed by EU FIUs, these FIUs have, on average, the highest access to databases. Data-mining systems are put in place to ensure that unstructured data can be processed quickly, accurately and with optimal results. These systems are diverse across the EU FIUs, as they need to adapt to national culture, language and the type of information that is available in each Member State.

No correlation is found between the size of a country or the general internet availability in a country and the IT intensity of the FIU. Similarly there seems to be no significant correlation between the FIU employing data-mining software and the number of reports it receives. Furthermore, whether or not FIUs use data-mining systems does not depend on the type of FIUs. FIUs have, however, recognized the benefits of receiving reports online, and most receive the majority of reports in electronic format.

Some arrangements for formal contact and feedback between the FIU and the reporting entities are in place in all countries. All FIUs meet with the reporting entities at least once a year, mostly through training sessions, and all FIUs publish annual reports to give the reporting entities general feedback, some of which is very comprehensive. Most EU FIUs provide reporting entities with acknowledgements of receipt of information, sometimes automatically through their IT system. The largest differences lie in the extent of training given by the FIUs, and in the nature of feedback given to the reporting entities. Some FIUs are able to offer individual feedback, whereas others prefer general feedback. No relationship is found between the size of the Member State or the type of FIU and the type of feedback the FIUs give to the reporting entities (see Chapter 7).

13.6   THE REPRESSIVE ENFORCEMENT OF AML POLICY

An effective criminal enforcement system is one that enforces criminal penalties in such a way that criminal behaviour is deterred. This study looked at the way criminal enforcement systems work and at the roles of the different institutions within these systems. The roles of the prosecution services were examined – with a particular interest in their interaction with other national law enforcement agencies and with the FIU.

In terms of criminal matters, there are large differences among the EU Member States. In some countries the public prosecutor also investigates, and can do so in money laundering cases; they may even settle money laundering cases outside court, thereby lowering the workload of the courts and allowing a more effective allocation of court resources.

When the prosecution cannot investigate, or has limited powers to investigate, the public prosecutor is dependent on law enforcement authorities with investigative powers to collect the necessary information. The effectiveness of the criminal enforcement system therefore depends upon good cooperation between the prosecution and the investigative authorities.

The type and severity of punishment that can be expected for ML differs significantly among states. The average expected imprisonment for money laundering in Luxembourg is approximately nine times larger than in Austria, Sweden, Finland and the Netherlands.

The probability that criminal behaviour will be punished in each Member State cannot be found in the statistics, so information theory was used to measure the value of the information chain that is present in each country. Information theory studies the decision-making process that underlies transactions where one party has more or better information than the other. Money launderers are aware of the illegality of their actions and have an incentive to hide this information from the national law enforcement units. A successful AML information framework, therefore, is one where government institutions can successfully identify money laundering and can sanction it accordingly. By contrast, an unsuccessful AML system is one which cannot trace or sanction the money laundering-related financial transactions happening in their own financial system. Intelligence gathering and effective communication is therefore the key to reducing this informational asymmetry.

The Information Flow index revealed that information flows are higher in Western Europe and comparatively lower in Southern and Eastern Europe, leading to a higher probability of repression in those Western European countries than in the South and East.

Some information flows are found to be more vulnerable because of the way they are constructed. However, there are examples of solutions that can be applied to reduce these inefficiencies/vulnerabilities (double reporting, changing the information flow setting, better feedback and use of liaison officers). Double disclosure of the reporting entities can reduce information loss, when this is due to 'bad intentions' and those countries with more effective information flows tend to have more ML prosecutions and convictions. However, the data could not determine any significant differences between countries with broad or narrow definitions of ML, or whether countries that have the same criminal law origins tend to have similar information flow systems and punishments, or whether countries with clusters of prosecutors specialized in money laundering have more money laundering prosecutions and convictions (see Chapter 8).

13.6.1. International Cooperation

This study shows that international cooperation takes place, in general, among homologue institutions. It is therefore the ministries that cooperate with other ministries via various EU platforms, the FIU with other FIUs through the use of various mechanisms, and the law enforcement authorities with their homologues: the police (law enforcement authorities) with police (law enforcement authorities) and public prosecutor's offices with public prosecutor's offices. There is one exception to this rule: in instances where the FIU belongs to the judicial or law enforcement model, cooperation from the FIU can be sought through judicial and/or law enforcement cooperation channels (Europol, Interpol or EuroJust). However, it should be noted that these FIUs cannot, strictly in their FIU capacity, formally make use of the other channels in international cooperation. These channels are augmented by informal networks of personal contacts and by MOUs and other devices.

The most common hindrances to international cooperation appear to be language barriers, time delays, generic information, differences in data protection standards, non-efficient *national* cooperation, and the lack of a legal basis in all EU Member States' legislation that would allow FIUs to block or freeze suspicious transactions on their own motion.

The extent of hindrances to international cooperation differs: while Western European Member States indicated that they do not encounter any serious hindrances in international cooperation, most Central and Eastern European Member States indicated that they faced a number of difficulties in international cooperation – particularly language difficulties. Time delays seem to be most commonly felt as the main hindrance to international cooperation, more commonly in international judicial cooperation than in international FIU cooperation. The translation of judicial documents, letters rogatory, and documentation that may serve as evidence takes considerable time. This is also why mutual legal assistance (MLA) takes a lot longer than FIU international cooperation. Non-efficient national cooperation in other countries was mentioned by various Member States' representatives as hampering international cooperation. Intra-national cooperation structures, by contrast, were quite often praised (see Chapter 9).

13.7   THE COLLECTION OF STATISTICS

Statistics on AML policy can be classified into two types: input statistics, which are the resources spent on AML policy (e.g. the budget of the FIU and other relevant institutions), and output statistics, which are the result of the AML policy (e.g. reports sent to the FIU, cash declarations at the border, the number of prosecutions and of convictions for money laundering and terrorist financing).

The most widely available statistic on anti-money laundering policy is the number of reports sent to the FIU. The EUROSTAT (2010) report on money laundering in Europe identifies the number of reports sent to the FIU as their first key indicator. However, it is still very hard to use this statistic as an actual indicator for anti-money laundering policy, because an increase in the number of reports can be the result of a greater anti-money laundering effort, a different counting rule, or an increase in the amount of money laundering. Moreover, an increased number of reports does not lead per se to better money laundering prevention or more convictions for money laundering, because it can also mean an overloading of the FIU with poor quality information, leading to an actual decrease in effectiveness. Concepts and counting rules are not uniform across the EU.

The most common type of report is the suspicious transaction report (STR). A suspicious activity report (SAR) differs from an STR by virtue of the fact that it may include other activities, such as opening a bank account under suspicious circumstances. An unusual transaction report (UTR) is also a broader concept than suspicious transactions, in which any unusual activity may be reported. Other standard types of reports include cash transaction reports, currency transaction reports and external transaction reports. An analysis of these types of reports shows inconsistencies in their usage: sometimes STRs are used for activities other than just transactions, and the practical application of UTRs and STRs is not always as different as might be expected. The names of these reports often do not fully reflect the actual differences between the reports, and in some countries multiple types of reports are used concurrently.

The reports used by various European countries in the prevention of money laundering and terrorist financing are of a very distinct nature in six different respects:

1. the type of report (some reports refer to only cash transactions, while others refer to all transactions; some reports only refer to only transactions, while others refer to any activity);
2. subjective grounds of suspicion (the level of necessary knowledge when defining a transaction as suspicious);
3. objective grounds of suspicion (the reporting threshold of the amount of money involved in a transaction, for which a report must be filed);
4. the definition of a transaction (specifying which activities constitute transactions);
5. the inclusion of attempt (including the attempt of a transaction even when stopped) and
6. the data collection methodology (making a report for each transaction or bundling the transactions of one money laundering operation together).

At present, the countries' statistics on the number of reports disclosed to FIUs cannot be compared and cannot be used as an indicator for money laundering or anti-money laundering policy. The most intuitive solution is to set up uniform legislation such that the notion of a report is a uniform concept in all the countries in the world. This of course would require legislative changes, which take time and effort, and in which political negotiations are involved. Changing the classification schemes of administration might involve other policy fields as well and might be very difficult.

Therefore, this policy option might be a long-term solution or even a utopian ambition. Alternatively, a restructuring of the data collection, to measure and compare the amount of money and the number of natural persons involved in the suspicion reports, instead of the number of reports, may be a better option. Clearly there will still be some degrees of freedom on how to interpret money laundering tasks and time devoted to it, but it at least takes away the differences in the data collection method, which is the least transparent characteristic of the current reports sent to the FIU.

Another statistic that seems to be a sensible choice when looking for an indicator for the effectiveness of the fight against money laundering is the number of persons prosecuted/convicted for money laundering. One of the main problems with this statistic is that when criminals are convicted for money laundering, they are often also convicted for the predicate crime in the same court case, and the convicted criminal may be registered as being convicted for the predicate crime only or for both. The same holds for the number of prosecutions. In addition, courts in different EU Member States interpret the term money laundering differently, particularly in relation to the criminalization of self-laundering, although this could be corrected for, since most Member States that have this statistic can differentiate whether the conviction is for self-laundering or third-party laundering.

An increase in the number of prosecutions and convictions for money laundering however does not necessarily indicate more effective anti-money laundering policies, since the increase could also be caused simply by an increase in money laundering. Even comparing this statistic with the number of STRs to measure the effectiveness of the investigation and prosecution stages might be problematic, for several reasons. First, many reports sent to the FIU could eventually result in only one conviction, and the opposite might also be possible. Second, the investigation and prosecution process of a money laundering case could be extremely time-consuming, especially when international cooperation is required, so that reports sent to the FIU in one year could be used to convict money launderers in some later year. Third, a report in one country might lead to a conviction in a different country. Fourth, convictions can also be the result of regular police work and therefore not originate from the reporting system at all.

Nevertheless, such statistics do exist, and this study examines the differences between Member States. Why are there so many convictions in the UK, Denmark and the Netherlands and why is the number of convictions in Lithuania and Slovenia so low? We find that the absolute number of convictions for money laundering is positively significantly related to the amount of threat, the corruption index of the World Bank, the number of suspicion reports sent to the FIU and the number of prosecutions for money laundering. The fact that the number of convictions is related to the amount of threat could suggest that it is driven more by the underlying unknown amount of money laundering in the country than by the effectiveness of the AML system itself.

The relation between money laundering and corruption has been debated in the literature. We found that in countries where corruption is better under control, there are more convictions for money laundering.

Since output statistics of anti-money laundering policy have the problem that an increase in the statistic can come from an increase in the amount of money laundering or from an improved policy response, it is perhaps better to use input statistics as an indicator for the amount of effort made by Member States in fighting money laundering. We conclude that the best available input statistic is the number of personnel in the FIU. All countries are able to provide such a statistic and, on the basis of countries that can also provide budget data, staff numbers are also found to be a good indicator of budget. When expressed as numbers of FIU personnel per million inhabitants, and FIU costs per population per year, these statistics indicate that FIUs have significant economies of scale, which means that the more inhabitants a country has, the lower the costs per inhabitant are. In this sense, having an FIU is relatively costly for the smaller countries.

These data form the basis for a cluster analysis, which shows that in terms of AML policy the 27 EU Member States consist of four groups which have their own distinct characteristics. We identify a group of countries (AT, DE, DK, FI, IE, SE) that experience or have experienced international pressure due to the fact that international standards did not fit well into their legal system, a group of countries (BE, EL, ES, FR, IT, PT, UK) in which domestic cooperation might be difficult, a group of relatively small countries with large transiting financial flows (CY, LU, NL), and a large group of mostly Eastern European countries that are relatively recent members of the EU (see Chapter 10).

13.8. POLICY EFFECTIVENESS

For measuring the effectiveness of anti-money laundering policy one has to take into account both the laundering threat a country faces and its policy response. This study took as a point of departure the existing FATF measures for the compliance of countries with regard to the forty FATF recommendations. We think that these compliance measures are a good start, but they still have two weaknesses. First, they do not relate the policy effort of a country to the threat it faces. We think it is important not only to measure the compliance of countries with FATF standards, but to set this in relation to the special threat the country faces. When doing so, we see that some small EU Member States (Estonia, Latvia and Luxembourg) that are highly threatened with being flooded with criminal money from abroad are close to what we define as the endangered black zone (see Chapter 11). These small Member States have to cope with huge amounts of criminal proceeds from abroad, which can quickly overburden them, even though they are highly compliant with FATF standards. With regard to large EU Member States one can see that the UK is the only country close to the endangered zone. The UK is a highly compliant country, but faces an enormous threat of laundering (see Chapter 12). Member States that are often in the news for insufficient compliance with FATF standards, such as Austria, Hungary, and Romania, are nevertheless in the white zone, indicating a low risk level. Compared to the threat they face, they do not do as badly as indicated by FATF compliance numbers alone. Second, in this study we have also tried to refine FATF compliance measures. We think that the effectiveness of an AML/CTF regime is multifaceted and is deeply rooted in the national institutions of the Member States: their legal system, their administrative system, their specific method of internal and external communication and their national information flows. In Chapter 11 we showed that Member States' policy effectiveness varies, depending on which criteria one takes. They all have strengths and weaknesses, and there is no one best and no one worst country.

13.9　COST-BENEFIT ANALYSIS

The costs of AML/CTF policy for a country can include:

- ongoing policy-making costs;
- sanction costs (repressive);
- costs of FIU;
- costs of supervision;
- costs for law enforcement agencies and judiciary;
- duties of the private sector;
- reduction in privacy;
- efficiency costs for society and the financial system.

The benefits of AML/CTF policy can include:

- fines (preventive and repressive);
- confiscated proceeds;
- reduction in the amount of ML;
- less predicate crime;
- reduced damage effect on the real economy;
- less risk for the financial sector.

However, the lack of hard data, even on the costs, makes any such country-by-country cost-benefit analysis impossible. The costs for institutions that are part of the fight against money laundering and terrorist financing are often hard to separate out for AML/CTF policy only, since these activities form only part of their workload (the FIU is an exception to this). In spite of often-repeated claims about the cost burden faced by the private sector, few real statistics are ever provided to support the claims. Measures of the costs imposed by the reduction of privacy not available. Even more problematic are estimates of the benefits, since these, too, are more often than not subsumed into more general data or impossible to estimate. This lack of data results in quite sensitive estimations.

By using the estimates that are available, and correcting these estimates for the price level and size of country, we were able to estimate almost all cost components and some benefits for each EU Member State. The duties of the private sector are the biggest cost component of AML/CTF policy, followed by the supervision of these obliged entities. We estimate that the total costs of the 27 EU countries are about 2 billion Euros, together with an immeasurable reduction in privacy and some inefficiency in the operation of society. Since most of the benefits of AML/CTF policy are hard or impossible to estimate, the cost-benefit dilemma is basically reduced to the question: does the EU want to spend about 2 billion Euros (compared to an EU GDP of 13 trillion) to obtain potential benefits, which include an unquantifiable reduction in money laundering, less crime in general, a reduced damage effect on the real economy and less risk for the financial sector? To answer in the words of Whitehouse (2003):[1] 'It would be a brave person who steps up to say that it is too high a price to pay for countering terrorism and serious crime.' (See Chapter 12.)

13.10 CONCLUSIONS

To use the same criteria for all countries, as the FATF does, tends to underestimate or to misperceive their AML policy performance. Europe's cultural inheritance is characterized by a variety of institutions, and asking for standards that are the same as the US standards for all European Member States can entail quite different tasks and costs for different Member States. In order to reach true compliance it is important to understand this variety of European institutions as Europe's strength.

---

[1]   Whitehouse (2003), p. 144.

The European model, as opposed to the US model, was always based on more variety and difference among institutions. Historically settled institutions, such as the diverse legal systems, in some cases date back more than a thousand years, for example the chamber system dating back to the medieval guilds. Some bar associations date back to the 1850s (and are still called chambers in some countries). In the internal and hybrid supervision models, some of these traditional professional associations are involved in anti-money laundering supervision because of their close relationship with their members. Notably different languages and history distinguish Europe from a one-size-fits-all US model.

With respect to AML policy, we performed a cluster analysis and found 'four Europes', *four groups of Member States which share among themselves similar legal or institutional characteristics for anti-money laundering policy. The first group of Member States* (Austria, Denmark, Finland, Germany, Ireland and Sweden) are countries that have on average significantly higher government effectiveness, low corruption, and more prosecutions for money laundering as a percentage of GDP. They almost all have a law enforcement type of FIU and a very narrowly interpreted money laundering definition. This group of quite rich EU Member States all experience or have experienced pressure from the FATF for not having criminalized self-laundering. *Their legal and institutional system does not match with the international standards of FATF AML policy.* For them, FATF pressure can mean a serious threat to the existing national set of legal and economic institutions. In particular the smaller Member States have given into FATF pressure and criminalized self-laundering recently, but especially in legalistic systems, double criminal punishment (one for the crime, one for the proceeds of crime) is considered a violation of fundamental legal principles. Criminalizing self-laundering can therefore mean an enormous change in the entire legal system. *One can therefore expect either resistance to the practice of anti-money laundering law or quite significant follow-up changes in the legal system of these Member States.* Which response occurs might still have to do with different cultures and attitudes towards Europe in these countries. Germany, as the only large Member State in this group, seems to face a double load: it faces particular legal problems with international AML standards, and it is a big country with a federal system where AML policy is '*Ländersache*' (regulated at the regional level), so that it shares domestic coordination problems with the second group of countries.

The second group of Member States (Belgium, France, Greece, Italy, Portugal, Spain and the UK) has on average significantly higher GDP and significantly more FIU staff. They almost all have an administrative FIU. Three founding members (Belgium, France, and Italy) are among them and there have been no newcomers since the Maastricht Treaty in 1992.

Thus, this is also a relatively established group of Member States within the EU. *Domestic cooperation might be more difficult* in this group than in the former, due to the large size of countries (France, Italy and Spain), combined with regional differences and social, religious or economic cleavages (Belgium, Spain, Italy and the UK). Here anti-money laundering policy might face more internal problems than external problems.

The third group of Member States consists of Cyprus, Luxembourg and the Netherlands. They share the fact that they are *small countries with large amounts of criminal money flowing through*. They are usually not affected by underlying crime, but only have to deal with the proceeds of crime. Their money laundering problem is, hence, not a domestically caused one. Their major concern is to maintain a *good international reputation* and to avoid criticism from abroad in order to avoid sanctions.

The fourth group of Member States (Bulgaria, Hungary, Romania, Czech Republic, Malta, Poland, Slovakia, Slovenia, Latvia, Estonia and Lithuania) are all *newcomers to the EU*. They have lower GDP per capita, most of them face less threat of laundering, and they face more corruption problems than the other groups. Their government effectiveness indicator is also significantly lower. They have to introduce all sorts of new EU laws; they have to build up institutions, adjust their country to EU norms, and therefore *might not consider combating money laundering as their first policy priority*. The EU should initiate and financially support more training and meetings of members and diverse actors of this group with other groups in order to facilitate information exchange and policy learning.

In order to reach true compliance of Member States it seems important to take into account the differences between these four country groups of European AML/CTF policy. *Pressures from abroad as in the first group, pressures from within the countries, as in the second group, pressures from large proceeds of crime for small Member States, as in the third group, and being a newcomer to the EU, as in the fourth group, might necessitate different policy measures and different ways of the evaluation of progress.*

Studying the FATF Mutual Evaluation Reports with regard to the most important predicate crimes that Member States combat with anti-money laundering policy, one finds that they list basically all predicate crimes for all countries. However, in practice we found different perceptions among Member States as to what anti-money laundering policy stood for. Their own understanding of what FIUs should do differed substantially. Some countries perceived anti-money laundering policy as anti-drug policy, others saw it as a fight against tax evasion and others as a fight against corruption. *The perception of whether the ultimate goal of anti-money laundering policy is to catch drug money, tax evasion money or corruption money clearly also means that policies to reach these goals will (and have to) differ.*

There also remain large differences in what is understood by money laundering in practice. Even when legal texts are harmonized, law in practice differs between the Member States. Different interpretations of what concealment means, different interpretations of the level of knowledge required, the evidence needed for prosecuting money laundering, the acceptance of the reversal of the burden of proof all showed us that law in practice still varies. *Interpretations of money laundering can also vary along the anti-money laundering chain within the same country.* The legislator might not have the same interpretation as the FIU, public prosecutor or the judge. The AML prosecution would result in no conviction if the judge does not accept the reversal of burden of proof, to give an example.

The Third EU Directive, the implementation of which we studied, was perceived as well-prepared and harmonious by the Member States. Some definitions, such as that of the ultimate beneficial owner, appeared to be too broad and had to be specified later. Some norms, such as simplified due diligence, turned out to be too expensive for the private sector and are hardly ever, or never, applied. Some extensions to scope, especially for gambling institutions other than casinos, were made by a large majority of Member States. From a legal effectiveness point of view they could therefore better have been included in the Directive. Notwithstanding these issues and considerable time delays in the implementation in some Member States, the *Third EU Directive as such can be considered a successful legal norm for anti-money laundering and combating terrorist financing policy.*

The *substantive norms* of the Third EU Directive, meaning the obligations of customer due diligence, reporting, record-keeping and internal policy *are to a large extent harmonized* in Europe – see Chapter 3. *The procedural norms however still differ a lot between the Member States.* The legal norms that regulate the supervision of obliged institutions and sanctioning in case of non-compliance with the preventive AML/CTF obligations in the Directive are minimal. The Directive only requires that obliged institutions and professionals are subject to adequate regulation and supervision and provide some very minimum requirements (see Chapter 5). Nevertheless, to combat international crime effectively, there needs to be a trade-off between the need for harmonization of procedures in order to close loopholes for money launderers and the need to maintain national autonomy. *The EU has to find the right balance here between accepting variety and harmonization.*

From the legal effectiveness point of view, a general point of criticism concerned the diverging standards between FATF Recommendations and EU norms. Member States that closely follow the text of the EU Directive can, therefore, nevertheless be criticized by the FATF for not fulfilling its soft law recommendations, for example with regard to which countries are suitable for third-party reliance. Conflicting standards are clearly bad for the legal security of countries and citizens. In particular, when FATF criticism and its impact on the reputation of a country can be very costly since blacklisting can mean serious economic sanctions, for example if no US bank is allowed to do business with the country. Conflicting standards should either be removed or accepted by both the FATF and the EU.

Combating money laundering requires the cooperation and compliance of many parties. *The major hindrance in international cooperation is time delays.* Fifteen out of 27 Member States have experienced this as the major difficulty in international cooperation. A further hindrance identified concerned conflicting *data protection systems* which do not allow the exchange of information. In addition, some of the international data exchange systems are too costly, especially for small, new Member States. We think that the way in which FIU.NET is technically established is a promising way of *facilitating data exchange and at the same time allowing the users to keep control over access to their information.* From our regional workshops it also became clear that *language is still a great barrier to international cooperation* especially for new Member States (group 4 of our 'four Europes'). In contrast to the US, Europe does not have a common language. Translation of legal texts and information requirements from other countries can cause delays in international cooperation and is costly.

At both an international and domestic level, fighting money laundering and terrorist financing depends on the acceptance and compliance of many actors. Governments, ministries, FIUs, the police, public prosecutors, judges, reporting entities like banks, dealers in high-value goods, notaries, accountants, lawyers and other groups in the private sector all have to comply in order to identify and catch money launderers and terrorist financiers. *To convince all these groups about the necessity and importance of anti-money laundering policy will certainly take time. Good communication, sharing information and feedback* to other entities are essential to reach true compliance. We found that the nature of feedback plays an important role. *Individual feedback* from the FIU is necessary to help reporting entities improve their reporting systems. Individual feedback from the public prosecutor to help FIUs filter out relevant transaction reports as suspicious is also important to improve effectiveness.

An important way to convince actors that anti-money laundering policy is meaningful is to show the success of anti-money laundering policy. For this it is important to produce *reliable comparative statistics.* Reliable statistics on convictions of launderers, and on confiscated proceeds, will help to demonstrate the success of anti-money laundering policy.

Reliable statistics however need true compliance from Member States.

European Member States are more used to a carrot than to a stick policy approach. This means that in many European countries compliance among actors is reached by convincing them about the necessity of the policy rather than threatening them with punishment. Blacklisting, as the FATF does, is a typical stick approach. And, moreover, this stick is held by an international organization which is not democratically legitimated and which cannot be sanctioned. This style of introducing anti-money laundering policy into Europe does not fit the European way of doing politics.

The reaction of EU Member States to this strange and unusual policy style may, and most likely will, be passive resistance. In comparing the effectiveness of Member States' anti-money laundering policy there is the danger that numbers are inflated. In principle, due to the diverse ways of archiving numbers, of compiling police files, of defining suspicious transactions and of collecting data, all Member States have the possibility to produce higher numbers and better outcomes on paper without changing their policy. We warn of the danger of inflated numbers, which might happen when Member States have to produce statistics without being convinced of the necessity of doing so. We have shown in our study how easily one could produce an increase in suspicious transaction reports just by making banks report each transaction separately rather than in bundles, to give an example. It seems, therefore, important from the very beginning to *avoid the number game* and compliance in the books and to aim at true compliance.

We recommend collecting input and output statistics, but first to concentrate on comparing input statistics. This means that we should start interpreting numbers on how much money was invested in AML/CTF policy, such as the number of staff employed in this policy field, the budget for FIUs and law enforcement. These numbers are easier to compare and less easy to manipulate than output statistics, which measure the outcome of the AML/CTF policy, such as the number of suspicious transaction reports or the number of convictions. *For comparing output statistics, some standardized ways of how to count and collect statistics on reporting and on convictions first have to be developed.*

We think that with regard to the AML/CTF policy, the *EU should become what political scientists call a global player*: it should take a lead in setting international standards in AML/CTF policy, as it does successfully with environmental policy and food regulation. But in contrast to these policy fields, where EU standards are much stricter than international standards, AML/CTF policy does not need stricter standards. It needs standards which allow EU Member States to adjust to these standards within their own institutional frameworks and which can be implemented according to a European policy style.

One way of taking such a global player lead would be to defend European interests against the FATF, for example with regard to the equivalence of EU Member States. The EU could also develop best-practice models, a *white list* showing Member States' strengths in anti-money laundering policy in creating voluntary and true compliance. Focusing on best practices rather than on failures would help to increase acceptance of AML/CTF policy among actors and in the Member States.

We are convinced that true compliance with fighting laundering can be reached in Europe with a carrot and not with a stick approach. Harmonizing AML/CTF policies in a Europe with diverse institutions will, and should, take time. The right balance between harmonization and the acceptance of variety seems crucial for fighting international crime and reaching true compliance of the majority of actors involved.

References

Addink, G.H. (2010), *Goed bestuur*, Kluwer: Deventer.

Addink, H., Anthony, G., Buyse, A. and Flinterman, C. (2010), 'Source Book on Human Rights and Good Governance', SIM Special no. 34.

Akerlof, G.A. (1970), 'The Market for "Lemons": Quality Uncertainty and the Market Mechanism', *Quarterly Journal of Economics*, 84 (3), 488–500.

Aldenderfer, M.S. and Blashfield, R.K. (1984), *Cluster Analysis*, vol. 44, edited by J.L. Sullivan and R.G. Niemi, Beverly Hills, London, New Delhi: Sage Publications.

Alexander, K. (2000), 'The International Anti-Money Laundering Regime: The Role of the Financial Action Task Force', *Financial Crime Review*, autumn, No. 1, 9–27.

Australian Institute of Criminology (2011), *Anti-money Laundering and Counter-terrorism Financing across the Globe: A Comparative Study of Regulatory Action*, AIC Reports Research and Public Policy Series, no. 113.

Backhaus, K., Erichson, B., Plinke, W. and Weiber, R. (2000), Clusteranalyse', in Backhaus, K., Erichson, B., Plinke, W. and Weiber, R., *Multivariate Analysemethoden. Eine anwendungsorientierte Einführung*, Heidelberg: Springer.

Baker, R.W. (2005), *Capitalism's Achilles Heel: Dirty Money and How to Renew the Free-market System*, Hoboken, NJ: John Wiley, pp. 173–4.

Bartlett, B.L. (2002), 'The Negative Effects of Money Laundering on Economic Development', *Platypus Magazine*, 77, 18 – 23.

Becker, G. (1968), 'Crime and Punishment: An Economic Approach', *The Journal of Political Economy*, 76, 169–217.

Bekkers, V., Bonnes, J., De Moor-van Vugt, A., Schoneveld, P. and Voermans, W. (1993), 'Succes- en faalfactoren bij de uitvoering van EG-beleid', *Bestuurskunde*, No. 4, 192–200.

Berglund, S.K., Gange, I. and van Waarden, F. (2005), 'Taking Institutions Seriously. A Sociological-Institutionalist Approach to Explaining Transposition Delays of European Food Safety and Utilities Directives', Paper presented at European Consortium for Political Research Granada, 14–19 April 2005, Workshop on 'Making EU policy work:

national strategies for implementing, postponing and evading EU legislation', organized by Marco Giuliani and Bernard Steunenberg.

Boerzel, T. (2001), 'Non Compliance in the European Union: Pathology or Statistical Artifact?', *Journal of European Public Policy*, 8(5), 803–24.

Bolle, A. (2004), 'Le Blanchiment des Capitaux de la Criminalité Organisée, in Francois, L., Chaigneau, P. and Chesney, M. (eds.), *Blanchiment et Financement du Terrorisme*, Paris: Sentinel.

Brettl, J., and Usov, A. (2010), 'Money Laundering Threat Assessment for EU 27', Mimeo.

Bruza, P.D. and Van der Weide, T.P. (1993), 'The Semantics of Data Flow Diagrams', University of Nijmegen.

Chaikin, D. and Sharman, J.C. (2009), *Corruption and Money Laundering: A Symbiotic Relationship*, New York: Palgrave Macmillan.

CTIF-CFI (2010), 'Annual Report', CTIF-CFI.

Cuellar, M.F. (2003), 'The Tenuous Relationship between the Fight against Money Laundering and the Disruption of Criminal Finance', *Journal of Criminal Law & Criminology*, 93 (2–3), 311–465.

Dawe, S. and Fleming, M.H. (2009), 'Apply Risk Management to Anti-Money Laundering at the National and Supra-national Level', Internal IMF Report (Working Draft of 27 March 2009).

Dawe, S. (2011), 'Conducting National Money Laundering or Financing of Terrorism Risk Assessment', in Unger, B. and Van der Linde, D. (eds.), *Handbook of Money Laundering*, Cheltenham, UK and Northampton, MA, USA: Edward Elgar Publishing, pp. 110–26.

De Bos, A. and Slagter, W.J. (2008), *Financieel recht: vanuit economisch en juridisch perspectief*, Deventer: Kluwer.

Deloitte (2011), 'Final Study on the Application of the Anti-Money Laundering Directive', Service Contract ETD/2009/IM/F2/90.

Dreher, A. and Schneider, F. (2010), 'Corruption and the Shadow Economy: An Empirical Analysis', *Public Choice*, 144, 215–38.

EBA, ESMA and EIOPA (2012), 'Report on the legal and regulatory provisions and supervisory expectations across EU Member States of Simplified Due Diligence requirements where the customers are credit and financial institutions under the Third Money Laundering Directive [2005/60/EC], JC/2011/097 and AMLTF/2011/07', accessed at: http://www.esma.europa.eu/system/files/jc_2011_097.pdf.

ECOLEF (2013), 'The Economic and Legal Effectiveness of Anti-Money Laundering and Combating Terrorist Financing Policy: Final Report', Utrecht, report prepared for the EC DG Home, JLS/2009/ISEC/AG/087.

Egmont (2004), 'Information Paper on Financial Intelligence Units and the Egmont Group', accessed at: www.egmontgroup.org/library/download/3.

Egmont, 'Annual Report 2010–2011', accessed at: http://www.egmont group.org/library/annual-reports

Egmont (2011), Newsletter, July, accessed at: http://www.egmontgroup. org/library/newsletters.

Ellison, G. and Glaeser, E.L. (1999), 'The Geographic Concentration of Industry: Does Natural Advantage Explain Agglomeration?', *American Economic Review*, 89 (2), 311–16.

European Commission (2010a), 'Report from the Commission to the European Parliament on the application of Regulation (EC) No 1889/2005 of the European Parliament and of the Council of 26 October 2005 on controls of cash entering or leaving the Community pursuant to article 10 of this Regulation', accessed at: http://eur-lex.europa.eu/ LexUriServ/LexUriServ.do?uri=CELEX:32005R1889:en:NOT.

European Commission (2010b), Communication to the European Parliament and the Council, No. 385/20/7/2010 on the 'Overview of information management in the area of freedom, security and justice', accessed at: http://eur-lex.europa.eu.

European Commission (2011), Staff Working Paper on Anti-money laundering supervision of and reporting by payment institutions in various cross-border situations, SEC(2011) 1178 Final, 4 October 2011.

European Commission (2013), *Proposal for a Directive of the European Parliament and of the Council on the prevention of the use of the finan- cial system for the purpose of money laundering and terrorist financing*, COM(2013) 45 final.

European Parliament – DG Internal Policies of the Union (2007), 'Comparative Study on the Transposition of EC Law in the Member States', PE378.294.

Europol SOCTA 2013 (2013), *EU Serious and Organised Crime Threat Assessment*, retrieved from: https://www.europol.europa.eu/sites/ default/files/publications/socta2013_0.pdf.

Eurostat Pocketbooks (2009), *Labour Market Statistics for the gross monthly earnings by occupation in Euro in 2006*, Luxembourg: Publications Office of the European Union, accessed at: http://epp.eurostat.ec.europa.eu/ cache/ITY_OFFPUB/KS-30-09-149/EN/KS-30-09-149-EN.PDF.

EUROSTAT (2010), *Money Laundering in Europe*, Report of work carried out by Eurostat and DG Home Affairs, by Cynthia Tavares, Geoffrey Thomas (Eurostat) and Mickaël Roudaut (DG Home Affairs), Luxembourg: Publications Office of the European Union.

EU FIU Platform (2008a), 'Report on Confidentiality and Data Protection in the Activity of FIUs', Brussels

EU FIU Platform (2008b), 'Report on Money Laundering and Terrorist

Financing Cases and Typologies', accessed at: www.ec.europa.eu/inter nal_market/company/ financial-crime/index_en.htm#fiu-platform.

Falkner, G., Treib, O. and Holzleithner, E. (2008), *Compliance in the Enlarged European Union, Living Rights or Dead Letters?*, UK: Ashgate.

FATF (1996), 'The Forty Recommendations', accessed at: www.fatf-gafi. org.

FATF (2002), 'Basic Facts about Money Laundering', accessed at: www. fatf-gafi.org.

FATF (2005), 'Third Mutual Evaluation on Belgium', accessed at: www. fatf-gafi.org.

FATF (2006a), 'Third Mutual Evaluation on Denmark', accessed at: www. fatf-gafi.org.

FATF (2006b), 'Third Mutual Evaluation on Ireland', accessed at: www. fatf-gafi.org.

FATF (2006c), 'Third Mutual Evaluation on Portugal', accessed at: www. fatf-gafi.org.

FATF (2006d), 'Third Mutual Evaluation on Sweden', accessed at: www. fatf-gafi.org.

FATF (2007a), 'Money Laundering and Terrorist Financing through the Real Estate Market', accessed at: www.fatf-gafi.org.

FATF (2007b), 'Third Mutual Evaluation on Finland', accessed at: www. fatf-gafi.org.

FATF (2007c), 'Third Mutual Evaluation on Greece', accessed at: www. fatf-gafi.org.

FATF (2007d), 'Third Mutual Evaluation on the United Kingdom', accessed at: www.fatf-gafi.org.

FATF (2009a), 'Fourth Follow Up Report on the United Kingdom', accessed at: www.fatf-gafi.org.

FATF (2009b), 'Third Follow Up Report on Italy', accessed at: www.fatf-gafi.org.

FATF (2009c), 'Third Mutual Evaluation on Austria', accessed at: www. fatf-gafi.org.

FATF (2009d), 'Third Mutual Evaluation Report Denmark', accessed at: www.fatf-gafi.org.

FATF (2010a), 'Executive Summary of the Third Mutual Evaluation of Luxembourg', accessed at: www.fatf-gafi.org.

FATF (2010b), 'Fourth Follow Up Report on Spain', accessed at: www. fatf-gafi.org.

FATF (2010c), 'Fourth Follow Up Report on Sweden', accessed at: www. fatf-gafi.org.

FATF (2010d), 'Third Follow Up Report on Denmark', accessed at: www. fatf-gafi.org.

FATF (2010e), 'Third Mutual Evaluation on Germany', accessed at: www. fatf-gafi.org.

FATF (2011a), 'Third Mutual Evaluation on France', accessed at: www. fatf-gafi.org.

FATF (2011b), 'Third Mutual Evaluation on the Netherlands', accessed at: www.fatf-gafi.org.

Faure, M.G., Nelen, H., Fernhout, F.J. and Philipsen, N.J. (2009), *Evaluatie tuchtrechtelijke handhaving Wwft*, The Hague: Boom Juridische Uitgevers.

Ferwerda, J., Kattenberg, M., Chang, H., Unger, B., Groot, L. and Bikker J. (2013), 'Gravity Models of Trade-Based Money Laundering', *Applied Economics*, 45 (22), 3170–82.

Financial and Capital Market Commission (2010), 'Combating Money Laundering in Latvia', June, accessed at: http://www.fktk.lv/texts_files/ Buklets_2009_final_v3.pdf.

FIU Poland (2011), 'Report of the General Inspector of Financial Information on the implementation of the Act of 16 November 2000 on counteracting money laundering and terrorism financing in 2011', accessed at: http://www.mf.gov.pl/en/documents/764034/1223641/ spr_2011_ANG.pdf.

FIU Slovakia (2010), 'Annual Report', accessed at: www.minv. sk/?oddelenia&subor=123604.

FIU Sweden (2009), 'Annual Report'.

Frankel, M.S. (1989), 'Professional Codes: Why, How and with What Impact?', *Journal of Business Ethics*, 8, 109–15.

Geiger, H. and Wunsch, O. (2007), 'The Fight against Money Laundering: An Economic Analysis of a Cost-benefit Paradox', *Journal of Money Laundering Control*, 10 (1), 91–105.

Gill, M. and Taylor, G. (2002), *'Tackling Money Laundering: The Experiences and Perspectives of the UK Financial Sector'*, a report by the Scarman Centre, University of Leicester.

Gilmore, W.C. (1999), *Dirty Money: The Evolution of Money-laundering Counter Measures*, 2nd edition, Strasbourg: Council of Europe Press.

Goodhart, C.A.E., Hartmann, P., Llewellyn, D., Rojas-Suaréz, M. and Weisbrod, S. (1998), *Financial Regulation: Why, How and Where Now?*, London: Routledge.

Goyal, S. (2007), *Connections: An Introduction to the Economics of Networks*, Princeton, NJ: Princeton University Press.

Greenberg, T.S., Gray, L., Schantz, D., Gardner, C. and Latham, M. (2010), 'Politically Exposed Persons: Preventive Measures for the Banking Sector', accessed at: http://star.worldbank.org/star/sites/star/ files/Politically%20Exposed%20Persons_0.pdf.

Group of Thirty (2008), 'The Structure of Financial Supervision: Approaches and Challenges in a Global Marketplace', October, accessed at: http://www.group30.org/images/PDF/The%20Structure%20of%20 Financial%20Supervision.pdf.

Harbaugh, W.T., Mocan, N.H. and Visser, M.S. (2011), 'Theft and Deterrence', NBER Working Papers 17059, National Bureau of Economic Research, Inc.

Harvey, J. (2004), 'Compliance and Reporting Issues Arising for Financial Institutions from Money Laundering Regulations: A Preliminary Cost Benefit Study', *Journal of Money Laundering Control*, 7 (4), 333–46.

Haverland, M. and Romeijn, M. (2007), 'Do Member States Make European Policies Work? Analysing the EU Transposition Deficit', *Public Administration*, 85 (3), 757–78.

Hawkins, K. and Thomas, J.M. (1984), *Enforcing Regulation*, Boston: Kluwer.

Head, K. (2003), 'Gravity for Beginners', version prepared for UBC Econ 590a students, Faculty of Commerce, University of British Columbia, Vancouver, Canada, 5 February.

Helliwell, J.F. (2000), 'Language and Trade, Gravity Modelling of Trade Flows and the Role of Language', Department of Canadian Heritage.

Hermelinski, W. (2005), 'Money Laundering and the Legal Profession', Paper presented at the ECBA Conference in Lisbon, 30 April 2005.

Heston, A., Summers, R. and Aten, B. (2011), Penn World Table Version 7.0, Center for International Comparisons of Production, Income and Prices at the University of Pennsylvania.

HM Treasury (2011), 'Supervision Report 2010–2011', November, accessed at: https://www.gov.uk/government/uploads/system/uploads/ attachment_data/file/204350/amlctf_supervision_report_201011.pdf.

IMF (2004), 'Financial Intelligence Units: An Overview', Washington, DC, accessed at: http://www.imf.org/external/pubs/ft/fiu/fiu.pdf.

Institut der deutschen Wirtschaft Köln, Consult GmbH (2006), Bürokratiekosten in der Kreditwirtschaft.

Irish Prison Service (2010), 'Annual Report', Dublin, accessed at: http:// www.justice.ie/en/JELR/Irish_Prison_Service_2010_Annual_Report.pd f/Files/Irish_Prison_Service_2010_Annual_Report.pdf.

Jans, J.H., De Lange, R., Prechal, S. and Widdershoven, R.J.G.M. (2007), *Europeanisation of Public Law*, Groningen: Europa Law Publishing.

Jehle, J.-M. and Wade, M. (2006), *Coping with Overloaded Criminal Justice Systems – The Rise of Prosecutorial Power*, New York: Springer.

Jehle, J.M., Wade, M. and Elsner, B. (2008) 'Prosecution and Diversion within Criminal Justice Systems in Europe. Aims and Design of a

Comparative Study', *European Journal of Criminal Policy Response*, 14, 93–99.

Kaeding, M. (2007), 'Active Transposition of EU Legislation', EIPASCOPE 3/2007, accessed at: http://www.eipa.eu/files/repository/eipascope/20080313162050_MKA_SCOPE2007-3_Internet-4.pdf.

Kaufmann, D., Kraay, A. and Mastruzzi, M. (2010), 'The Worldwide Governance Indicators: Methodology and Analytical Issues', World Bank Policy Research Working Paper No. 5430.

Keefer, P. and Stasavage, D. (2002), 'Checks and Balances, Private Information, and the Credibility of Monetary Commitments', *International Organisation*, 56 (4), 751–74.

Komárek, J. (2008), 'Legal Professional Privilege and the EU's Fight against Money Laundering', *Civil Justice Quarterly*, 27 (1), 13–22.

Law Society of England and Wales (2013), 'Fourth European Money Laundering Directive Proposals Released Today', accessed at: http://www.lawsociety.org.uk/advice/articles/new-money-laundering-directive/

Leschke, J. (2005), 'Is it Useful to Cluster Countries? Analysis on the Example of Unemployment Insurance Coverage of Non-standard Employed', TLM.NET Conference Paper, Budapest, accessed at: http://www.siswo.uva.nl/tlm/confbuda/papers/papers_files/WP8%20Janine%20Leschke%20-%20Is%20it%20useful%20to%20cluster%20countries.pdf.

Levi, M. and Reuter, P. (2006), *Money Laundering, Crime and Justice*, 34, 289–375.

Luchtman, M. and van der Hoeven, R. (2009), 'Case Comment to Case C-305/05, Ordre des barreaux francophones and germanophones & Others v. Conseil des Ministres', *Common Market Law Review*, 46 (1), 301–18.

Lumpkin, S. (2002), 'Supervision of Financial Services in the OECD Area', OECD Working Paper.

Mansfield, G. and Peay, J. (1987) 'The Director of Public Prosecutions: Principles and Practices for the Crown Prosecutor', London: Tavistock Publications.

Masciandaro, D. (1998), 'Crime, Money Laundering and Regulation: The Microeconomics', *Journal of Financial Crime*, 8 (2), 103–12.

Mastenbroek, E. (2003), 'Surviving the Deadline: The Transposition of EU Directives in the Netherlands', *European Union Politics*, 4 (4), 371–95.

McDowell, J. and Novis, G. (2001), 'The Consequences of Money Laundering and Financial Crime', *Economic Perspectives*, 6 (2), 6–8.

MONEYVAL (2005), 'Third Round Report on Hungary', accessed at: http://www.coe.int/t/dghl/monitoring/moneyval/Evaluations/Evaluation_reports_en.asp.

MONEYVAL (2006), 'Third Mutual Evaluation on Cyprus', accessed at: http://www.coe.int/t/dghl/monitoring/moneyval/Evaluations/Evaluation_reports_en.asp.

MONEYVAL (2007a), 'Third Mutual Evaluation Report on Poland', accessed at: http://www.coe.int/t/dghl/monitoring/moneyval/Evaluations/Evaluation_reports_en.asp.

MONEYVAL (2007b), 'Third Mutual Evaluation on Czech Republic', accessed at: http://www.coe.int/t/dghl/monitoring/moneyval/Evaluations/Evaluation_reports_en.asp.

MONEYVAL (2008a), 'Third Mutual Evaluation on Bulgaria', accessed at: http://www.coe.int/t/dghl/monitoring/moneyval/Evaluations/Evaluation_reports_en.asp.

MONEYVAL (2008b), 'Third Mutual Evaluation on Estonia', accessed at: http://www.coe.int/t/dghl/monitoring/moneyval/Evaluations/Evaluation_reports_en.asp.

MONEYVAL (2008c), 'Third Mutual Evaluation on Romania', accessed at: http://www.coe.int/t/dghl/monitoring/moneyval/Evaluations/Evaluation_reports_en.asp.

MONEYVAL (2009a), 'Second Progress Report on Latvia', accessed at: http://www.coe.int/t/dghl/monitoring/moneyval/Evaluations/Evaluation_reports_en.asp.

MONEYVAL (2009b), 'First Progress Report on Czech Republic', accessed at: http://www.coe.int/t/dghl/monitoring/moneyval/Evaluations/Evaluation_reports_en.asp.

MONEYVAL (2010a), 'Second Progress Report on Poland', accessed at: http://www.coe.int/t/dghl/monitoring/moneyval/Evaluations/Evaluation_reports_en.asp.

MONEYVAL (2010b), 'Report on Fourth Assessment Visit Report of Hungary', accessed at: http://www.coe.int/t/dghl/monitoring/moneyval/Evaluations/Evaluation_reports_en.asp.

MONEYVAL (2010c), 'Fourth Mutual Evaluation Report on Hungary', accessed at: http://www.coe.int/t/dghl/monitoring/moneyval/Evaluations/Evaluation_reports_en.asp.

MONEYVAL (2011a), 'Report on Fourth Assessment Visit Report of Slovakia', accessed at: http://www.coe.int/t/dghl/monitoring/moneyval/Evaluations/Evaluation_reports_en.asp.

MONEYVAL (2011b), 'Report on Fourth Assessment Visit to Slovenia', accessed at: http://www.coe.int/t/dghl/monitoring/moneyval/Evaluations/Evaluation_reports_en.asp.

MONEYVAL (2011c), 'Report on Fourth Assessment Visit Report of Czech Republic', accessed at: http://www.coe.int/t/dghl/monitoring/moneyval/Evaluations/Evaluation_reports_en.asp.

MONEYVAL (2011d), 'Report on Fourth Assessment Visit Report of Cyprus', accessed at: http://www.coe.int/t/dghl/monitoring/moneyval/ Evaluations/Evaluation_reports_en.asp.

MONEYVAL (2011e), 'Second Follow Up Report on Romania', accessed at: http://www.coe.int/t/dghl/monitoring/moneyval/Evaluations/Evalua tion_reports_en.asp.

MONEYVAL (2012), 'Fourth Assessment Visit Report on Malta', accessed at: http://www.coe.int/t/dghl/monitoring/moneyval/Evaluations/Evalua tion_reports_en.asp.

Navarro, P.E. and Moreso, J.J. (1997), 'Applicability and Effectiveness of Legal Norms', *Law and Philosophy*, 16 (2), 201–19.

Nooteboom, B. (2002), *Trust: Forms, Foundations, Functions, Failures and Figures*, Cheltenham, UK and Northampton, MA, USA: Edward Elgar Publishing.

Ottow, A. (2006), *Telecommunicatietoezicht: De invloed van het Europese en Nederlandse bestuurs(proces)recht*, The Hague: Sdu Uitgevers.

Polish FIU (2012), 'Report of the General Inspector of Financial Information on the implementation of the Act of 16 November 2000 on counteracting money laundering and terrorism financing in 2011', accessed at: http://www.mf.gov.pl/en/documents/764034/1223641/ spr_2011_ANG.pdf.

Prechal, S. and Van den Brink, T. (2010), 'Methoden van omzetting van EU-recht in het Nederlandse recht: onderzoeksrapport ten behoeve van de Raad van State', accessed at: http://www.raadvanstate.nl/publicaties/ publicaties/pdf/rvs_methoden_omzetting.pdf.

PriceWaterhouseCoopers LLP (2003), 'Anti-money laundering current customer review cost benefit analysis', Retrieved from http://www.fsa. gov.uk/pubs/other/ml_cost-benefit.pdf.

Rauhut, H. and Junker, M. (2009), 'Punishment Deters Crime Because Humans are Bounded in their Strategic Decision-making', *Journal of Artificial Social Systems and Societies*, 12(3)

Reuter, P. and Truman, E.M. (2004), 'Chasing Dirty Money: The Fight Against Money Laundering', Washington, DC: Institute for International Economics.

Schott, P.A. (2003), *Reference Guide to Anti-Money Laundering and Combating the Financing of Terrorism*, Washington, DC: World Bank and International Monetary Fund.

Sinn, H.-W. (2003), *The New Systems Competition*, Oxford: Blackwell Publishing.

Stessens, G. (2000), *Money Laundering: A New International Law Enforcement Model*, New York: Cambridge University Press.

Steunenberg, B. (2004), 'EU Policy, Domestic Interests, and the

Transposition of Directives', accessed at: http://repub.eur.nl/res/pub/1747/NIG1-08.pdf.

Steunenberg, B. (2006), 'Turning Swift-Policy Making into Deadlock and Delay: National Policy Coordination and the Transposition of EU Directives', *European Union Politics*, 7 (3), 293–319.

Steunenberg, B. and Voermans, W. (2006), 'The Transposition of EC Directives: A Comparative Study of Instruments, Techniques and Processes in Six Member States', accessed at: https://openaccess.leidenuniv.nl/bitstream/handle/1887/ 4933/5_360_361.pdf?sequence=1.

Stouten, M. (2012), *De witwasmeldplicht: Omvang en handhaving van de Wwft-meldplicht voor juridische en fiscale dienstverleners*, The Hague: Boom Juridisch Uitgevers.

Stouten, M. and Tilleman, A. (2013), 'Reporting Duty for Lawyers versus Legal Privilege: Unresolved Tension', in Unger, B. and Van der Linde, D. (eds.), *Research Handbook on Money Laundering*, Cheltenham, UK and Northampton, MA, USA: Edward Elgar Publishing.

Tak, P.J.P. (2005), *Tasks and Powers of the Prosecution Services in the EU Member States*, Nijmegen: Wolf Legal Publishers.

Takáts, E. (2007), 'A Theory of "Crying Wolf": The Economics of Money Laundering Enforcement', IMF Working Paper, WP/07/81.

Thony, J.F. (1996), 'Processing Financial Information in Money Laundering Matters, The Financial Intelligence Units', *European Journal of Crime, Criminal Law and Criminal Justice*, 257–82.

Tinbergen, J. (1962), *Shaping the World Economy: Suggestions for an International Economic Policy*, New York: Twentieth Century Fund.

Transcrime (2007), 'Cost Benefit Analysis of Transparency Requirements in the Company/Corporate Field and Banking Sector Relevant for the Fight Against Money Laundering and Other Financial Crime', a study financed by the European Commission – DG JLS (contract no. DG.JLS/D2/2005/01 30-CE-0073549/00-93).

Tweede Kamer, vergaderjaar 2007–2008, 31 200 IXB, nr. 2. The Hague: Sdu.

Unger, B., Siegel, M., Ferwerda, J., de Kruijf, W., Busuioc, M., Wokke, K. and Rawlings, G. (2006), *The Amounts and the Effects of Money Laundering*, Amsterdam: Ministry of Finance.

UNODC (2011), 'Estimating Illicit Financial Flows Resulting from Drug Trafficking and Other Transnational Organised Crimes', accessed at: http://www.unodc.org/documents/data-and-analysis/Studies/Illicit_financial_flows_2011_web.pdf.

Van den Broek, M. (2010), 'The EU's Preventive AML/CFT Policy: Asymmetrical Harmonisation', *Journal of Money Laundering Control*, 14 (2), 170–82.

Van den Broek, M. (2011), 'Gelijkwaardigheid in the anti-witwasbeleid: de FATF en de EU', *SEW Tijdschrift voor Europees en economisch recht*, October.

Van den Broek, M. and Addink, G.H. (2013), 'Prevention of Money Laundering and Terrorist Financing from a Good Governance Perspective', in Unger, B. and Van der Linde, D. (eds.), *Research Handbook on Money Laundering*, Cheltenham, UK and Northampton, MA, USA: Edward Elgar Publishing, pp. 659–81.

Versluis, E. (2007), 'Even Rules, Uneven Practices: Opening the "Black Box" of EU Law in Action', *West European Politics*, 30(1), 50–67.

Vervloet, K.A.E. (2000), 'Transposition of EC Directives in the United Kingdom and in the Netherlands', thesis, Utrecht University Law Department.

Walker, J. (1995), 'Estimates of the Extent of Money Laundering in and throughout Australia', report for the Australian Financial Intelligence Unit, AUSTRAC.

Walker, J. (1999), 'How Big is Global Money Laundering?', *Journal of Money Laundering Control*, 3 (4), 25–37.

Walker, J. and Unger, B. (2010), 'Measuring Global Money Laundering: "The Walker Gravity Model"', *Review of Law & Economics*, 5 (2), 821–53.

Whitehouse, A. (2003), 'A Brave New World: The Impact of Domestic and International Regulation on Money Laundering Prevention in the UK', *Journal of Financial Regulation and Compliance*, 11 (2), 138–45.

CASES

Belgian Constitutional Court, 23 January 2008, No. 10/2008 (Case nos. 3064 and 3065).

ECJ, Case 33/76, *Rewe* [1976] ECR-1989.

ECJ, Case 45/76, *Comet* [1976] ECR-2043.

ECJ, Case C-305/05, *Ordre des barreaux francophones et germanophones and Others v Conseil des ministres* [2007] I-5305.

French Conseil d'Etat, Lecture du 10 avril 2008, Nos. 296845, 296907 (Conseil National des Barreaux et autres).

Trybunał Konstytucyjny (Polish Constitutional Court), 2 July 2007, Judgment, 72/7/A/2007.

Index